RATTLE SNAKE UNDER HIS HAT
THE LIFE & TIMES OF EARL BROCKELSBY

BY SAM HURST

© 2016 by Reptile Gardens, Vantage Point Historical Services, Inc.
and Sam Hurst. All rights reserved.

Published by Vantage Point Historical Services, Inc.,
1422 Clark Street, Rapid City, SD 57701.
www.vantagepointhistory.com.

Book design by Kyle Read at Badson Studio
and Matt McInerney at Motel.
Printing by Primary Color.

ISBN 978-0-9903972-0-5

Cover and interior photos used with permission of
Reptile Gardens. All rights reserved.

TABLE OF CONTENTS

9	*Introduction*
16	*Chapter 1: A Governor's Dream*
26	*Chapter 2: The End of the Frontier*
54	*Chapter 3: Retreat to the City*
79	*Chapter 4: The Showman and the Tourist*
102	*Chapter 5: A Spectacular Dare*
119	*Chapter 6: The Mentality of War*
134	*Chapter 7: War Behind the Lines*
152	*Chapter 8: Home is Where the Work Is*
168	*Chapter 9: Politics and Civic Leadership*
175	*Chapter 10: The Breakdown*
184	*Chapter 11: Return to Business*
195	*Chapter 12: Mixing Family, Friends and Business*
211	*Chapter 13: Moving the Highway and Moving On*
221	*Chapter 14: A Perfect Life*
234	*Chapter 15: Traveling Man*
245	*Chapter 16: Through Mexico and Central America*
252	*Chapter 17: The Treasure of Cocos Island*
264	*Chapter 18: The Dark Side of Paradise*
282	*Chapter 19: The Flood*
289	*Chapter 20: Roller Coaster '70s*
304	*Chapter 21: Passing the Torch*
314	*Conclusion*
323	*Acknowledgments*
327	*Sources*
335	*Index*

And the LORD God said unto the woman, What is this that thou hast done? And the woman said, The serpent beguiled me, and I did eat.

And the LORD God said unto the serpent, Because thou hast done this, thou art cursed above all cattle, and above every beast of the field; upon thy belly shalt thou go, and dust shalt thou eat all the days of thy life.

— Genesis 3: 13-14

INTRODUCTION

— A Rattlesnake Under His Hat —

Earl Brockelsby believed that he could find a place in the badlands of South Dakota where the foot of man had never stepped. He imagined a place of perfect solitude, where no hunter had ever taken aim at a fleeing antelope, where no windmill had ever broken the silence of a hot summer day and the dens of a thousand tangled, writhing rattlesnakes guarded the fossil boneyard of the Cretaceous.

Brockelsby was a badlands boy, born on the eastern edge of the American West, in the small village of Kadoka. He grew up tall, lean and angular, with a long stride that carried him effortlessly up and over the sculpted buttes. He was a disciple of Teddy Roosevelt's "strenuous life," and he measured his fitness by the stamina of his gait in the blast furnace of dry creeks and the maze of wildlife trails that led ever deeper into the rattlesnake's lair. While most people stood on the pinnacles overlooking the badlands and saw breathtaking loneliness, Brockelsby saw renewal where the ridges ran wild with color and the creeks raged with a deafening roar during spring floods only to retreat into silence by summer.

The badlands did not give themselves up easily. Lakota ghost dancers had retreated into the solitude of the steep canyons of the Stronghold to escape the prying eyes of federal Indian agents and call forth the restoration of the buffalo nation. Cowboys of the open range had warned homesteaders that, "This country warn't made for humans—just Indians and rattlesnakes and cowhands is all it was intended for."

By the time he was a teenager, Earl was steeped in the treacherous vagaries of the badlands, whose beauty was carved by hundred-year droughts and deadly winter blizzards and human folly. He returned throughout his life in search of inspiration and escape from his own bedeviling demons. In his yearning for solitude, Brockelsby tapped into one of the great themes of American westward expansion: the obsession with a perfect freedom and escape from the complexities and suffocation of modern, industrial, urban life.

By 1935, with dust storms blowing over the wreckage of the last failed homesteads, no one claimed that the badlands could sustain a modern economy. But for an enterprising rockhound who knew where to look, a day of digging in the red and yellow geology of Sheep Mountain Table or the Stronghold offered a bounty of geodes, agates and minerals and a treasure chest of small fossils that could be sold to passing tourists for a quarter a piece.

And so, it was not uncommon to see Earl ascend from the chalky crags, smelling of juniper and sage and covered in alkali dust, his winsome smile undaunted and shaded beneath the sweat-stained brim of his Stetson hat. He carried a canvas bag, slung over his shoulder, and a hopeful expectation that Bill Harvey at the Phillips 66 gas station in the town of Wall might offer him a cold glass of water and a few dollars for a day's work with a rock hammer.

Harvey made his living in the service of cross-country travelers who stopped for gas and relief after trailing dust for 300 miles across the gravel roads of South Dakota. Despite the Depression, 200,000 tourists crossed South Dakota in 1935, most on their way to Yellowstone Park and destinations west. They came with images from dime novels and Wild West shows fresh in their minds. By the time the prairie gave way to the badlands, they knew instinctively that they had arrived at the gateway to the American West.

Behind the gas station, Harvey kept a pit filled with prairie rattlesnakes for the tourists to gawk at while they stretched their legs. Among local ranchers, he had a reputation as a "snake man" that was magnified by his casual association with Frank Buck, the celebrity adventurer, international wildlife trader and author of the best-selling memoir, *Bring 'Em Back Alive*. Buck regaled readers with stories of death-defying safaris to capture rogue elephants, man-eating tigers and King Cobras.

Prairie rattlers were no King Cobras, but Bill Harvey did the best he could to promote the frenetic guardians of the badlands, and for tourists the insistent rattle of agitated snakes suddenly made the adventure of a western vacation very real. As Earl stood over the snake pit, he was mesmerized. No matter the danger, like a man who had stared too long into a fire, he wanted to reach out and touch.

When Harvey offered Earl only a nickel a piece for the rocks in his bag, Earl made a counteroffer—all the rocks for two rattlesnakes. "With a long pole, which had a hook on the end, Bill stirred the pile of rattlers, picked a large one up with the hook, and passed it to me," Earl remembered many years later in an unpublished autobiography.

"I took hold of it in the middle of its body. Another quick dip into the pit and up came a second rattler, which I held in my other hand. There I stood, holding a twisting, turning rattler in each hand with their heads hitting my arms. They were frightened and continually rattling, but made no attempt to bite." Remarkably, Earl believed he could turn these two creatures into pets.

With the snakes in a bag, Brockelsby returned to his job and his bunk at Hidden City, a popular tourist attraction south of Rapid City. Located on the road to Mount Rushmore, Hidden City consisted of a small bunkhouse, a ticket shed and a worn dirt path beneath a series of rock outcroppings where the geology of the plains butted against the uplift of the eastern slope of the Black Hills. In just the right light, the rocks took on the appearance of ancient ruins. Explorers of the Great Plains had searched for the lost Cities of Gold for centuries, and the owners of Hidden City made the most of this mythology.

Earl worked as a guide at this roadside attraction in the summer after his freshman year of college, but it was a miserable experience. When he arrived for his first day of work, he was greeted by the resident cook and two teenage guides who had started a few days earlier. The whole group slept in a bunkhouse that doubled as a storage shed for animal food. Earl and his new colleagues gagged on the smell of cracked eggs, abandoned chicken entrails and waste. The shed had little ventilation and the workers slept on rough planks of wood nailed to the wall bunk-bed style, with ragged wool blankets to keep them warm.

The blankets were thick with bedbugs, fleas and lice. "I would awaken with red itching bites every morning," Earl remembered. "I would have swollen red spots from my face to my feet; but my abdomen seemed to be their favorite feeding place…I noticed that the skin under the hair of my genital region was gray; and when I scratched it with my fingernails, it would come off in loose patches. On close examination these gray patches had hundreds of wildly moving legs." In the mornings, he washed himself with kerosene and went to work.

While the cook and both guides fled the miserable conditions within a week, Earl persevered as Hidden City's only employee. A gifted talker who was not afraid to embellish, he worked 15 hours a day, seven days a week, for $6 a week, leading tourists through the site. He picked up extra cash making rock art at night from crystals and geodes that he collected in the badlands and sold to tourists as paperweights, ashtrays and keepsakes.

It was not the life he imagined for himself. Ever since he was a child, he had dreamed of becoming a famous artist or author—a man of intellect, whose creativity would make him a millionaire by the age of 30. The hand-to-mouth existence at Hidden City did not approach his dreams of fame and fortune. At the height of the Depression, with jobs hard to find, he was in no position to be choosy about work, but he was always searching for opportunity.

At Hidden City, Earl built a cage for his snakes behind the bunkhouse. In the quiet evenings, after the last gullible tourist had asked the last question about ancient ruins, Earl got to know his new pets. "Every time I came near their cage, they would coil up into a striking position with the neck in an 'S'…and rattle vigorously," Earl wrote years later. "Still, when I reached into the box to lift one out, it wouldn't strike and would quit rattling once it was in my hand. Then it would crawl up my shirt sleeve, out the collar at my neck, then over my ear, and force its way under my hat where it would then coil tightly on top of my head."

The idea that the reptilian brain of a rattlesnake could be tamed, that they could be pets in any traditional sense, was absurd. But there was no denying Earl's fearlessness. As the summer progressed, he began to hide one of the rattlesnakes beneath his cowboy hat while guiding tourist families through the Hidden City. At the end of his tour, he would thank his guests, graciously accept their small tips and remove his Stetson to wipe his brow. The rattlesnake, quietly absorbing the warmth of Earl's head, would rise from its slumber, rattle and spit its forked tongue.

The tourists shrieked in terror and delight, and assailed Earl with a barrage of questions. Was it a real snake? Was it deadly? Why didn't it bite him? He soon realized that the tourists were more interested in the rattlesnake than the phony pretensions of the Hidden City.

Earl knew next to nothing about rattlesnakes. But he quickly grasped their cultural significance and the deeply embedded obsession and terror they inspired. These were Midwestern, Christian farm families, raised with the Bible, whose fear and curiosity were rooted in the serpent of Genesis. "Cursed are you above all livestock and above all beasts of the field." God had condemned the serpent for his seduction of Eve: "On your belly you shall go. And dust you shall eat all the days of your life."

What they did not learn from the Bible, the tourists knew from schoolbooks and literature. Since the first days of Puritan settlement, the rattlesnake had permeated American history as guardian of the wilderness—a malevolent manifestation of the dangers that lurked beyond the edge of civilization. When the British Crown banished criminals to the American colonies, Benjamin Franklin suggested that colonists return the favor by sending rattlesnakes back to the King. The coiled snake, with 13 rattles, over the warning, "Don't Tread on Me," became a battle flag of the American Revolution. As American settlers moved west, they discovered that almost all Native American tribes included the rattlesnake in their traditions and ceremonies. Rattlesnakes became central participants in some Christian Pentecostal ceremonies when members of the congregation, moved by the Holy Spirit, grabbed snakes and held them over their heads as witness to God's protection.

All of these historical and cultural reactions came into play when Earl Brockelsby revealed the rattlesnake under his hat. But in the moment, what the 19-year-old would-be entrepreneur saw was opportunity—the chance to leverage the beauty of the badlands and Black Hills, the adventurous spirit of the American West, the coming golden age of automobile tourism and, most of all, the attractive power of Mount Rushmore—to realize his own fame and fortune.

Though he may not have known it at the time, that opportunity derived from an improbable adventure that began more than a decade before Earl was born, when a 35-year-old well-driller from Redfield, South Dakota, set out to become the first person to drive an automobile across the state.

A GOVERNOR'S DREAM

— Chapter 1 —

In April of 1905, before the spring thaw had turned the old buffalo trails to swampy mush, but late enough to take the winter bite out of the air, a young South Dakota businessman named Peter Norbeck climbed behind the wheel of a single-cylinder, open-topped Cadillac and drove west from the small farm town of Redfield toward the Missouri River. At the time, there were only 480 automobiles registered in South Dakota and not a single mile of paved road. But the stout Norwegian well-driller and his two friends, Oscar Nicholson and Ole Iverson, were determined to be the first explorers to drive a motorcar across western South Dakota. It was a trip of almost 300 miles from the prairie pothole glacial plain in the east, through the rugged badlands escarpment, across the unpredictable Cheyenne River, to the Black Hills in the far southwestern corner of the state.

The expanse of farm fields in eastern South Dakota had not yet been tiled and drained. There were no tree lines to break the wind. The rivers and streams had not been bridged. All of that was imagination. In fact, the wagon trails that Norbeck and his friends navigated were not roads at all. Over the centuries, buffalo trails had hardened into cattle trails and cattle trails into wagon trails. None had ever felt a tire. No pothole had ever been filled. No steel blade had graded the deep ruts left by wagon wheels. All the old wildlife trails meandered toward water; shallow lakes and streams that flooded in spring, ran dry in summer, froze in winter and waited menacingly for a foolish muleskinner to find his fate.

Eastern South Dakota did offer one redeeming quality for both farmers and automobile pioneers. From the Minnesota border to the Missouri River the prairie was flat—tabletop flat, as if thousands of years of retreating glaciers had scraped the land with a razor. The land was so flat that the James River, which flowed only a few miles east of Norbeck's home, was one of the slowest draining rivers in North America. Mosquitoes dancing on the water moved the current faster than the grade. Easy driving. Norbeck's Cadillac effortlessly swallowed the first 120 miles and cruised into Pierre, on the banks of the Missouri River, in just two days.

The second leg of his trip was an altogether different challenge. The neat, linear, Scandinavian order of eastern South Dakota crumbled and the *true* West began on the western shore of the Missouri. This was buffalo country—blue grama and buffalo grass prairie, badlands, high plateaus and deep river bottoms of gumbo clay.

The great paradox of twentieth-century South Dakota began at the river. Statehood suggested settlement, Christian civilization and picket fences, but beyond the river lay a vast, unsettled, arid, inhospitable emptiness that only a generation earlier had been the heart of the Lakota nation.

On the third day, Norbeck and his friends crossed the Missouri on a ferry and headed west on well-worn wagon trails. They kept to the high ground and resisted the temptation to follow buffalo trails that descended into the Bad River breaks. Past noon, they turned south by west toward the badlands. They had traveled 88 miles from Ft. Pierre when a torrential spring thunderstorm brought them to a halt near Grindstone Butte. Gumbo coated their tires. The more they accelerated, the deeper Norbeck's Cadillac dug into the mud.

This was the Great American Desert of Coronado's imagination. John Wesley Powell had warned against trying to mimic the family farms of Indiana and Iowa on these arid plains. Only the courageous, or desperate, even tried. "This was not the West as I had dreamed of it," Edith Eudora Kohl wrote in her homestead memoir *Land of the Burnt Thigh*. "It was a desolate, forgotten land, without vegetation save for the dry, crackling grass, without visible tokens of fertility. Drab, gray and empty. Stubborn, resisting land. Heroics wouldn't count for much here."

The Black Hills may have been the spiritual heart of Lakota culture, but the shortgrass prairie that Norbeck intended to drive through was the economic muscle of Lakota life. And then, in a blink, the web of relationships that had shaped the economy of the plains for thousands of years was destroyed. Bison were slaughtered to the edge of extinction and small herds of elk were driven off the plains and into the mountains. Lakotas were harassed onto reservations and the ecosystem of the plains was cut to shreds. Farmers plowed the bottomlands into improbable farms while beef cattle and sheep laid waste to the last corners of open range. Rattlesnakes and prairie dogs thrived where the bones of the old way bleached in the sun.

Many years later, Norbeck reflected on his trip through the Bad River valley. "After the rain quit and the sun came out, we attempted to go but the gumbo was too heavy so we hired a ranchman to hitch on to the car." A team of horses dragged the Cadillac 30 miles to the Cheyenne River, where yet another problem presented itself—crossing the river in the throes of the spring melt. "The Cheyenne River looked bad, but fortunately there were three riders about to cross when we reached the bank… They hitched their ropes to the machine and took up through the stream on a gallop, the machine pounding onto the rocks in the river bed." It was an ignominious opening act for the internal combustion engine.

BLACK HILLS HORIZON

As Norbeck's mud-splattered Cadillac ascended out of the Cheyenne River breaks, the Black Hills came into dark relief. Verdant meadows, bursting with wildflowers, rose out of the plains. Mountain springs offered a salvation from the flat ocean of grass that stretched 500 miles in every direction. It was obvious to anyone who explored the spider web of buffalo trails into the Black Hills, and became lost in the old growth ponderosa forests and granite spires, that the Hills were mystical, otherworldly, sacred and well used by the Lakotas. Primordial granite, *Inyan*, rocks of ages, suggested that the Hills had been present at the Creation—an act of the First Day.

When Colonel George Armstrong Custer entered the Black Hills in 1874, at the head of a thousand soldiers, scientific explorers and a gaggle of reporters, he was not interested in Lakota mysteries. His report suggested that he had discovered a Garden of Eden. "The country has generally been open and extremely fertile…consisting of beautiful parks and valleys, streams of clear, cold water and unlimited supplies of timber where Americans could build homes, grow crops, raise cattle and enjoy nature's plenty."

Custer found specks of gold in French Creek. Americans read news of his discoveries and rose up in a spasm of euphoria. With the nation mired in the bank panic of 1875, telegraph wires hummed from the first reports and newsboys hawked newspapers with sensational headlines: "Gold discovered in the Black Hills. National debt to be paid."

For the first generation of white settlers, the Black Hills was a lonely, inaccessible cathedral. All its potential, both real and imagined, lay at the end of the earth, its connection to eastern South Dakota a fiction of the cartographer's pen. In the 1870s, territorial maps placed the Black Hills at the western edge of Dakota Territory, but by geology, climate, economy and culture, the Black Hills and its people, Lakotas and Cheyennes, gold miners, open range ranchers, cowboys, adventurers and gamblers, were nothing like the farm families taking root east of the Missouri River.

No matter the scattered settlements and rugged conditions, after Congress expropriated the Black Hills from the Lakotas in 1876, wealthy investors rushed to explore the tourism potential of this "last American wilderness." They arrived in the southern Hills by train from Omaha and Cheyenne. Enterprising developers built hotels and imagined a spa retreat for easterners who would be drawn to local hot springs and mysterious caves that exhaled ghostly groans every time the barometric pressure changed. But it was a sparse adventure. As a destination, towns like Hot Springs had potential for tuberculosis patients and aging or infirmed veterans of the Civil War, but were too remote to sustain the dreams of railroad sponsored township boosters.

The fastest route from the edge of civilization to the Black Hills was across the western frontier from the riverside capital at Pierre to the mining camps. This was Norbeck's route. But the trip evoked the eighteenth century, not the twentieth. For the fathers of South Dakota statehood, the paradox of the twentieth century lay in the unbridgeable distances at the center of the state. The future of the Black Hills was too important to abandon to transient mining camps or open range ranchers, but too far from the booming farm communities east of the river to be easily integrated. The fate of the West rested on the slow, calculated expansion of the railroads.

Homesteaders followed the rails and moved in the shadow of the track builders, unsure of whether they were in farm country or ranch country or uninhabitable desert. Railroads were not just the primary mode of transportation. They were lifelines. Settlers eagerly awaited the arrival of "next year's" stretch of new track, and town building was driven as much by railroad promoters, land speculators and government concessions as it was by the initiative of homesteaders.

Railroad tracks tied one town to the next, but they could not tie a hundred scattered homesteads into a community. Once a traveler arrived at the depot, he returned to the horse and buggy age to travel the last mile, or ten, to his homestead. Rail tracks often flooded, and when they did, everything from the east, including mail and news, commerce, food supplies, even the travelling circus, stalled at the Missouri River. On the scale of the Great Plains, railroads were a grim compromise. "The Western railroads had to get *across* the Plains," Walter Prescott Webb would later write in his epic history of the Great Plains. "To stop on the Plains would have been fatal, because there was nothing to stop for."

None of this reality dampened Peter Norbeck's enthusiasm. He imagined that the automobile might someday leapfrog the railroad as the primary means of American transportation and in the process develop western South Dakota.

The challenge of tying two disparate halves of South Dakota into a fully integrated economy came into sharp relief when Norbeck and his Cadillac were trapped in Rapid City by a fast moving spring blizzard. He left the automobile in the hands of Ole Iverson and escaped south to Chadron, Nebraska, by train, then east to Sioux City, Iowa. Diagonally across the South Dakota prairie, Norbeck had traveled 289 miles by automobile over impassable prairie from Redfield to Rapid City. The trip home by train was more than twice as long. Therein lay the difference between the reality of railroad travel and the visionary promise of the automobile.

A POLITICAL VISIONARY

In 1905, Norbeck would never have described himself as a politician. Since its territorial days, South Dakota had been led by competing land speculators and town builders with deeper connections to railroad companies than immigrant homesteaders. But Norbeck was a new kind of leader, an authentic inventor, and entrepreneur. At the age of 35, he was one of the most successful businessmen in South Dakota. He had designed a new kind of gasoline-powered deep-well drilling rig and grown wealthy by bringing water from the artesian aquifers of eastern South Dakota to small farms and towns. He was a solid Republican, with prairie populist sympathies. He developed a progressive approach to government wrapped in the economics of enterprise and hard work. He was culturally conservative, the son of an itinerant Christian minister, but his economic populism was nurtured at the kitchen tables of a hundred farm clients, listening to complaints about railroad monopolies, rigged markets, the high cost of money and the petty corruption of state officials.

Even before Teddy Roosevelt articulated his "trust busting" brand of progressive Republicanism, Norbeck understood the essential conflict between farmers and the concentrated economic power of big banks and railroads, especially as the conflict played out on the isolated, under-populated, economically powerless Great Plains. Farmers on the Great Plains "were far from markets, burned by drought, beaten by hail, withered by hot winds, frozen by blizzards, eaten out by grasshoppers, exploited by capitalists and cozened by politicians," Walter Prescott Webb wrote about the spirit of agrarian radicalism at the beginning of the twentieth century. From the successes and failures of the populist movement, Norbeck fashioned an authentic American blend of home grown Christian socialism and enterprise.

In the spectacular granite outcroppings and thick stands of Black Hills pine, Norbeck imagined a new economy for the Black Hills built upon automobile tourism. It was a bold leap, comical for a man whose best efforts had left him stuck in the mud at Grindstone Butte. Even if there had been hardtop roads, and even if Americans could afford a family automobile or a family vacation, why would they drive to the desolate Black Hills of South Dakota? There was no way to get there and nothing to do when they arrived.

Norbeck's thinking galvanized around the idea of a state wildlife preserve, where buffalo, elk, deer, pronghorn and mountain sheep, along with clear mountain streams and wide alpine meadows, would draw restless tourists to the easternmost edge of the frontier West. The Black Hills were 500 miles closer to civilization than Yellowstone and the high Rockies. But in 1905, the idea seemed an improbable stretch. The Black Hills were not as majestic as the Rocky Mountains, and there were no exotic geysers or wildlife to fascinate tourists. The gold rush and early settlers had ravaged the local wildlife. Norbeck believed that the region of the game preserve could support 4,000 deer, 1,000 buffalo, 1,000 elk, 500 antelope and 150 mountain goats. But when he conducted a survey, he found no buffalo, no elk and only 15 to 50 deer in the general area.

A year after Norbeck's trip, the Chicago and North Western Railway began to lay track along the Bad River from Ft. Pierre to Rapid City. A flood of homesteaders loaded their life possessions onto freight cars, and boarded the immigrant trains for the new depot towns of Midland, Phillip, Cottonwood, Wall and Wasta.

Two years later, Henry Ford rolled the first Model T off the assembly line. High volume production kept costs and retail prices low. Almost equally important, Ford increased the wages he paid his workers so that they could afford to buy a Model T. With these innovations, the emerging American middle class accumulated the wealth to explore America beyond their communities, unfettered by train routes and schedules. In 1905, Norbeck's Cadillac had been an exotic curiosity. Only five years later there were 10,000 automobiles registered in South Dakota, and by 1920, there were 100,000.

Visitors to the Great Plains began to comment on the irony of seeing new automobiles parked outside tarpaper homestead shacks and weathered Indian tipis. Even the poorest farm families grasped the transformation that the automobile made possible. When one farmwoman was asked why her family owned a car when they had no bathtub in the house, she replied, "Why you can't go to town in a bathtub!"

Norbeck's political career ascended with the automobile. He was elected to the state legislature in 1908, and after three terms became lieutenant governor in 1914 in a Progressive landslide. When he ran for governor in 1916, he stormed the conservative ramparts of the old Republican Party and swept into office on a progressive platform. "Boys, let's quit the politicians for once and elect a businessman Governor," exclaimed the *Kadoka Press* in its endorsement editorial. Reporting on his first speech to the legislature, the *Pierre Daily Journal* editorialized, without a hint of irony, that Norbeck's message was the "most business like document ever presented to a legislature of South Dakota," despite the fact that Norbeck's policies were "in reality somewhat socialistic."

No policy in Norbeck's platform symbolized the strange, pragmatic mixture of enterprise and socialism as much as his call to build a state-owned cement plant. Economic development in the West required automobile roads, not knee-deep gumbo wagon trails. Tourism demanded paved roads. If it was too expensive to purchase cement and ship it into South Dakota, Norbeck insisted, then the state would make its own. He enlisted Paul E. Bellamy, a conservative young businessman in Rapid City, to bring his dream into reality.

Peter Norbeck became the first native-born governor of South Dakota and led an entire generation of young leaders to positions of power in state and local government. One of those young progressives was John Earl Brockelsby, the newly elected treasurer of Jackson County. A recent immigrant from Iowa, Brockelsby had settled on a homestead claim near the railroad depot town of Cottonwood, just a few miles from where Norbeck's Cadillac had been stuck in the gumbo.

THE END OF THE FRONTIER

— Chapter 2 —

Over the generations, the name came to fit the character of a tenacious breed of men who bent themselves to the plow: farmworkers from the small agricultural parish of Lincolnshire, England, who became expendable in the early days of the Industrial Revolution. *"Brock"* the badger. *"By"* the village. Brockelsby: the men of Badgertown.

Were it not for mid-nineteenth-century innovations in the mechanical reaper that drove farm workers off the land and into English factories, John R. Brockelsby might never have immigrated to the fertile black soil of Clinton, Iowa. John was 22 when he joined his brother William on the American prairie in 1868. The landscape fit John's eye, and the young Englishman embraced the enterprise required of a frontier farmer.

After six years in Clinton, John moved west to a farm near the village of Vail in Crawford County, Iowa, pushing himself closer and closer to the imaginary meridian where the best farmland in the world gave way to the worst. In Crawford County,

John purchased 80 acres, and soon added another 80. He built a cottage, and took pride in recording its dimensions—16 by 22 feet, large by frontier standards. Soon after, he built another 16-by-40-foot addition. He joined the Republican Party of Lincoln and Grant, and became a party stalwart and local leader. *The Biographical History of Crawford, Iowa* recorded that John "spent 30 years on the Crawford County school board, 25 as president, performing his duty with the strictest fidelity. He was reared in the faith of the Episcopal Church. He is now in the prime of life, is frank and jovial, and is popular with all who know him."

Survival on the western prairies of Iowa required a kind of toughness that had no precedent in the tightknit villages of England, and no one was cut from thicker sod than John's wife. Brockelsby men had a history of marrying cousins who were Cousins. John's own mother had been a Cousins from Lincolnshire, and in 1870, 26-year-old John married 13-year-old Alice Ann Cousins.

Alice Ann had lost her left arm in a farm accident at the age of nine, but she rose to the responsibilities of a farm wife with graceful dignity. Each morning, she pulled her hair tight into a bun and handled her daily chores with resolution. She sewed with her one good arm, carried water from the well, milked cows, washed clothes, cooked the family meals and joined the Presbyterian Church to provide proper spiritual guidance to her family. She gave birth to her first child at 15, endured ten pregnancies, lost four children in infancy and nurtured six to adulthood. On May 1, 1885, Alice gave birth to John Earl Brockelsby, her fourth surviving child.

The economic laws of farming in the nineteenth century were universal and immutable, on the cleared forest pastures of England or the wide-open prairies of Iowa, and they quickly caught up with the Brockelsby family. Nineteenth-century farms required everyone in the family to work the land, but as the Industrial Revolution mechanized farm labor it became more and more difficult for an entire family to sustain itself on the produce of a single farm. The nobility of the yeoman farmer had deep roots in American culture, but non-mechanized farms, like most of those on the homestead frontier in the 1870s, required the work of ten to provide economic security for two. Prairie farmers quickly learned that small-scale farming was no way to make a living for the second son—or, in John Earl's case, the fourth.

Large families who held on to their land learned to diversify their interests and their income. The Brockelsby children took this hard truth to heart. Two of John and Alice Ann's sons stayed in the Vail area and bought their own farms. One son became a cattle buyer in Omaha. Another went to work in a local hardware store. Daughter Alice married and moved to nearby Dunlap, Iowa. John Earl Brockelsby went to school, completed the eighth grade and enrolled in business college in Carroll, Iowa, to become an accountant. Within one generation, the Americanized Brockelsby clan was in the wind.

After he completed a three-month course at business college, John Earl took to the rails as a hobo and explored the American West. Jobs were hard to find and adventure served his future goals more than a return to the family farm. In winter, he told his children years later, he hid inside cattle cars, laying on top of cows with his fingers buried deep in their thick winter hides to keep from frostbite.

When the Chicago and North Western Railway laid track west of Fort Pierre in 1906, along the same Bad River route that Peter Norbeck had driven, John Earl made his way to the federal land office in Chamberlain, South Dakota, put $14 in cash on the counter and claimed 160 acres near Cottonwood on March 21, 1907.

John proved up his homestead by erecting a sod home. "Soddies" were well insulated, but impermanent, and required constant attention lest they be recycled as bird and mice nests with the homesteaders still living in them. More common were the flimsy tarpaper shacks, which were occasionally built onto sleds as a practical way for a team of horses to drag a shack from town to a distant homestead. The shacks provided evidence of a homesteader's residence when meddling officials from the federal Land Office came nosing around—a sly recognition that life on the frontier was transient and deserved only a transient's commitment to a permanent dwelling. These frail, black, 8-by-10-foot monuments to folly, with their slight windblown lean to the southeast, littered the countryside in a neat grid, every quarter mile, in every direction, spreading out from the rail depots and Main Streets of a dozen small railroad towns like Cottonwood. At night, lanterns in the windows created the impression that the heavens had touched the earth.

The largest number of immigrants to ever land on American shores came across the Atlantic Ocean in 1906: 1,100,735 optimistic souls crowded out of Europe. Stanley County, South Dakota, boomed. In 1905, it claimed 2,649 citizens. Most lived near Fort Pierre on the Missouri River. Five years later, the population had grown to almost 15,000. Some of these new residents came to farm the arid prairie, site unseen. Others were speculators—filing a claim, living on the homestead just long enough to prove up, then selling and moving on. The surge was a mirage created by the press of immigration and the outsized claims of railroad township companies.

Homesteading the northern plains was a desperate, lonely enterprise. The soil was poor, the winters long and the growing season short. In the first years after being opened to settlement, homesteaders found the prairie scattered with a thousand years of buffalo bones. When harvests fell short, which they almost always did, families survived on the cash they could earn by filling wagons with old, bleached bones and selling them to agents who shipped trainloads east to be crushed into fertilizer. When the buffalo bones were gone, the homesteaders faced a lonesome, inevitable fate.

Of all the perils, the most difficult challenge was water.

Agronomists reported that the average rainfall at John Earl's Cottonwood homestead was 16.45 inches, just above the standard for dryland wheat farming. But Cottonwood almost never experienced the average. In 1910, the village recorded only 9.95 inches of rain, and the crops burned in the late summer drought. In 1915, the community recorded 27.62 inches and farmers thrived. Not even the most disciplined farmers could survive on a good harvest two out of every five years. Successful farmers and small ranchers had second jobs in the depot towns and enough capital to survive the bad years. But the homestead laws had not been written for those who had college educations or money in the bank. They had been written for dreamers with no assets other than strong backs and a willingness to work. They were the first to fail.

The homestead claim near Cottonwood set John Earl Brockelsby's anchor in the community, but he was sober about his future and more interested in business and Republican Party politics than farming. In 1910, he sold his homestead and settled in Cottonwood, where he opened a hardware store on Main Street with Sam Davis, who was also from Iowa. In the 1910 census, John described himself not as a farmer or rancher, but as a "merchant."

Homesteading on the plains nurtured a democratic impulse. For young women, a land claim also offered a chance at independence that they could never achieve in the settled regions of the East. Young women came to South Dakota by the hundreds, trainloads of teachers, enterprising journalists, women in search of husbands and women escaping husbands, and suffragettes who saw in the egalitarian spirit of the West an opportunity that did not exist in the East. "Some of the girls we knew talked about 'going homesteading' as a wild adventure," Edith Eudora Kohl wrote in her memoir. "They boasted of friends or relatives who had gone to live on a claim as though they had gone lion-hunting in Africa or gold hunting in Alaska." As the decades passed, and women married and moved to the cities, being a woman who had homesteaded on her own became a badge of honor.

Edith Kohl and her sister Ida Mary Ammons homesteaded on a strip of land west of the Lower Brulé Indian Reservation. Edith became a reporter for the local penny newspaper. Ida Mary became a schoolteacher and then owner of a general store. She married a local rancher. The sisters lost their homestead in a fire that burned the home, land and Edith's newspaper office just months before they were proved up.

Carrie Peterson, a Norwegian girl from Fairfax, South Dakota, left her family and moved 50 miles west, where she homesteaded 18 months by herself. "The only thing my grandmother had on her homestead was a horse," her granddaughter Ruth Ahl remembered. "When the storms hit all she could do was hide under the belly of her horse." After she had proved up, Carrie married a young Sicangu Lakota, John Scissons, who was from an influential family on the Rosebud reservation.

When Beila Cohen filed her patent at the land office, she was required to sign her "full Christian name," but she was unable to speak English. The land office agent simply changed her name to Bertha. She filed a homestead claim near the badlands town of Interior, on the edge of what is now Badlands National Park. The land was miserable. She failed almost immediately, moved to Interior and opened a bakery. She failed again and moved to Kadoka, where she opened a successful general store and boarding house.

Sara Emmaline Kingsbury, known within her family as "Emma," homesteaded near John Earl Brockelsby, along Cottonwood Creek. She lived with her mother in a small home in town, near the Chicago and North Western tracks. Her brother, Alton Kingsbury, owned lumberyards and hardware stores in several towns along the railroad. While good men and women struggled to prove up their claims and extract enough profit from their homesteads to plant another crop, Alton Kingsbury grew wealthy supplying their daily needs.

In 1913, John Earl Brockelsby and Sara "Emma" Kingsbury were married at the small Presbyterian church in Cottonwood. Like other young couples, they became part of the progressive Republican movement on the frontier.

When Peter Norbeck won his race for lieutenant governor in a landslide in 1914, men like Chester Leedom and John Earl Brockelsby rode his coattails into public office. Leedom, who was editor of the *Cottonwood Republican* and president of the Stanley County Land Company, was elected to the state legislature. With 338 votes, Brockelsby was elected county treasurer of newly created Jackson County. The two aspiring political leaders moved their families to the new county seat in Kadoka.

Like Cottonwood, Kadoka was just as new as the railroad track that ran through it. John took a job as cashier at the Kadoka State Bank and settled into his responsibilities as Jackson County treasurer. His friend "Chet" Leedom became editor and publisher of the *Kadoka Press* and the local boss of the Republican Party.

In addition to the political patronage that flowed to Kadoka with its designation as a county seat, the small village of 200 had all the practical assets necessary to stamp itself on the map of South Dakota. It was a depot town on the Chicago, Milwaukee and Saint Paul rail line that ran from Sioux Falls to Rapid City. It was a trade center for homesteaders and ranchers in the White River valley and for Lakota Indians from the Pine Ridge and Rosebud reservations. Kadoka was a gateway to the starkly beautiful geological wonderland of the badlands, which became a tourist attraction long before it was designated a national monument in 1929. Early automobile pioneers, eager to drive a straight line from Sioux Falls to Rapid City, camped in Kadoka's roadside parks to watch a sunrise over the badlands. Locals claimed that there was also something "magical" about the town of Kadoka.

In Kadoka and the surrounding countryside, the absolute dependence of every homesteader on his or her neighbor created a culture of tolerance and interdependence. Bertha Cohen, for example, was Jewish. She married twice, raised six children and took the name of her second husband, Martinsky. She was *frum*, very religious, and kept kosher, even though she was surrounded by anti-Semitism and even occasional parades by the Ku Klux Klan. But she also believed that a spirit of tolerance surrounded Kadoka.

Bertha's store on Main Street was a center of the town's social life, and when she observed the Sabbath on Saturdays, her neighbors, the good Christian ladies of Kadoka, took turns managing the store for her. There were only two houses of worship in Kadoka: the Catholic and the Presbyterian churches. Bertha, a lonesome Jew on the prairie, began to invite the local Catholic priest to engage in theological conversations. Over time, their conversations became informal community gatherings, with neighbors quietly huddled around the stove at the Kadoka Mercantile, listening to the town's two religious intellectuals debate the finer qualities of Jewish and Catholic teachings. For a child growing up in this isolated small town, exotic places and ideas came alive in the stories and debates shared by this community of transplants.

ENCOUNTERS WITH THE LAKOTAS

Nothing symbolized the "magical" character of Kadoka like the caravans of Lakota families who rode from the badlands every Saturday. They arrived in horse-drawn wagons with empty water barrels, followed by colts and dogs and children, with men in the lead and women walking quietly behind. Their hair was long and braided. Their ears were pierced. The women were wrapped modestly in shawls. Everyone wore moccasins. They rode straight to Bertha Martinsky's store. It was a time when Lakotas still needed permission to leave the reservations to come to town, and border towns like Kadoka had reputations for racism. Few Lakota children attended school with white children. But on Saturdays, during the long days of summer, Lakota families stayed the weekends in Kadoka to dance and celebrate and trade with local townspeople.

Bertha was a fluent Lakota speaker. As a Jew, she had a heightened sensitivity to the poverty and discriminations endured by her Indian customers. "She joked many times that when Indians were in the store she always felt comfortable about stepping out to take a break," her grandson Stanford Adelstein remembered. "When transient whites were in the store, she knew she couldn't leave. They would steal her blind." Some Indians paid in cash for their supplies, others traded crafts. Mrs. Martinsky stocked beads and shawls and blankets specifically for her Lakota customers. But one of the images that set itself deep in Earl Brockelsby's memory was how much the Indians loved the exotic taste and texture of bananas.

John Brockelsby joined the Masons in Cottonwood and tolerated the Ku Klux Klan in Kadoka, but he was not a joiner, and refused to belong to business associations like the Kadoka Kommercial Klub. He had a strong instinct for social justice and slowly came to the conclusion that the popular secret lodge societies "didn't make for brotherly love and understanding."

Earl Brockelsby's views on race were shaped by these early experiences passed on from his father. When Earl was chosen to represent his fifth grade class in a school debate on the question: "Was the Indian treated fairly by the white man?", he chose to argue that the Indians had been treated unfairly. For him, the personal, intimate relations between Indians and whites in Kadoka made it possible to imagine that the "magic" of his hometown might be replicated in other border communities.

HANNIBAL ON THE PLAINS

John Earl and Emma Brockelsby settled into a three-bedroom home on the outskirts of this "magical" town, and on May 11, 1916, their first child was born. They named him Earl John Brockelsby.

There was an aspiring middle class dignity to the Brockelsby household. John Earl dressed each day in the suit and tie of a banker. Emma wore a full-length, white dress with lace trim that betrayed the inescapable presence of wind and dust and mud. The first photographs of baby Earl show a smiling, fat and happy child, bundled against the cold in a wicker bassinette. As he grew older, Emma dressed him in pantaloons and sailor's outfits, always with a stylish cap and scarf. One of Earl's first memories of Christmas was Santa's gift of a little green wooden wagon with red wheels, in the middle of which sat a huge red apple. Throughout his childhood, Earl's wagon doubled as a child's toy and an essential cart for the boy's odd jobs.

Life in Kadoka was distinctly western, complete with wild horse roundups and Lakota dances in the streets on summer weekends. The town was one step removed from the frantic insecurity of homesteading, and Earl grew up a town boy rather than a homestead boy. His father's job at the bank was secure, and as World War I battlefields destroyed the foundations of European agriculture, wheat farmers and ranchers on the flat plateaus overlooking the badlands were doing the best they would ever do. They took out new loans at the bank and poured their profits into expansion at a time when the Brockelsby family was growing as well.

Around 1920, Earl's mother encouraged him to pray for a sister. "I would lie on the couch and pray over and over every night for a baby sister, really hoping but only one-half believing, that my prayers would be answered," he wrote in his journal. One morning, she invited Earl into the bedroom and introduced him to his newborn sister Reta Mae, who was wrapped in a blanket. "My prayers had been answered," he judged.

With "concrete evidence of God fulfilling my prayers," Earl came to the deeply held, but short-lived, conviction that God might answer more practical prayers. He prayed that God would make him a famous writer and painter. He prayed that God would bring him barrels of paint and leave them on the front porch. When Christmas arrived and Santa Claus brought him a small box of watercolor paints, he counted it a fair settlement and stopped praying to God for earthly prizes.

THE CIRCUS AND THE RAILROAD

Earl grew up in the tradition of Tom Sawyer and Huck Finn. It was a life of mud-between-the-toes mischief, pranks and endless summers. By the time he was four, he was liberated from his pantaloons, and spent his summers in denim coveralls and an oversized cowboy hat. Kadoka was remote, but just as the Mississippi River brought the outside world to Mark Twain's Hannibal, Missouri, the railroad brought the outside world to Kadoka. "Trains played an important role in village life," Earl remembered years later. "All supplies and merchandise arrived by train, and grain and livestock were shipped by rail from Kadoka. It was always exciting to see the steam locomotive puffing its way across the prairie, and many locals made a habit of being at the depot when the train stopped."

Earl stood by the tracks as a child and read the brightly painted signs on the boxcars, dreaming of places he might someday visit. The trains brought all things ancient and modern. Traveling evangelists arrived and pitched their tents at the edge of town. Old Testament exhortations for sinners to find their way to God echoed through the quiet country nights. Circuses, flashy new automobiles, patent medicine salesmen, caravans of gypsies and hoboes with every kind of exotic tale of the world beyond passed through Kadoka on the rails and settled in young Earl's imagination.

Each summer the railroad brought theater troupes and traveling Chautauqua. "The most American thing in America," Teddy Roosevelt proclaimed about these traveling theater and debate societies. Even in old age, Earl could remember scenes from a theatrical adaptation of *Uncle Tom's Cabin*, the dramatic crescendo of Eliza's escape across an icy river, acted out beneath the dome of a circus tent illuminated by kerosene lanterns.

Earl's childhood years coincided with the golden age of the American circus. Almost a hundred circuses crisscrossed the nation by rail, coast to coast, stopping in small towns like Kadoka. They offered a "celebration of diversity" on the isolated prairie. Hamlin Garland captured the influence of the Big Top in *Son of the Middle Border*, his classic memoir of growing up on a homestead in western Iowa:

> It was India and Arabia and the jungle to us. History and the magic and pomp of chivalry mingled in the parade of the morning, and the crowds, the clanging band, the haughty and alien beauty of the women, the gold embroidered housings, the stark majesty of the acrobats subdued us into silent worship…It was our brief season of imaginative life. In one day—in part of one day—we gained a thousand new conceptions of the world and of human nature. It was an embodiment of all that was skillful and beautiful in manly action. It was a compendium of biologic research but more important still, it brought to our ears the latest band pieces and taught us the most popular songs. It furnished us with jokes. It relieved our dullness. It gave us something to talk about.

At every stop along the rail line, schools were closed when the circus whistle sounded. As the train groaned to a halt at the town depot, children crowded the rails for hours to watch a menagerie of circus animals, magicians, musclemen, bearded ladies, thin men, fat babies, acrobats, daredevils, sword swallowers, lion tamers and snake charmers disembark and cast a spell of fantasy and wonderment over the town. From the lanterns of the circus tent, a warm, enchanting, otherworldly glow emanated across the nighttime prairie.

At the age of four, watching the circus performers parade along Kadoka's Main Street, Earl found himself looking up at an elephant. The elephant trainer beckoned the animal, and before the boy could gather his wits, the elephant had wrapped its trunk around Earl's waist and lifted him onto its back. "It was a long way to the ground but once seated up so high on its back I felt pretty safe," Earl wrote years later. "I didn't feel all that secure being held by the trunk of an elephant that couldn't even see exactly where I was. The trunk felt me out perfectly as if it were looking right at me and gently picked me up and set me back safely on the ground."

Of all the circus sideshows, the most thrilling was the performance of an Amazon explorer who unrolled the slick skin of a 20-foot anaconda snake and told tales of the jungle and a vast river as far removed from the treeless plains of South Dakota as a young boy could imagine.

THE YOUNG ENTREPRENEUR AND HIS PETS

If the Amazon symbolized a world of endless water and wild things that lived beneath the currents, Kadoka was a world where water was always precious. At the Brockelsby home, water was collected in a cistern beside the house. When a thunderstorm struck, Earl waited a few minutes for the rain to pour down the drainpipe and then raced through the lightning and deluge to the cistern to flip a switch that would send water from the gutters cascading through layers of rock, sand and charcoal filters to trickle into the dark, cool cistern. A small kitchen pump brought drinking and cooking water from the cistern to the sink. The Brockelsby family proudly bathed once a week, and washed clothes on Monday with the bathwater.

After a long day at the bank, John Brockelsby found comfort in a small garden beside the house, onto which the family poured the wastewater from baths and laundry, salty water from cooking, water from melting ice and water from the fleeting, turbulent rainstorms that swept over Kadoka in the summer. It was never enough. John planted trees. They died. He planted the yard to grass. It died. In a moment of optimism, he planted strawberries in the garden. All were lost by August. Edith Kohl's admonition echoed across the scorched grass: "It was a desolate, forgotten land, without vegetation save for the dry, crackling grass." Finally, John reconciled himself to a lawn of alfalfa and honeysuckle vines that could survive both winter blizzard and summer drought.

While the family tended to water, young Earl weeded the garden. In the mornings before school, he milked the family cow, shoveled manure, raked it into the garden and delivered milk to the neighbors. He earned his wage from the sale of each season's calf, which he dutifully deposited in a savings account at his father's Kadoka State Bank.

Along with the values of hard work and thrift, Earl developed an instinct for enterprise at a very early age. While homestead boys filled their days with backbreaking manual labor, Earl honed his skills as a bootstrap capitalist and entrepreneur. At the age of five, he used a small axe to chop kindling for the stove—five cents a bushel. When his little metal bank was filled with nickels and dimes, he marched down to the bank and made a deposit.

He scoured the city dump and the garbage piles that collected in ravines behind people's homes for glass bottles that he could clean and sell to the drugstore to be reused for medicine. He scrounged old lath left over from homebuilding and crafted it into doll furniture, which he sold to neighborhood girls. His profits were small, but his savings account at the bank grew steadily.

Mail-order catalogs connected the young entrepreneur to the outside world. Their glossy pages supplied his imagination with get-rich schemes (and met more basic needs in the family's three-hole outhouse). He combed the catalogs in search of interesting business opportunities, and one day settled on a set of three rabbit traps. The badlands abounded with rabbits, and Earl imagined himself trapping and breeding rabbits for a local market—to what end he had not quite determined since his enterprise faced the challenge of creating a local market as well as supplying it. He trapped a cottontail the very first night, but the next morning he discovered, to his horror, that the rabbit had chewed its leg to the bone trying to escape. "I took the poor little rabbit, its eyes filled with terror and its heart visibly pounding in its side, home to my father who killed it quickly with a wooden club." In despair, Earl threw the traps in the corner of the barn and never used them again. "I retired to my room, broken-hearted and hating myself," he wrote 50 years later, confessing that he still could not shake the memory or forgive himself.

Disturbed, but not defeated, Earl decided that, instead of engaging in the gory task of trapping rabbits, he would order his rabbits from a catalog. He settled on two New Zealand Whites; large, ten-pound muscular mainstays of the mail-order catalog. John helped Earl build a rabbit pen, complete with an underground den, where the rabbits could breed and escape the winter. Once again, the seven-year-old came face to face with his own limitations. He enjoyed raising the rabbits, but had no heart for skinning them. In exasperation, he sold his two adults and their litter to a local farmer, who was more willing to do the brutal work.

Stubbornness is a valuable quality in an entrepreneur, and when Earl turned eight, he tried again, this time with chickens. He studied the pages of the Gurney Company catalog and settled on an order of light Brahmas. Well-tended adults were large, often 12 pounds. They were white, with a stark necklace of black around the neck and on the tips of their tail feathers. When his order of 50 chicks arrived, Earl warmed them in a cardboard box next to the kitchen stove. "One by one my little chicks died, one or two a day until I was down to only twenty-three." He agonized over his losses, but the strongest chickens survived and thrived to produce eggs. He built a chicken roost and fed the birds all summer. Through his childhood eyes, "they were the most beautiful chickens in the world; I had never known that any chicken could get so large and handsome."

One autumn afternoon, he returned home to discover his mother and aunt busily choking, boiling and canning his chickens. He was heartbroken. It was the price of his parents' investment in months of chickenfeed, and an early lesson in the hidden costs of business. Earl's tears saved five chickens from the axe, but John convinced him to sell the survivors to the local market and put the money in the bank—nine cents a pound live weight, five chickens at 12 pounds each: $5.40 in his savings account.

It seemed that no matter how many times Earl tried to engage the animal world, with pets, or business schemes, or simple curiosity, his efforts ended in trauma and the chopping block. One summer, when Emma planted cosmos on the east side of the house, Earl discovered that a brightly colored garter snake had made its home in the shade of the flowers. What a wonderful pet a docile, friendly snake would make. He took to tying a length of thread gently around the neck of the snake and parading his reluctant companion up and down the boardwalk on Main Street.

"It didn't seem to want to go where I did," Earl remembered. "When I would drag it over the wooden sidewalk it got slivers in its belly. I took tweezers and spent an hour removing all the splinters."

Earl returned the snake to its flowers and decided that the best plan would be to visit his pet amid the cosmos rather than dragging it through town. All went well for a few days until the snake haplessly slithered in front of Earl's father one morning and was summarily chopped in half. Earl was distraught by what he considered his father's callow indifference toward "such a bright bit of graceful life."

SNAKES AND THE GREAT PLAINS

Snakes filled a complicated niche in the superstitions of Great Plains settlements. They were everywhere, a dozen species, indistinguishable to the settlers, lurking silently beneath slivers of shade, coiled beneath bales of hay, lounging under the floor boards of homestead cabins. Their camouflage made them virtually invisible.

Prairie rattlesnakes could be especially terrifying. They wintered deep below the frost line in enormous dens and lethargically sunned themselves on south-facing rocks during the warm days in autumn and spring. Their dens were far from the rolling pastures and wheat fields. But in the summer, rattlesnakes became hobos, occasionally travelling ten or twelve miles from their dens in search of food. It was common for ranchers to discover a small, but agitated, rattlesnake defending its turf beneath the hooves of a bucking cow pony that wanted no part of a rattlesnake's bite. At harvest time, homesteaders encountered rattlesnakes in their freshly thrashed hay piles or sometimes in the shade of a sod wall.

Field mice, voles, baby prairie dogs and the occasional grassland songbird were the natural prey of rattlesnakes, whose venom combined both hemotoxic and neurotoxic qualities that could stop a ground squirrel in its tracks. No one knows how many homesteaders died from the bite of a prairie rattlesnake during the homestead era, but those who were bitten, and lived to describe their agony, often claimed that the month of pain that followed a bite was so excruciating that they wished they had died.

Snakes were an essential part of plains ecology, but few homesteaders understood ecology in the first decades of the twentieth century. See a snake, kill a snake. Poisonous or harmless, the species didn't really matter. Better safe than sorry. In Genesis, the Bible exhorted believers to "smite them on their head," and homesteaders stayed true to the command.

Once, on a family trip to Emma's brother's farm in Chamberlain, South Dakota, Earl discovered a coiled snake in the barn. His uncle described the snake as a puff adder, one of the most poisonous snakes in the world. Terror swept through the gathered family, which retreated a dozen paces from the hissing viper while Uncle August whacked the snake to death with a hoe and buried it a foot underground so that no one would accidentally step on the fangs and die a painful, tortured death.

Uncle August never explained how a puff adder, native to the deserts of northern Africa, ended up in a South Dakota barn. In fact, the hissing hognose snake in the barn was harmless and a blessing to every farm family threatened by exploding mice populations. But hiss and slither sparks a universal terror in the human psyche, especially when embellished by a mischievous uncle.

FATHER AND MOTHER

The trauma that accompanied Earl's childhood experiences with animals was not limited to rabbits, chickens and snakes. One spring Sunday after church, clusters of parishioners gathered in the middle of the street, where Earl's faithful Airedale, Rex, began to fight with a neighbor's collie. The owner of the collie started his car and deliberately ran over the two dogs, breaking Rex's back. Earl was in tears, and pleaded with his father to come to the rescue, but John refused to intervene with the driver or to help Rex.

"Well, the dogs shouldn't have been fighting," he explained to his son.

"I felt so all alone," Earl later recalled, "and now when the only thing in the world that loved me lay dying, my father would do nothing."

John's passive response to Earl's feelings, his inability to act in defense of his son or himself, scarred Earl in ways that never healed.

Earl's parents were not sentimental or outwardly romantic. They had gone about the business of raising a family with cool deliberation, but there had never been a spark between them. "There was no loving relationship between myself and either of my parents," Earl remembered with blunt honesty. "I cannot remember ever hearing kind and loving words; never once was there a hug or the words, 'I love you.'"

Earl's mother Emma was fragile. Later in life, she would become more confident, more secure and trusting, and her grandchildren remembered her as generous and patient. But as a young mother on the frontier, she was frightened of strangers, hobos, gypsies and, most of all, Emma was afraid of illness.

To some extent, her fears were well founded. It was the age of the great flu pandemic of 1918, when almost 700,000 Americans died of influenza. Childhood diseases had not yet been conquered. A snakebite, or accident, could end in a runaway infection and fever. Emma obsessed about her children's health and diseases both real and imagined. She acquired a crude electric shock contraption, a "therapeutic electric battery," to cure every sickness from Earl's severe migraine headaches to stomachaches, common colds, flu and fever. The battery had been given to Emma by her brother Mason, a chiropractor of dubious reputation, but Emma became a true believer. "Each electrode would be wrapped in a wet cloth; one was placed at the back of your neck and the other in a damp cloth at your feet," Earl wrote in his journal. "Thus you could feel the electrical current running through your body. Sometimes she set it so strong you could feel the muscles in your neck jerking and popping. How I hated to see my mother coming with that wooden box." The treatments lasted an agonizing two hours, and after the first half hour Earl was more than willing to pronounce himself cured. From his mother's point of view, the health effects of electric shock therapy were miraculous and undeniable. After all, the more she threatened to use it, the less Earl complained of being sick.

Earl described his mother as judgmental and suspicious of neighbors. She held herself apart from the "miracle" of Kadoka, and was quick to criticize neighbors from Germany and Ireland, even the kind-hearted Bertha Martinsky. But mostly he remembered that she was critical of her husband John, who endured her judgments in silence. She confided to Earl that she had been in love with another man, and had made a mistake in marrying John Brockelsby. It was hard for a boy to hear. "A small misbehavior on my part might make her throw herself on the bed, yelling, screaming and crying all at the same time," Earl remembered. "Sometimes when things didn't go her way, she would rush into the closet that separated the two bedrooms and try to hang herself. Dad would try to calm her down and get her out of the closet. He probably knew that she couldn't or wouldn't hang herself, but it was a terrifying experience for a little boy."

At the age of four, Earl began to experience painful, debilitating migraine headaches that regularly occurred on weekends when both his parents were at home and quarreling. Later in life, he concluded that the tension between his parents had a huge influence on him as a young boy. Emotionally distant from his parents, Earl became protective of his little sister, and learned to navigate through life by avoiding confrontation and conflict.

Earl had other boyhood friends, including Chet Leedom's son, Boyd. Leedom later became a member of the South Dakota Supreme Court and chairman of the National Labor Relations

Board during Dwight Eisenhower's presidency. He remained Earl's close friend for life, preserving Earl's connection to Kadoka. But neither his sister Reta Mae nor his boyhood friends earned Earl's deepest affections. He reserved his deepest emotional connection for the badlands wilderness.

IMMERSED IN THE WILD

The eroded valley of the White River twisted its way through spectacular geology. Bright strata of yellow, red and brown rock, weathered by torrential storms, were transformed each year by mudslides and flash floods. The geological wonderland gave up a wild array of rocks, geodes, agates and dinosaur fossils to catch the imagination of a young boy.

For most children, the deepest memories of freedom and exploration take place in the summer, but Earl loved the badlands most in the bitter, cold, white winter. It was counterintuitive. There is no peril on the plains like a blizzard, no threat like the plunging temperatures of a treacherous winter cold front. It is a central theme of Great Plains literature: herds of frozen cattle smothered beneath the snow along a fence line, frostbitten homesteaders curled beneath their buffalo-hide robes while the last embers of their fire burn out, children frozen to death and buried in snow on their way home from school. Ole Edvart Rolvaag's classic novel *Giants in the Earth,* first published in 1924, ends with the protagonist lost in a winter storm, skiing across the prairie to a neighbor's home. His body is discovered the next spring. And yet, for young Earl, "Nothing seemed to compare with the beautiful white snow of winter, the silence of a winter night, and the thrill of skiing down the small hills around Kadoka."

He fashioned skis from old barrel staves that had been used to transport everything from crackers to coffee beans. He sanded the rough wood smooth and then rubbed his mother's paraffin into the grain. He held his feet in place with leather straps cut from old shoes. Off he went into the hills and valleys south of town.

At the age of eight, John and Emma gave Earl a pair of real $1.98 skis. The new skis presented an immediate problem. None of his friends, struggling along on barrel staves, could keep up, so Earl decided to keep one ski and gave the other to his friend. The boys would use their free leg to push along the flats, then glide down the hills, two feet planted on one ski—snowboarders before their time.

Only once was Earl lost in a blizzard, fighting the cold and oncoming night, squinting to find dim lights on the horizon. He was a badlands boy: lost but not afraid, and after an hour of gliding by instinct, feeling his way through the blowing snow, he found his way home.

EDUCATION AT THE HEARTH

Earl described himself as an indifferent student, drawn more to the outdoors than the classroom. But the Kadoka newspaper regularly listed him as an honor student throughout his elementary school years, often with perfect attendance. School was never as demanding as his own mother, who set up a blackboard in the family dining room and taught him to read and write at the age of three.

He was argumentative and stubborn in class. Once, in the second grade, he drew on his considerable powers of observation to argue that his teacher could not be right that the world was a sphere. Looking out the window, he argued, anyone could see that the world was flat, and any reasonable person could understand that if the world was a sphere, a person on the other side of the world would be upside down.

By the time he was five, he wanted to be a writer and an artist.

Almost all public school classrooms on the prairie were adorned with art, including the ubiquitous print of Gilbert

Stuart's portrait of George Washington. But Earl was drawn more to other prints on the classroom walls. He loved Jean-François Millet's portrayal of three French peasant women collecting seed after the harvest in *The Gleaners*. Earl's attraction to the painting suggested that an awareness of poverty and the subsistence struggle of farmers was still deeply embedded in Brockelsby family memory. He was captivated by the bold brushstrokes of Landseer's *Newfoundland Dog* and Bonheur's *The Horse Fair*: animals, nature, outdoors. Like a shallow badlands creek that goes underground at the slightest temptation, Earl's love of art would reemerge constantly throughout his life, although he never became a painter. Artists and writers were immortal, Earl concluded, and he wanted to be immortal.

THE OVERLAND RUNABOUT

In a world where cowboys on horseback and Indian wagons took a young boy back to the nineteenth century and the railroad was a steel thread into the twentieth, the automobile burst onto the scene as a great liberator that allowed prairie families, including the Brockelsbys, to escape their isolation and explore the world. Most of the first images of automobiles on the prairie were incongruous: cowboys using their cars to round up cattle, or Indians with automobiles parked beside their tipis. Emma's brother, Alton Kingsbury, drove his expensive Packard over dirt trails at five miles per hour, just to prove it could be done. Tourists began to arrive in Kadoka by automobile rather than the train, and makeshift tourist campsites sprang up on the outskirts of town, one of them owned by the ever-enterprising Bertha Martinsky.

When John purchased a used Overland Runabout in 1919, life in the Brockelsby household changed forever. The Overland was put to daily use rounding up the family milk cow and the neighbors' cattle when they drifted too far from town. There were still no paved roads in western South Dakota, and the

30-mile automobile trip from Kadoka to the regional shopping center in Philip took two hours on a road that Earl described as "a tooth-shattering washboard." The 120-mile trip to visit cousins on their farm north of Chamberlain took all day—hours longer if the ferry across the Missouri River was delayed or the trip was hijacked by a storm. The family took long drives to Omaha and to visit relatives in Iowa that would have been unthinkable only a few years before John purchased the car.

In the summer of 1924, John and Emma loaded the children into the Overland and took off for the Black Hills on the family's first vacation. For a growing class of Americans, the "family vacation" was a novel idea that reflected not only the increasing mobility of the automobile era, but also the prosperity of the new American middle class. An escape from the daily demands of farm life, the office or business, coupled with new and exotic scenery, was invigorating and suggested financial security. It also brought the family together for experiences that made lifelong memories.

The Brockelsby family camped in a canvas tent at the state game preserve for $1 a night. Earl's fondest memory of the week was being able "to lie on your stomach and drink from the sparkling stream that flowed so fast." He and Reta Mae fashioned finger-sized birchbark canoes from nearby trees, tied them to strings and floated them in the rapids of Squaw Creek (later renamed Grace Coolidge Creek).

While the Brockelsby family was enjoying the fresh air and cool mountain streams of Peter Norbeck's wildlife park, state leaders were putting Norbeck's larger vision into action. By 1924, Norbeck had ascended to the United States Senate, where he and allies, including state historian Doane Robinson, began to imagine tourism in western South Dakota in national terms.

The Black Hills had great potential to draw farm families from the parched prairies and perhaps even from Omaha and

Minneapolis. But to attract tourists from Chicago or the East Coast, the Black Hills needed more than granite spires. Robinson had been an ardent supporter of the Black and Yellow Trail, the proposed 1,600-mile highway from Chicago to Yellowstone National Park that he had routed directly through the Black Hills, but a single road and wildlife were not enough. Robinson believed that western South Dakota needed a bold reason for tourist families to visit. "Scenery alone will not sell the Black Hills to the world," he wrote the secretary of the Rapid City Commercial Club. "Tourists soon get fed up on scenery, unless it has something of special interest connected with it to make it impressive."

Robinson proposed to carve massive busts of great characters from Western history into the inaccessible granite spires of the Black Hills, in a region known as the Needles. True to the spirit of the Progressive Era, Robinson believed that human ingenuity and engineering could be blended with the conservation of wilderness, and would be applauded by visitors as a conquest of nature. Sculpture on a mammoth scale would not detract from the wildlife park, Robinson argued. It would enhance the tourist experience. He reached out to the Danish-American sculptor Gutzon Borglum in January 1924, and what the historian John Taliaferro called the "obsessive quest to create Mt. Rushmore" was put into motion.

There is no record that John Brockelsby, sitting behind the teller's window at the bank in Kadoka, knew anything about the plans of Norbeck and Robinson. But he was active in the Republican Party and the business community. The coincidence of the family trip to the Black Hills taking place in the same summer that Borglum first visited the Black Hills is provocative. Borglum's interest in the sculpture project was widely reported, and may have suggested to John that the future of the region lay in tourism and the Hills, not along the railroad tracks of small, homestead towns like Kadoka. This point was driven home soon after the

Brockelsby family returned to Kadoka. The Farmers State Bank suddenly collapsed, eviscerating the savings of many in the community, including young Earl.

During World War I, American agricultural markets had boomed. Farmers moved from the small, rocky farms of New England to the prairies of Indiana and Iowa. As they did, farmers in western Iowa cashed out and moved even farther west to South Dakota. In South Dakota, established farmers in the James River Valley sold out and moved accross the Missouri River. Moving ever westward, they settled on marginal land that had been broken and brought into production to compensate for the wartime ruin of European agriculture. With wartime demand, commodity prices exploded. Even on the improbable edges of American agriculture, farmers reaped huge profits. To finance this expansion, banks loaned to farmers and ranchers in the boom times. When the war ended and European agriculture recovered, the bottom dropped out of American wheat and cattle markets. Long before the Great Depression, rural banks on the Great Plains began to fail, beginning with those on the frontier edge of prosperity. In 1921, there were 566 state chartered banks in South Dakota. Five years later, 200 had closed.

John must have had some foreboding. The Farmers State Bank of Kadoka had been in a death spiral for over a year before it closed its doors. He was stoic about his losses, but young Earl grieved over the sudden evaporation of his rabbit and chicken money, his bottle money and his calf profits: his life savings of $88 ($1,208 in 2015 dollars) had disappeared.

Earl's father found a new job down the street at the Dakota State Bank, where he worked as a clerk and member of the management team. But the collapse of Farmers State Bank changed him. He became more conservative and increasingly distant from his family, but the collapse also forced him to take greater risks to recover greater losses. He speculated in land and sold crop insurance. He purchased several thousand acres of badlands for 25 cents an acre, and sold them in Chicago for $1.50 an acre, sight unseen.

DRIVER TRAINING

Despite the collapse of land and crop prices, nothing could hold back the automobile. Even in the badlands, where every mile of trail was gumbo and a brief summer storm could force an automobile to the side of the trail for hours, people continued to purchase automobiles. With his friend Neil Rounds, John acquired the Chevrolet dealership in Kadoka. He kept the accounts and ranged far into the surrounding country, selling automobiles to anyone who still had disposable income.

Automobiles were so new that John found himself giving driving lessons to first-time buyers. "One day Dad had to give such a lesson to a farmer by the name of Hand, who lived about 15 miles east of town," Earl remembered. "This lesson, as most that Dad gave, took place not on a road but in a pasture where there was no danger of running into anything. Mr. Hand was doing pretty good on the level, but when he started down a hill in the pasture and kept going faster and faster, Mr. Hand lost all control. Instead of applying the brakes, he started pulling back on the steering wheel and shouting, 'Whoa, Whoa' as though he was driving a team of horses. Fortunately, when we reached the bottom of the hill and the driver had lost all control, we started up the other side and gravity finally stopped the car."

John held on for two years at the Dakota State Bank, and Earl opened a new savings account. One evening, after work, John walked into the house and announced that the bank had failed and been put into receivership. John had known for months that the bank was going under, he explained, but he thought that it would be unfair to withdraw the family savings and leave his friends and neighbors to take the beating by themselves.

Once again, John had gone broke with Kadoka, and for the second time in as many years, young Earl lost his life savings. John tossed a quarter onto the kitchen table and told his son, "This is all the money we have in the world."

RETREAT TO THE CITY

— Chapter 3 —

Eleven-year-old Earl Brockelsby could not imagine moving from Kadoka. But after the Dakota State Bank closed its doors, it was hard to imagine a future in a town whose economic foundations were collapsing. One day in August 1927, John announced to the family that he had been offered a job at the Chevrolet dealership in Rapid City: a hundred miles to the west.

The Brockelsbys were not alone. As the small farming towns surrounding Rapid City sank deeper and deeper into depression in the 1920s, and homesteaders abandoned or sold their failing farms and moved into town, it became apparent that the automobile and highway economy was depression-resistant. As governor, Peter Norbeck matched federal highway funds with state funds, and the washboard gravel roads began to be conquered by asphalt and oil. The trip from Kadoka to Rapid City was reduced from five hours to two, and small railroad depot communities like Kadoka were transformed into automobile satellites of Rapid City. In the last decade of the nineteenth century, it would have been rare for a homestead family to visit Rapid City. By 1927, families like the Brockelsbys could look west to the Black Hills as a vacation destination.

In the old days, Lakotas camped in the valley of the fast moving creek that descended out of the mountains and ran east to the Cheyenne River. They called the area *Mniluzahan Otonwahe*, "Swift Running Water City." When gold was discovered in the Hills, the valley of Rapid Creek became a service and supply center for local ranches and the mines 40 miles to the north. Between 1880 and 1920, Rapid City had experienced a series of booms and busts. By the late '20s, it was growing again, with a population of 10,000. But most important, for that brief summer, it became the capital of the nation.

Like many presidents before him, Calvin Coolidge had little desire to remain in Washington during the hot, humid summer months. By outward appearance, Coolidge was a Massachusetts lawyer raised at the knee of New England politics. But he had been born into a Vermont farm family, and the Green Mountain ethos of rugged individualism shared much in common with the values of Black Hills pioneers. In 1927, at Peter Norbeck's suggestion, the President and his wife, Grace, made the Black Hills their summer White House.

The President and first lady arrived at the train station in Rapid City in late June and were met by an enormous crowd. An honor guard of cowboys and Indian cavalry escorted them south to the State Game Lodge. Over the next ten weeks, Coolidge traveled to Rapid City to conduct business from a temporary office in the high school. In the afternoon, he was chauffeured back to the State Game Lodge to greet visitors and relax.

Throughout the summer, the President was trailed by reporters from big-city newspapers. Desperate to file stories every day, even when the news was thin, they promoted the charms of Western living to readers trapped in cities like Chicago, New

York and Washington, D.C., helping to feed a growing interest in the Black Hills. They snapped pictures as the innocent, gullible president fished mountain streams that had been stocked with corn-fed trout, and the press corps quickly spread the word that huge, hungry Black Hills trout jumped out of the water and onto hooks baited with corn. Dressed as a Hollywood cowboy and riding a horse, Coolidge was even adopted into the tribe by Lakota elders. In August, around the time that John Brockelsby announced to his family that they were moving to Rapid City, Coolidge attended the dedication of Mount Rushmore.

The dedication marked a turning point in the history of Rapid City and the Black Hills. Before a crowd of a thousand local boosters, the President set the monument firmly in the context of American 'manifest destiny,' guided by the "hand of the Almighty." Coolidge described Mount Rushmore as a "national shrine to which future generations will repair to declare their continuing allegiance to independence, to self-government, to freedom and economic justice."

Shortly thereafter, Gutzon Borglum's crew set their chisels to the rock. Within a couple of years, a hundred thousand tourists a year began visiting the faces as they emerged from the granite. In a foreshadowing of what was to come, most made the trek from Rapid City to the construction site by bus or automobile.

SETTLING IN TO CITY LIFE

Rapid City was not Chicago or New York, but the move changed the Brockelsby family's life just as dramatically as a move to a big city. John worked ten- and twelve-hour days, six days a week, at the Chevrolet dealership. He earned $200 a month managing the accounts as well as the service and sales departments. His salary restored the family to the ranks of the middle class. He purchased a small two-bedroom home on Quincy Street. When Emma gave birth to her third child, William, the Brockelsby home was crowded, but for the first time in a decade, the family was secure.

For the boy whose backyard paradise had been the badlands, the move to Rapid City did not go so smoothly. Earl felt like a country bumpkin. While other boys in school had made the transition to long pants, Earl was still in knickers, to his everlasting embarrassment. "Sissy clothes," his classmates joked. Earl was shy and self-conscious about his appearance. The more insecure he felt, the larger the mole on his cheek seemed to grow in the mirror. One day, in a fit of self-consciousness, he twisted the mole until it came off. The wound bled profusely and he rode his bicycle around town for hours waiting for the bleeding to stop before going home.

Earl earned above-average grades in school. He became a Boy Scout. He joined the debate team. By outward appearance, he was a conventional young man. He wrote a class essay in the seventh grade about "The Cause of Preventable Fires," in which he bemoaned the irresponsibility of careless citizens who refused to clean up their yards, heating pipes and stove flues. But inside, he was not as compliant and conventional as he appeared. Years later, he described himself in his youth as being in rebellion with "a fierce need to be independent from all of society."

In Rapid City, he gave free rein to the habits that were already starting to emerge in Kadoka but had been kept in check by the tight constraints of a small community. He skipped school so regularly that his principal called him into the office to say that he was giving up on Earl but was concerned that other boys had begun to follow his example. When Earl did come to school, he talked back to his teachers. When one teacher punished him by rapping his knuckles with a ruler, he stared back and smiled, even as his hands began to bleed. The only check on his behavior was a deep sentimentality that made him cringe when his resistance to authority made one of his female teachers cry. "I could stand the pain (of the ruler) but never the tears," he remembered.

The more rebellious he became, the more he turned in on himself. He built a secret fort in the backyard from old scraps of lumber. The only way into the fort was through a small window in the garage. "I had a craving desire to have a place of privacy," he said. "Any place that was just mine."

Inside his cave, he stored packs of cigarettes, his rifle, a pepperbox pistol and other assorted treasure that he scrounged from the back alleys of town. When he was satisfied with the cave's privacy, he turned his attention to a treehouse and carved his name in the highest branches he could reach in a silver poplar. Most of all, he channeled his anxious energy into long bicycle rides; west to Hangman's Hill and Dark Canyon and south to a makeshift village where poor Indians camped beside the city dump. Occasionally he found himself in street fights, but most often he quenched his need to explore by riding ever farther beyond the outskirts of town.

In Kadoka, Earl's experiences with Indians had been shaped by their dignity and their commitment to family and tradition. They were poor, but proud and self-reliant. But in the Indian camp, he discovered a tragically different way of life. Unmoored from traditional Lakota communities, the self-reliance and confidence were gone. Extended families of a dozen or more lived in flimsy canvas tents that blew apart in blizzards. There were no city services: no water, no electricity and no sewers. The small town intimacy of relations between whites and Lakotas that Earl had grown up with in Kadoka was breaking down.

"There was a sad sight at the city dump where Indians, many of them very old, could be seen picking through the trash, looking for bits of food that had been hauled from the restaurants and garbage cans in the city," he wrote. "Each Indian would use a stick to pick through the garbage, and on finding anything that could be considered even remotely eatable, would put a rotting potato, or whatever, into a sack and take it back to camp to eat. Some you would see nibbling on a lemon rind or discarded steak bone."

From Earl's perspective, children in the Indian camp almost never went to school. Their parents preferred to hold what was left of the family together in desperate poverty rather than lose the children to the city and its schools.

There were exceptions. One Lakota boy, Kenny Scissons, became one of Earl's best friends. Kenny was a year older than Earl, but otherwise the lives of the two boys were remarkably similar. Kenny was Sicangu Lakota, an enrolled member of the Rosebud Sioux Tribe. His grandfather had emigrated from England a decade before the first Brockelsby had left Lincolnshire. His grandmother Hannah was the twin sister of the Lakota warrior Little Big Man, who had ridden with Crazy Horse. John Scissons and Hannah Flesh had married at Fort Laramie, Wyoming, in 1860. In the early days of reservation life, they built a sprawling ranch and farm near Colome, South Dakota, east of the Rosebud reservation, where they became influential among both the Lakotas and homesteaders. Hannah's son, John Jr., married a solid Norwegian homestead woman, the same Carrie Peterson who had lived alone on a homestead south of Colome and waited out hailstorms by hiding under the belly of her horse.

Kenny was born into this proud, mixed-blood family in 1915. When the Depression struck rural South Dakota, the bank in Colome was shuttered and the family lost its farm. Kenny's parents moved to Rapid City where his father took a job in the local sawmill. "Our friends were Indians and whites," Kenny's oldest daughter remembered. "We didn't know the difference. We played with everybody. I never thought of being different."

Earl and Kenny played on the same junior high school basketball team and won the city seventh grade championship. Kenny was the star, while Earl was a silent, skinny benchwarmer. They competed for the attentions of the same blond, blue-eyed girl, though neither of them knew exactly what it meant to have a girlfriend. They marauded through town on their bicycles, huffing and puffing their way up the steep hill to Skyline Drive, then speeding down to the bottom, launching themselves off a small bump in the road and soaring head over heels into the yards of exasperated mothers, who gazed out their windows at the daredevils and warned their own young sons, "Never do that!" Over and over for many years, Kenny Scissons would return to Earl's life, and he remained a close friend until Kenny's early death in 1973.

In Kadoka, Earl had nurtured his entrepreneurial instinct within a narrow window of opportunity, but in Rapid City a 12-year-old boy had many other ways to make money. Earl hustled subscriptions to *The Literary Digest*. He scavenged for scrap metal in downtown alleys. He became the janitor in a small theater for 25 cents a day and the small change and half-full chewing tobacco tins he cleaned off the floor. When the theater burned down, he collected scraps of brass and copper that he could bundle and sell. He discovered an abandoned box of knife sharpeners in a back alley and went door to door selling them for a quarter each. He took a mail order course in illustration from the London School of Cartooning, and he began to collect stamps, not as a hobby, but as a potential source of profit. He spent hours studying the "missionary mixture" of stamps he received in his start-up collection, soaking the stamps off of the envelopes while he searched for the rare value stamp that never arrived.

Occasionally, Earl's zeal to make money crossed over the thin line between entrepreneurial drive and petty theft. In his search for metal that could be recycled, he discovered that families put the ashes from their coal stoves and furnaces in copper-bottom buckets and left them at the curb for the garbage truck. Earl became adept at dumping the ashes in the alleys and stomping the center of the bucket until the copper bottom could be pried loose. He stored his stash of copper plates in his cave behind the house until he had enough to sell to the Rapid City Hide and Fur Company for 15 cents a pound. "I guess that is the way I was really amoral," Earl concluded. "I was living a carefree happy thoughtless life."

The nation slipped into an unprecedented economic depression in 1929, when Earl was 13 years old, and it seemed like everyone was hustling to make ends meet. But the scramble for money also fueled a powerful longing for success. "Although I was timid and shy, another part of me made me aggressively competitive, and kept me busy looking for any way to make money," he wrote. "It seemed that when it came to earning money I could force myself to overcome my bashfulness."

HIGH SCHOOL IN SPEARFISH

In 1929, the federal bill to fund the construction of Mount Rushmore finally passed Congress. A year later, 2,000 people hiked and motored to the site of the monument to dedicate the face of George Washington. Despite the stagnation of the national economy, the federal commitment to Mount Rushmore held the promise that Rapid City might grow while the rest of the nation sank into depression. But John Brockelsby determined that his future lay to the north, in the college town of Spearfish, South Dakota. He formed a partnership with another automobile salesman and a local banker, and they took over the local Chevrolet dealership.

Spearfish was a sleepy town of 1,500 people set against the sheer cliffs and cascading waters of Spearfish Canyon. Frank Lloyd Wright visited the town in 1935 and declared the canyon's waterfalls and red rock canyon walls a spectacular "miracle" and hidden treasure. But for the most part, Spearfish was not a tourist destination. It was located 75 miles from the chisels and ruckus of Mount Rushmore. It served the gold mines in Lead and Deadwood and became a trading center for dozens of small ranching communities flung across the prairie for a hundred miles in every direction. The most important difference between Spearfish and the towns around it was the regional teachers college. While the nation foundered in the Depression, gold and education kept Spearfish alive.

In Spearfish, Earl renewed his participation in the Boy Scouts. He attended Presbyterian church socials. He continued to skip school when he lost interest, but he settled in as a good student. He took a modest role in the senior class play, "Miss Collegiate." As the anchor for the high school debate team, he overcame his shyness by partnering with his ever-loyal sidekick, Joe Garrett. In isolated, rural towns, high school debaters, "the silver tongued orators," drew on the deepest traditions of oratory in American history. They debated rival schools on issues of national importance with all the enthusiasm and community participation of Friday night football games.

There was one hobby that set Earl apart from his peers. He developed a fascination with snakes and collected a dozen hissing, slithering garters and bull snakes, bright blue racers and blunt-headed hognose. He kept them in boxes hidden underneath the front porch, which occasionally made for startled visitors, who knocked at the door only to hear a cacophony of hissing beneath their feet. For curious friends and neighbors, Earl would empty his boxes onto the front lawn. One day, he came home from school and discovered the boxes empty and the snakes disappeared. "I thought that someone had deliberately turned them loose," he wrote in his journals. "The truth, too terrible to think about, had happened. Yes, my mother had taken them all out and killed them."

The crowning achievement of Earl's high school years in Spearfish came in the summer of 1933 when the *Rapid City Journal* offered a free trip to the "Century of Progress" World's

Fair in Chicago to the newsboy who could sell the most subscriptions. Earl was a relentless competitor. When he fell behind other boys in the contest, he closed the gap by organizing his own sales network, recruiting neighborhood boys to solicit subscriptions door to door in his name for a cut of the profit from the sales. Earl didn't mind giving up the revenue. It was the trip to Chicago that he coveted.

On August 18, 1933, Earl and four other prizewinners boarded the Chicago and North Western train for a two-day trip to Chicago. They roomed at the glamorous Palmer House and reported their activities to *Journal* patrons. "In the afternoon we saw the Hearst gold cup races from the lagoon grandstand," young Earl wrote in one of his dispatches. He visited the Golden Temple of Jehol and the Japanese and Chinese pavilions. He was particularly impressed by the Chinese pavilion, "with its intoxicating incenses and fine hand-carved ivory" as well as "the Chinese acrobats whose stunts seem almost impossible." Even as a teenager, the boy from the badlands who had loved the travelling circus found himself drawn to the most exotic corners of the world.

Earl graduated from Spearfish High School in 1934, while the nation was still in the deepest trough of the Great Depression. Thanks to his father's success as an automobile salesman and accountant, he was able to start college at the South Dakota School of Mines in Rapid City. By his own description, he had no interest in engineering or mining, and made a concerted effort to enroll in every class that was not required of an engineer. Much of the curriculum at the college was based on badlands geology, but Earl's passion for the badlands was not scholarly. It was spiritual, aesthetic and commercial. He was less interested in the geology and paleontology of the wilderness, and more interested in roaming the draws and hillsides in search of geodes and fossils that he might sell to tourists as "Indian rattle rocks."

By the end of his first year, Earl knew he had had enough of college. He wasn't cut out for school, and he needed to get a job. The national economy was stagnant. The farm economy was worse. Many of the policies of the New Deal had not yet been put into action. National unemployment at the end of 1933 was at the highest level it had ever been, over 22 percent, and it did not decline throughout 1934.

In rural western states like South Dakota, where the farm economy had already been in a free fall for a decade, conditions were even worse. The Plains soils were adrift in dust storms. Farmers and ranchers took to describing the short grass prairie as "*no grass* country." Farm families with no industrial skills fled the land to live in small South Dakota cities. Once proud, independent, conservative families went on relief. "Nearly everyone was dependent on government projects and aid," one homesteader remembered. Those who were able moved west once more to California, Oregon and Washington. Unemployment figures were not scientific, but the best guess was that South Dakota's unemployment rate was close to 40 percent.

Earl took a job thinning and blocking sugar beets in Rapid Valley, seven miles east of the City. He worked with a Mexican immigrant whose relentless pace and work ethic put the young college boy to shame. He worked with hobos who labored just hard enough to make their wage. He innocently shared his food with the crew and quickly discovered that every dollar he earned was consumed by food bills. He found himself purchasing extravagant foods, like canned peaches, that the crew devoured as dessert. When he challenged the wild stories of a hobo, he found himself staring at a straight razor. "I was told that if I ever dared to call him a liar again, I would find my head neatly severed from my body."

Earl tended the rows of beets for 15 hours a day, bent over the kind of short-handled hoe that would be outlawed in the 1970s.

After two weeks on the job, his back ached, he could not stand straight and he crawled to his bed. His hands were blistered and swollen, and after the food bills were calculated and subtracted from his wage, he estimated that he had earned four cents an hour. Great Depression or not, he quit and took the job as a guide at The Hidden City that changed his life forever.

As ragged as the work conditions were at The Hidden City, Earl discovered that he loved talking to tourists. Even if he had trouble escaping his own small world, the tourists brought the outside world to him. The idea of a "family vacation" was still new, almost an abstraction, but Earl came to realize that he loved the engagement with other people and wanted to spend his life in the tourism business. When he recognized how fascinated his guests were with the rattlesnake under his hat, he knew just what kind of business he wanted to create. But to start a business, he needed cash.

SITTING BULL CRYSTAL CAVERNS

In August, the owners of Hidden City told Earl that they had not collected enough entry fees to pay his final month of wages. He accepted a sampling of fossils from the gift shop as partial payment and returned to the School of Mines for his sophomore year. By day, he attended classes without enthusiasm. By night, he made rock art, hundreds of pieces to sell to summer tourists: paperweights, ashtrays, bookends, flower pots and vases covered with rose quartz, purple and yellow lepidolite, and other native stones and minerals. Most of all, he plotted how he might make a fortune in tourism and retire at 30 to a life of adventure. He was a terrible student, by his own admission, but he was also a precocious intellectual who imagined that he might spend his wealth exploring the outer boundaries of human psychology and the paranormal.

While Earl was contemplating his future, the South Dakota tourism economy was beginning to feel a wind at its back. President Coolidge's summer vacation in the Black Hills had been the spark that ignited federal funding for Mount Rushmore, and by the mid-1930s, Borglum's chisels and dynamite blasts were hard at work on Abraham Lincoln's massive forehead.

In the summer of 1936, President Franklin Delano Roosevelt visited the Black Hills on an entirely different mission. He came west by train and open-topped automobile to survey the impact of drought on American agriculture. He visited farmers whose topsoil had eroded and blown away. He toured small towns that had been buried in dust storms and listened patiently to boosters who resented the suggestion that their region was dying. On August 29, he surveyed the progress of Mount Rushmore, and 3,000 people turned out to celebrate his dedication of the Jefferson bust. It was clear from both the dust-covered prairies and the images of the President grinning from the backseat of his sedan that the economic future of western South Dakota had shifted from agriculture to tourism.

By April 1936, Earl could not wait for the snow to melt and the temperature to rise. After a winter of hard work, he had created several hundred pieces of rock art. Rather than selling them wholesale to local businesses, he convinced Alex Duhamel to allow him to build a log cabin at the entrance to Sitting Bull Crystal Caverns where he could sell directly to tourists.

Duhamel was scion to one of the most important families in Rapid City. His father, Peter Duhamel, a French Canadian, had emigrated from Quebec Province to the United States in 1857. He spoke only French. Within a year, he was on the Dakota frontier. He navigated his way through the worst of the Indian Wars by studiously avoiding confrontation with Lakotas and showing a respectful deference to those he met. On more than one occasion, he survived by dumb luck. Over three decades, he built an open-range cattle empire. When the range was closed and fenced to homestead farms and small ranches, Duhamel sold out, moved to Rapid City and became a banker and a businessman.

The fate of the Duhamel family fortune had been tied to the boom and bust of the frontier since Peter first crossed the Missouri. He had built and lost his cattle empire several times. He founded the Pennington County Bank and made it into one of the most profitable banks in South Dakota, only to lose it in 1932 during the Depression. Each time, the family rebounded and redoubled its commitment to the community.

Peter's son, Alex, built a sprawling store on the corner of St. Joseph and Sixth Street where he sold hardware, clothing, furniture, general merchandise and tourist souvenirs. Outside his store on summer evenings, Lakotas would dance for the tourists. But the store was most renowned for its famous saddles. Tourists newly arrived at the gateway to the American West could gaze out the windows of the Hotel Alex Johnson and watch five, ten, sometimes even twenty saddle makers hard at work in the Duhamel storefront windows.

At the store, Alex Duhamel extended credit to local ranchers and farmers who were already underwater. When many of these borrowers failed to repay their loans, Duhamel himself sank deeper into debt. In the middle of the Depression, he owed $40,000 and carried a half million dollars in uncollectable debts.

It was Alex Duhamel's daughter-in-law, Helen, who saved the family empire. Tall and attractive, she towered over her husband Francis "Bud" Duhamel, both physically and by personality. Bud was gentle, soft-spoken and kind to a fault. By all accounts, he was a tremendous citizen of the community but a poor businessman. Helen was a ruthless, fierce competitor who abhorred debt and refused credit to even the most sympathetic customers. When she approached her father-in-law with a request to take over the family business, it was so deep in debt that most bankers believed it could not be salvaged. Five years later, by sheer force of will and a tight fist, Helen had pushed the company into the black.

In 1929, the Duhamel family purchased the land surrounding one of the most beautiful caves in the Black Hills, a complex of stalactite and stalagmite limestone that dripped calcite and dogtooth crystals. The cave had been formed before the Ice Age. Diamond Lake, a swimming-pool-sized pond of clear mineral water, lay 1,256 feet beneath the surface. The Duhamels named the cave after the Lakota warrior and medicine man, Sitting Bull, who, legend had it, camped at the entrance to the cave when he visited the Black Hills.

The location of the cave was perfect for tourism. It sat directly along Highway 16 from Rapid City to Mount Rushmore. At the entrance, the Duhamels erected an octagonal barn where they sponsored the region's most spirited summer attraction, the Sioux Indian Pageant. The nightly program, led by the Black Elk family, included Lakota dancing, songs and prayers set among the pines and tipis of a small Lakota campsite. Tourists were encouraged to join the Omaha Dance and roam among the tipis, where they could listen to "real Indians" describe the traditional nomadic life and ceremonies of the Plains. There was no denying the energy and spirit of the encampment, but the pageant bore all the contradictory qualities of kitsch and sincerity that was common to American Indian-themed tourism.

Next to the Sioux campsite, Earl built a log cabin and began to sell his rock art. As the summer days grew longer, and a steady stream of tourist families flowed past Spring Creek and over the hill to the Sioux Indian Pageant, Earl made his home among the eclectic community of Lakotas, tourism entrepreneurs and college students working summer jobs.

For the third time in his life, Earl was presented with the opportunity to develop intimate personal relationships with Lakotas. That was, in itself, rare. Generally, Lakotas lived on the reservations and moved within prescribed neighborhoods in Rapid City or small reservation border towns. Many whites in western South Dakota passed a lifetime without developing any Indian friendships. As a child, Earl had watched Lakota families shop at Bertha Martinsky's general store and powwow in the streets of Kadoka. These families were nameless, but in a child's eyes they left an impression of poverty wrapped in dignity and integrity.

When he moved to Rapid City as a teenager, Earl experienced Indian Camp on the south end of town. He was repelled by the squalor. These families seemed unable to adapt to modern life and hopeless to fend for themselves during the Depression. If the Lakota people from the reservation were dignified and honest, the families of Indian Camp left him with feelings of pathos and resignation. And yet, at the same time, he had developed a close friendship with Kenny Scissons where boyhood adventure and the common experience of public school transcended race and culture.

At the Sioux Indian Pageant, Earl met Indians who, like the white entrepreneurs at Hidden City and Keystone, were struggling to turn the emerging tourism economy of the region to their own advantage. His friendships allowed him to know Lakota people beyond the romantic image they showed to tourists.

Ben Black Elk was one of the most important of these friendships. The son of the famous Lakota medicine man Black Elk, Ben had been born in 1899. His father had fought with Crazy Horse, witnessed the massacre at Wounded Knee and later rode in Buffalo Bill's Wild West show. When Ben was in his early thirties, he helped his father collaborate with author John Neihardt to write the book *Black Elk Speaks*. Published in 1932, the book became a classic piece of American literature. Ben was a disciple of his father. At the Caverns and in travels throughout the United States and in Europe, he shared his insights into Lakota spirituality and culture. Black Elk was 16 years older than Earl, but from their encounters at Sitting Bull Caverns they formed a lifelong friendship.

THE PETRIFIED WOODS

Earl struggled to make a living and cobbled together jobs as he could find them. He sold his rock art and gave tours at the Caverns to feed himself. When he encountered a 30-inch rattlesnake near the pageant grounds he put it in a barrel and charged a quarter for tourists to look at it. True to his experiences at Hidden City, the tourists had more questions about Earl's snake than Lakota culture. Despite his best efforts, the rock shop at the Sioux village delivered only meager returns.

In early June, Earl found a new opportunity. A half-mile east of the Pageant, a roadside attraction offered tourists the opportunity to see and touch real petrified wood. Given the chance to lease the Petrified Woods and run the attraction as his own business, Earl recruited his high school debate partner Joe Garrett, and the two of them went to work. They cut down slender lodgepole pines and wrapped them in canvas to make a tipi where they could sell tickets. Godfrey Broken Rope painted a large sign for the entrance and smaller signs that could be nailed to fence posts along the road.

The Black Hills held many caches of petrified wood, but none were at the entrance to their new enterprise, so Earl and Joe gathered petrified wood from other locations and brought it to their new establishment, where they buried the pieces and encouraged tourists to borrow a shovel and dig up the ancient fossilized wood—an act of participation and engagement that made the experience more rugged and real.

Every morning, they drove to town at five a.m. and ran through the parking lots of local motels, plastering brightly colored, hand-written advertisements on the windshields of cars with out-of-state license plates. Then they scurried back to their tipi to await the tourists.

Earl and Joe charged a dime for children and a quarter for adults. They worked seven days a week, 15 hours a day, and they made $15 to $35 dollars a day in gate receipts. To make ends meet, they lived on pork and beans, cans of Franco-American Spaghetti and day-old bread. They were not getting rich, but it beat working the sugar beet fields.

Petrified Woods also gave Earl a venue to test his ideas about tourists and snakes. "Sometimes I stood next to the highway holding a rattlesnake, and one of the men would hold a camera and pretend to take my picture," Earl remembered years later. "Cars were going slowly up Spring Creek Hill and would often stop to see what kind of a snake I was holding. This would give an opportunity for another guide to step on the running board of the car, say a few words about the rattlesnake, and then make a 'pitch' to get the tourists to go through The Petrified Woods. Again, I was learning the ways of tourists and, most importantly, how much a rattlesnake could interest them."

The shy, reserved boy from Kadoka was becoming a showman. His public personality—the debate champion, the adventurer—came to the fore. When the Associated Press ran a funny story under the headline "Man Bites Dog," a *Rapid City Daily Journal* reporter telephoned Earl and asked to take a photo of Earl biting a rattlesnake. Earl jumped at the opportunity, and the postcard, sold to tourists under the title, "Man Bites Snake," became an instant classic.

THE WOOLWORTH'S SALESGIRL

As the summer of 1936 wound down, as Labor Day neared, as the last performances of the Sioux Indian Pageant approached, Earl and Joe decided to host an end-of-season party, complete with beer keg, Indian dances and a midnight tour of Sitting Bull

Crystal Caverns. They each resolved to ask a girl, but Earl had no girlfriend. He barely had women acquaintances. He hadn't had a date since he attended church sponsored socials in Spearfish, and those strictly chaperoned events hardly qualified as a real date. After much handwringing, Earl decided that he would invite a Woolworth's salesgirl whom he had met at a church social.

With small, bright eyes, a tentative smile and brown wavy hair that was sculpted around her open, round face, Maude Millicent Wagner caught Earl Brockelsby's attention. Raised on a farm near Lake Andes, South Dakota, until the drought forced her family to give up the land and move to the small town of Wood, she had grown up only 70 miles south and east of Kadoka, on the northern border of the Rosebud Indian Reservation, in the heart of traditional Sicangu Lakota country. At the height of the homestead movement, Wood had been a depot on the Chicago and North Western Railway line, but like so many villages on the rail line, the railroad was no help beyond the depot. Homesteaders walked and rode their wagons dozens of miles to get their mail and have a drink at the Bloody Bucket Saloon. Everyone in Wood was poor, especially the Indians.

Maude's father Charlie Wagner was a drayman who scratched out a living by unloading railroad cars and hauling the goods by wagon to outlying homesteads. Her mother supplemented the family income by washing other people's laundry and taking in boarders. At the same time, she had to care for her five children. Years later, Maude confessed to her children that she had only two dresses as a girl: "The one she wore, and one on a hook in the closet."

After graduating from Wood High School, Maude moved to Rapid City with her mother and sister. Hoping to earn enough money to support her family and save for college, she found a job as a salesgirl at the Woolworth's five-and-dime store on Main Street and began attending First Presbyterian Church. Between the job and church, Maude led an active social life. Woolworth's was one of the biggest retail chains in the country, and on Saturdays it was packed with locals and farm families who came to town to buy everything from clothes to toiletries. For a farm girl from Wood, the glamorous interiors and lighted displays in Woolworth's windows were symbols of prosperity and relief from the grinding poverty she had grown up with. It was not surprising that when she met the flamboyant and charismatic Earl Brockelsby, she said yes to Earl's invitation.

A SEASON OF DOUBT

When Earl first leased the Petrified Woods, the owner signed him to a four-month contract and promised that tourists would continue to arrive well past Labor Day. None did. The last week in August, business was robust. By the second week in September, days passed without a single paying customer. Local boosters understood all too well the consequences of winter. Winter could last five months or eight. No one could plan the first blizzard or the last. Winter came abrupt, destructive, final upon the landscape. In winter, no one tried to get in to South Dakota. South Dakotans tried to get out.

For the cluster of summer tourist businesses that had begun to spring up in Keystone and along the road to Mount Rushmore, winter was an existential threat. Borglum's drills went silent, and the unfinished granite faces had only their resolution to protect them from blowing snow and frigid nights. If they hadn't made enough money to last them through the winter, tourism operators had to look for other ways to earn a living and hope that they would save enough of their summer profits to reopen the next spring.

For Earl, and for the nation in 1936, the prospects were not good. After three years of New Deal programs, the American economy slipped back into stagnation. Across the country, unemployment began to rise again.

Earl considered returning to the School of Mines, but his heart was not in it. When he met the vice president of the college on the street one day, the professor bluntly discouraged him. Earl also realized that he was a "doer" and not a scholar. He was drawn to adventure more than an engineer's slide rule. What he needed to learn from books he could do by reading, and he was a voracious reader. Besides, in 1936, college was a luxury. Nonetheless, the vice president's lack of faith in his ability stung, and Earl shouldered a grudge that lasted for years.

As winter approached, Earl had no idea what he would do to make a living. He liked Maude, and the two had begun to spend more time together, but his childhood experiences had made him anxious about love, marriage and intimate relationships. Besides, without any money, he didn't feel he could offer Maude a future. Beyond marriage and domesticity, Earl fantasized about going to a city where the opportunities would match his ambitions.

With the tourist season winding down, Earl's small world suddenly became large when Jack Plumb and Bob Hall wheeled their new gray Dodge Phaeton into the parking lot of the Petrified Woods and asked for a place to sleep for the night. Joe and Earl took their guests to the Indian dances, and the four men talked late into the night. Hall and Plumb were older and more worldly than Joe and Earl. Both were married but cavalier about the wives they had left in Chicago and expected to never see again. They struck Earl as "likeable con men," but their profanity unnerved him. They encouraged Earl and Joe to make the trek to California with them, and by morning, the four had agreed to travel together.

Earl didn't know if he would ever come back to the Black Hills. He knew only that he wanted to escape winter and explore what was on the other side of the mountains. He put money into a group cache to cover the cost of food and gasoline, and kept his last few hundred dollars—his rock art earnings from the summer—in his pocket. He had learned a hard lesson from the bank failures in Kadoka. He kept his cash close.

Their first night on the road, the cache of shared funds mysteriously disappeared from Jack's bedroll. Earl pointed no fingers. He simply agreed to share his remaining money with the group, and they all agreed to reduce the food ration. For three days, they ate canned beans and slept on the ground. They swam in the Great Salt Lake and combed salt out of their hair and clothing for days. On the California border, they slept in irrigation ditches that flooded in the early morning. They rolled into the home of Bob Hall's parents in Alhambra, California, exhausted but excited about the possibility of beginning new lives and landing jobs in the "City of Angels."

Bob Hall's parents accepted the young Westerners with open arms. Much like Earl's father, Cary Hall had been a banker and accountant in Kentucky and Illinois. Middle-aged, handsome and patriarchal, he had suffered the collapse of his banks with stoic grace and moved west to start over, establishing a new career as a mid-level accountant for Paramount Pictures. After dinner, Cary and Eloise Hall would settle next to each other on the piano bench and sing for their guests.

The intimacy of the Hall family carved itself deeply into Earl's memory. "Here, for the first time in my life, I saw a husband and wife who truly loved each other and showed it in a dozen little ways every day," Earl wrote in his journal years later. "I had thought that I would never get married as my parents didn't get along and, as far as I could see, none of the parents of my friends showed any real love or affection for each other. Now I saw a couple who loved each other and were happily married. Perhaps some day I, too, would marry now that I knew that a marriage could work."

Bob's Aunt Phoebe lived with the Halls and took Earl under her wing. By night, she listened to Earl talk about his life, his dreams and his curious fascination with snakes and Black Hills tourism. Phoebe had never been to the Black Hills, but she was patient, curious and a good listener. Without ever saying she was giving advice, she slowly steered Earl to his own insights about what he wanted to do with his life.

By day, Earl and Joe pounded the streets of Southern California looking for work. They tried to sign on as merchant seamen on a freighter bound for Asia, but they missed the cut. They tried to land jobs at a new Studebaker automobile assembly plant, but the plant was not scheduled to open for six weeks. Soon they were flat out of money and reluctant to impose on the Halls for much longer.

Finally, Earl took a job as a glazer at the Vernon Pottery Works. He woke in the morning at four a.m., packed a sandwich that Eloise Hall had made the night before and hitchhiked 40 miles to work. More often than not, he arrived early. "My work didn't start until eight o'clock, but I would start so early to prevent myself from ever being late for my job."

Having a job and a wage was fulfilling, but the work itself was a nightmare. Wearing a gas mask and long rubber gloves, he sprayed toxic glazes onto an endless stream of production pottery. The job was tedious and dangerous. On his long hitchhikes home, he could not get snakes out of his mind, and he could not stop thinking about the difference between working in the gorgeous Black Hills and the toxic soup of industry. At a time when farm families were fleeing the Dust Bowl by the tens of thousands, heading west to the sun and opportunity of Southern California, Earl dreamed of going home.

With Aunt Phoebe encouraging him to follow his dream, Earl resolved to return to the Black Hills. In the weeks between his decision and actually leaving, he made a second fateful choice that would have a lasting impact on his life. With Joe, he hitchhiked to Tijuana, Mexico. In 1936, Tijuana was a sleepy fishing village of just over 16,000 that served weekend tourists and seamen from the U.S. Navy base at San Diego. In Tijuana, Earl wandered the tourist shops along Avenida Revolución, studying the quality of merchandise and the tastes of American tourists. But there was something else about Tijuana that stuck in Earl's subconscious. He loved the way that the desert chaparral hugged the coast. He fell in love with Baja California. This was his first time south of the border, but it would not be his last.

COMING HOME

Earl boarded a bus in Los Angeles with four dollars in his pocket. He arrived home bursting with ideas and resolved to spend the winter frantically making rockwork souvenirs to build inventory for the coming summer. Meanwhile, he worked odd jobs unloading boxcars. He lived cheap, and he rekindled his romance with Maude Wagner.

In the spring of 1937, the Rapid City business community was small. Almost all the families of importance had migrated from farms and ranches, and still kept a romantic attachment, if not an ownership tie, to the land. The Duhamel ranching empire was firmly entrenched on Sixth Street. Art Dahl was kingpin of a local banking group. Morris Adelstein, the son of Bertha Martinsky in Kadoka, had come home from World War I and launched a successful civil engineering company, building roads and bridges for the expanding automobile economy. Boyd Leedom, Earl's childhood friend from Kadoka, had gone to law school and become legal counsel to the Rapid City business community. John Knecht owned the local lumberyard and hardware store.

The first among equals boosting tourism in the Black Hills was Peter Norbeck's old friend, Paul Bellamy. Bellamy's family, like that of John Brockelsby, had migrated west from a small farm in Iowa that could not support three sons. Bellamy had worked with Peter Norbeck on the state cement plant in Rapid City and helped design the Iron Mountain Road through Custer State Park. He had built his Black Hills Transportation Company into a fleet of taxis, trucks and buses that met tourists at the train station and then took them on a guided tour around the Hills in open-top luxury. He had hosted both President Coolidge and President Roosevelt on their trips to the Black Hills. He had written popular pamphlets on the importance of tourism for the local economy. Bellamy was a generation older, but when Earl came to him with an idea for a new business, the older man listened.

THE SHOWMAN AND THE TOURIST

— Chapter 4 —

At the ceramics factory in Los Angeles and in late night conversations with Aunt Phoebe, Earl had spent hours thinking about the business he might start in the Black Hills. He remembered the fascination and fear in the eyes of tourists at Hidden City who had stared at the rattlesnake coiled on his head. He thought about the way they leaned out of the car window to watch as he handled a rattlesnake at the side of the road beside the Petrified Woods. Gradually, he began to formulate a plan.

Earl envisioned a reptile zoo with rattlesnakes as the main attraction. He would call it Reptile Gardens. By trapping hundreds of rattlesnakes in their badlands dens, he could collect enough rattlesnakes to put on a spectacular show. From all of his experiences at Hidden City and Petrified Woods, he knew that tourists were fascinated by snakes; repelled, yes, but drawn by some powerful force so deeply hardwired that it overwhelmed their fear. If tourists could be enthralled by watching one rattlesnake, they would be spellbound by a hundred or two hundred.

Earl gathered a group of friends who were like him—young, energetic and hopelessly naive about business (and about snakes). They had no families, mortgages or history of failure, but they had the ability to trade their labor for credit. These friends included Joe Garrett, who returned from Los Angeles in February; Maude Wagner's brother Gerald and Marvin Basham, who had spent the summer of '36 guiding tourists at the Petrified Woods. "We became four partners in a new enterprise with not a dollar to spare between us and no idea of a location for The Great New Reptile Gardens," Earl later wrote.

He searched the southern edges of Rapid City for a location along the route to Mount Rushmore. Long before Peter Norbeck had ever imagined Custer State Park, tourists, ranchers and hunters had used Highway 79 to enter the Black Hills from the east. The road traveled south across the prairie, following the route of the railroad from Rapid City to Buffalo Gap and on to Hot Springs. Side roads followed creeks and valleys up into the forests. From Highway 79, adventurous tourists could take Peter Norbeck's breathtakingly beautiful Iron Mountain Road deep into the Hills. It had taken Norbeck three years and tons of dynamite to blast the narrow switchbacks and tunnels of the Iron Mountain Road. The road itself was a piece of grand sculpture to match Mount Rushmore. It was slow and treacherous but an aesthetic masterpiece.

As Rapid City grew and the pace of Borglum's crews quickened, most tourists in the late 1930s chose U.S. Highway 16, which traveled south from Rapid City through Keystone and offered the route of least resistance to Mount Rushmore. Increasingly, Highway 16 was dotted with secondary tourist attractions aiming to capture the passing automobile traffic, including the Sioux Indian Pageant, Sitting Bull Crystal Caverns and the Petrified Woods. Earl believed that Highway 16 would eventually become the main tourist route into the Black Hills.

From downtown Rapid City, Highway 16 ascended for almost three straight miles over Rockerville Hill. At the top of the hill, the view of endless prairie to the east and mountains to the west was spectacular, but the grade was a nightmare for automobiles. Tourists invariably stopped at the top of the hill to cool their engines and admire the views. That's where cars would naturally slow enough to allow Earl to pull a rattlesnake from under his hat. That's where guides could jump on the slow-moving running boards and make their pitch. That's where Earl wanted to build his new Reptile Gardens.

Eugene Raymond owned 360 acres of land on top of Rockerville Hill, including a three-story lookout tower with a small telescope. Raymond charged tourists ten cents to climb the tower and use the telescope. When Earl approached him about purchasing a few acres for Reptile Gardens, Raymond made a counteroffer: lease 12 acres of land, including the lookout tower, and pay a rent of $300 for the season. Without a dime in his pocket, Earl agreed to the lease and the promise to pay in July.

With Maude at his side quietly working on rock art inventory, Earl spent his nights designing every detail of the small building he planned to construct with his own hands. He thought about the carpentry and how to stucco the exterior. He had a plan to use rock art as accents in the flowerboxes. He thought about how to place the snake cages so that they could be easily cleaned but safe for tourists. After he had worked through every detail, he went to John Knecht at the lumberyard.

"I explained that I had no money and that he would have to trust me to pay him by autumn when the tourist season ended," Earl remembered. Knecht loaned the young entrepreneur $150 of construction pine on a handshake.

Earl was now $450 into his project. To raise cash, he turned to his father. By 1937, John Brockelsby had become the mayor of Spearfish. His investment in the car dealership had paid off.

With his intimate knowledge of the increasing importance of the automobile, he should have seen the opportunity that Earl envisioned. But he didn't.

John ridiculed the idea of a reptile park. "He told me that he thought my idea was crazy and no one would pay to see snakes," Earl wrote. "Having gone broke twice in his life when he had worked in two different banks…he was forever after very conservative and cautious." Unwilling to invest his own money, John suggested that Earl visit Roy Dean and Art Dahl at the Rapid City National Bank. "Banks are where you get money—that's what they are for," he bluntly told his son.

"With knees shaking, I visited [Roy Dean] at the bank …. He wanted to know what I had for collateral." Earl was stuck. "I had nothing, of course." Dean was not encouraging, but Earl returned to the bank three times, each time facing the cold stares of Dean and Art Dahl. Eventually he wore the bankers down. They offered him a $400 loan without collateral "based on the fine reputation of my father." John Brockelsby may have believed his son was embarking on a wild adventure, but he faithfully and quietly cosigned the note.

Earl was not as naive as the bankers undoubtedly imagined. He had known all along that he needed at least $600 to finish building Reptile Gardens and get the business underway. He settled on the $400 offer from the bankers and resolved not to press the issue until he had spent the first $400. He also guessed that with construction partially completed, the bank would have a hard time turning down a request for another $200 to finish the job and open the doors.

For years, Earl felt guilty about blackmailing his elders, but he had learned how to game the system. His approach may even have annoyed Dean and Dahl, but banking leaders had long since cast their lot with the tourism economy, and that meant backing a lot of crazy ideas, including a "snake farm."

Back in the 1920s, when Gutzon Borglum and the boosters of Mount Rushmore were unable to raise money to begin the carving, Doane Robinson had turned, in desperation, to the Rapid City business community. Like many local residents, leaders in the business community had been ambivalent about carving up the Black Hills. Some believed that the Hills were sublime in their natural state. Some thought that Borglum would never be able to raise enough money to complete his project and would leave an ugly pile of granite tailings in his wake.

When the federal government agreed to underwrite the project, everything changed. Borglum's progress also calmed local nerves. As Robinson pointed out, the bankers in Rapid City were "hard boiled business men who have their eye only for the material side of it." Nearly three decades after Peter Norbeck's Cadillac journey across the state over wagon routes and rutted trails, the carving of Mount Rushmore, combined with the growing popularity of the automobile, promised to turn his dream into reality.

OPPORTUNITY AND THE AUTOMOBILE

Even before the first Model T rolled off of Henry Ford's assembly line, the nascent tourism industry in the Black Hills benefitted from a national effort to promote travel by car. The automobile industry sponsored cross-country races and caravans and marketed photographs of daring pioneers stuck in river mud or navigating narrow mountain passes. As reliability improved and the cost of ownership plummeted, middle-class families rushed to buy automobiles. By 1930, there were nearly 23 million cars registered in the United States. Seizing this opportunity, oil companies formed tourism councils that appropriated the "See America First" slogan of the railroads to promote automobile tourism, suggesting that the car offered greater adventure and a more intimate encounter with "real Americans" and landscape.

By the 1920s, these messages and the growing popularity of the automobile had led to a dramatic shift in travel patterns. In 1916, railroads still carried the majority of tourists to Yellowstone and other national parks. By 1926, automobiles accounted for more than three out of four of the park's nearly 182,000 visitors. Ten years later, as Earl Brockelsby coaxed tourists into the Petrified Woods, cars brought 409,471 tourists to Yellowstone, while the railroad accounted for only 19,472.

Along the route to Yellowstone and across the country, the automobile transformed the tourism industry. In the nineteenth century, most tourists were relatively affluent. They traveled by rail to spas and resorts where they tended to stay for weeks in luxury hotels. With the advent of the automobile, middle-class Americans took to the road, creating a market for a host of new businesses that catered to their pocketbooks, including auto camps, motor courts, motels and diners as well as new roadside attractions like Hidden City, Sitting Bull Crystal Caverns and the Petrified Woods.

Local business leaders in the Black Hills leveraged these national trends. By 1937, the business and banking leaders of Rapid City had recognized the opportunity on the horizon and were committed to the development of a tourism economy. Through automobile dealerships, road and bridge construction, and their own tourist attractions and services, they supported businesses that would complement the Rushmore experience. To help entrepreneurs like Earl, the Rapid City Chamber of Commerce hosted seminars for small business owners about how to market their attractions.

Paul Bellamy, whose luxury open-topped tour buses carried many of the tourists to Mount Rushmore, wrote a series of booklets promoting the wonders of a Black Hills vacation. The booklets were sponsored by an association of local chambers of commerce, but advertising by oil companies paid for the printing. "Enjoy a new, entirely different kind of vacation," one full-page Standard Oil advertisement promised in 1937. "With your car at hand you are free to go when and where you will. Fine, skillfully engineered highways traverse the hills, luring you on to mild adventures and pleasant surprises."

The booklets were packed with photographs: former President Calvin Coolidge smiled holding a trout; a band of Lakota dancers appeared under the headline "See the Big War Dance." The booklets promised "700 miles of trout streams and pine and spruce forests a half century from primeval" and plenty of activities for a complete family vacation, such as "Gold Discovery Days Pageant and Rodeo," which, they said, "Depicts With Vivid Reality the Indian Legend of the Creation of the World."

The very week that Earl and his partners began hammering away on construction of the new building, Paul Bellamy hosted a meeting of community leaders with the Denver manager of the Conoco Travel Bureau to discuss the future of tourism in the Black Hills. The *Rapid City Daily Journal* reported that the Conoco agent "predicted that within the next 10 or 15 years 'tourism' will be the United States' number one industry, and likewise the greatest in South Dakota."

The agent described the United States as a "traveling nation." He promised that "more leisure time is going to result in more travel and that within six or seven years, every family in the United States will have a car and will travel." Setting his conclusion squarely in the language of agriculture that local businessmen and bankers understood, the agent told the assembly, "The Black Hills must have a vision and be prepared to reap its share of the increased travel harvest."

OPENING THE GARDENS

Tourism got a boost in early June 1937 when highway workers finished laying an oil surface on Highway 16 "almost all the way across South Dakota." The *Journal* enthusiastically reported that the highway improvements had "put South Dakota back on the maps of automobile associations who are now sending thousands of tourists through the state instead of around as formerly."

Tourists began to arrive in mid-May even though Reptile Gardens was not yet open for business. One can imagine the frantic group of young men, along with Maude Wagner and Earl's teenage sister, Reta Mae, pounding hammers and plastering walls as the first tourists wheeled into the parking lot. For two weeks, the workers scrambled up and down their ladders to share with early tourists the attraction that was almost ready. "Come back in a week!" they might have shouted as they watched automobiles turn south out of the parking lot and head toward Mount Rushmore. It was not the nature of tourism in the Black Hills to come back in a week. A week was a lifetime, and almost all the tourists were on their way somewhere else. Earl learned the hard lesson that every tourism business in the Hills had to learn: be ready to open on May 15, or lose revenue.

Eight days after Earl's 21st birthday, on May 19, 1937, the crew sold several colored postcards for 30 cents. On the 24th, Reta Mae began giving tours at the lookout tower. Earl kept a precise ledger of his expenses and revenue. As tourists clambered up the steps and gazed east for 50 miles, revenues rose to one dollar on the 25th, then fell to 70 cents on the 26th and then 50 cents on the 27th. On the 1st of June, receipts spiked to $1.60.

Waiting for construction to be completed on Reptile Gardens, Earl made money by selling his rock art. He wholesaled his surplus to a dozen tourist shops throughout the Black Hills, but he kept the best pieces that he and Maude created to sell at the Gardens. Tourists wanted to return home with something practical to remember their trip. They couldn't pack a rattlesnake into the trunk of the car, but in an era when millions of Americans smoked, a souvenir ashtray adorned with sparkling quartz, a vase with polished rock trim, or polished agates represented real memories that could be shared with friends. By the time Reptile Gardens opened for its first tour on June 3, Earl had pocketed $35 from rock art sales, and the summer had not even begun. On opening day, Earl collected $3.85 in admissions fees and sold $8.35 worth of rock art. Meanwhile, Reta Mae earned $3.10 at the Tower. They sold pictures and postcards worth $3.35. All told, the day's gross receipts amounted to $18.65.

Almost immediately, Earl's project faced the hurdles of South Dakota weather. High winds ignited a wildfire near Deadwood only days before Reptile Gardens opened. A thousand men rushed to fight the flames that rampaged through the dry timber. Although the fire was 50 miles from the Gardens, smoke colored the sunsets bright orange and gave an otherworldly quality to the Hills. As news spread, tourists stayed home or simply drove past the Black Hills. Fortunately, rain came on May 20. The *Rapid City Journal* reported "Heaviest Rain Fall Since '35 Received in Rapid City." Over the next two weeks, to the delight of firefighters and farmers, the rains continued and by early June the newspaper declared that the drought was broken. For farmers, the rain foreshadowed good profits, but it was bad news for the tourist economy. In early June, rain turned to snow, and the Black Hills were blanketed in white. For two days, Earl recorded no revenues for Reptile Gardens.

Despite this adversity, Earl and his partners were hardly discouraged. When the sun came out, receipts shot back up. On July 5, with tourist families swarming the Hills, Reptile Gardens hauled in the largest gate of the summer—$75.90 in a single day.

As the money flowed in, Earl made payments on his loan from the bank. By July 29, he had paid back the entire balance and converted hard work into credit. In the coming years, this credit would prove a powerful asset.

BUYING SNAKES

As scrupulously as he kept track of his revenues, Earl also recorded his expenses. Every nickel and dime that he spent on building supplies was dutifully noted. Every bag of groceries for the crew and every gallon of gasoline was entered in the ledger, along with every dollar spent on iguanas, turtles, mice, toads and snakes.

Each day, the crew force-fed dozens of snakes a mixture of hamburger, eggs and cod-liver oil, using a rubber hose attached to a grease gun. It was a two-man job. One man would catch and hold the snake just behind the head, while the other inserted the feeding tube and operated the grease gun. The routine was tedious and demanded exact discipline. But even with the personal attention of the staff and force-feeding, most of the snakes died before the summer was over.

Ironically, while Earl and his crew were struggling to keep rattlesnakes alive, the State of South Dakota had begun "the greatest slaughter of rattlesnakes in the history of the United States." The general in charge of this campaign was 53-year-old Albert M. Jackley. Around the time that Earl Brockelsby was born, two children that Jackley knew had died of rattlesnake bites. Jackley resolved to do what he could to eradicate these vipers. He spent more than 30 years learning to locate rattlesnake dens and perfecting ways to pour gasoline into crevices in rocks and kill the snakes as they slithered into sunlight. In 1937, he convinced the South Dakota Legislature to hire him as a fulltime exterminator, becoming the only official state rattlesnake killer in the country.

Jackley's efforts were encouraged and aided by farmers and ranchers in western South Dakota who killed rattlesnakes on sight, but every once in a while, a farmer or rancher caught a snake and carried it to Reptile Gardens in a box or flour sack. Local boys also trapped them behind their homes and brought them to Earl as a testament to their bravery. Earl accepted and occasionally paid for these specimens. In 1937, he recorded spending $275 for these catches.

Earl soon realized that these purchases wouldn't begin to meet the Gardens' need for specimens. Prairie rattlesnakes were small and shy and never reached the intimidating six- and seven-foot lengths of eastern diamondback rattlers, with girths thicker than a man's bicep. Prairie rattlesnakes packed a venomous punch, but they did not look the part. As Earl developed his showmanship and pushed the boundaries of snake handling to thrill the tourists, he began to look for opportunities to bring truly dangerous, lethal snakes to the Gardens.

To find exotic snakes—like Amazonian anacondas, Indian cobras or exuberantly colored rainforest coral snakes, Earl turned to *Billboard* magazine. Founded in 1894 as a trade publication for what was then called the "bill-posting industry," *Billboard* had repositioned itself in 1900 as "The Official Organ of the Great Out-Door Amusement World." Its articles focused on fairs, carnivals, circuses, game parks, vaudeville and burlesque shows, including big names like Ringling Bros. and Barnum & Bailey Circus and Buffalo Bill. The classified advertisements in the back included a section titled "Freaks to Order," as well as suppliers for exotic animals. As the recording industry for sound and motion pictures developed in the 1910s and 1920s, the magazine added coverage of music and the movies to its pages. But in the late 1930s, when Earl Brockelsby began combing the classified advertisements for exotic reptiles, the world of the sideshow was still a major element of *Billboard*.

The pages of *Billboard* took Earl back to the world of circus sideshows that he had loved as a boy and introduced him to the subculture of zoos and animal attractions. Everyone from Raymond Ditmars at the New York Zoological Society to Frank Buck and "Kafoozelum, The Snake Eater" competed in the market for exotic snakes. Sometimes the dealers were as exotic as the snakes.

One of the first dealers that Earl bought snakes from was a short Jewish man from New York who had moved to Texas and called himself the Snake King. "He wore an enormous cowboy hat," Earl remembered, "and with his tiny body he looked like a mushroom."

In the *Billboard* ads, no one bought one snake at a time. Snakes were bought and sold by the pound. Earl could buy ten six- or seven-foot diamondbacks from the "Snake King" for two dollars a pound. Smaller, lower quality snakes from a roundup in Texas or Oklahoma might fetch only 85 cents a pound.

In later years, Earl placed weekly orders to stay one step ahead of the high mortality rates. Even the most poisonous snakes were shipped in old flour sacks inside wooden boxes, and no one could guarantee what the customer would find when they opened the sacks.

"Railway Express charged us three times first-class rates for shipping charges on live snakes," Earl remembered. "In hot weather, the snakes would die the first day they started out on the train. They would quickly turn to liquid, and the odor was the most rotten smell that one could imagine."

The Snake King had even improved on nature to offer his most exotic snake: "the horned rattler." He would take an average prairie rattlesnake, cut tiny slits on top of the snake's head with a razor and slip rooster spurs under the skin. After a few days of healing, the Snake King could turn a dollar snake into a five-dollar exotic rattler that no other snake hunter could ever find.

The competition between snake brokers was ferocious, and as Reptile Gardens grew, Earl developed close relationships with several Mexican snake dealers. Jesus Figueroa lived in Colima, a thousand miles south of El Paso. It was not illegal in the 1930s to import snakes into the United States, but it was against Mexican law to export snakes. Figueroa would ride the bus to the border with his bags of snakes, proclaiming to the bus drivers that he was carrying chickens. On several occasions, when the chickens started to rattle, he would be thrown off the bus in the middle of the Mexican desert. At the nearest village, he would wipe the rattles with a thick coating of lard to muffle the sound and be on his way. On the Mexican side of the border, Jesus would hand his cargo off to an American friend who worked in the Reptile House at the El Paso Zoo. The American would then drive the snake boxes across the border in the backseat of his car, waving casually to American Customs.

All of these efforts ensured that Reptiles Gardens had a sufficient supply of writhing, hissing and rattling snakes to keep the families from Minnesota, Wisconsin and Illinois mesmerized with the ancient and primal fear of the serpent.

CAMARADERIE

For Earl and his partners and employees, Reptile Gardens was not just a place to work. It was *the* place to be young and independent in Rapid City in 1937. Earl played Peter Pan to a host of Lost Boys—a tightly knit community of young adults adrift in the Depression who lived, ate and worked together seven days a week for a dollar a day, room and board.

Earl was boss, but there was little hierarchy. When they were too exhausted to go back down the hill to their own homes, they slept on the ground. Ever loyal Reta Mae cooked lunch and dinner and bore the brunt of "kid sister" pranks. The Gardens became a subculture unto itself, staffed by dreamers and risk-takers, adventurers and shade-tree philosophers. The days were thick with flirtation. By the end of the summer, Earl and Maude were a steady couple. Reta Mae and Maude's brother Gerald had also kindled a romance, and more than one young woman tourist spent the rest of her summer writing love letters to the guide she had met at the Gardens.

No one doubted Earl's affinity for life's slithering, cursed reptiles, but neither Earl nor his crew had any training or any formal knowledge about how to handle snakes. They purchased a copy of Raymond Ditmars's *Reptiles of the World* to inform their presentations, but their idea of fun was to poke walking sticks in snake holes in the badlands and see what hissed. If someone was bitten, they used razors to cut an X across the fang marks, and sucked the venom from the wound, but they had no formal medical training and no idea how to handle a tourist who might be bitten.

One day, Gerry Wagner was giving a tour when a woman squatted low to the ground to peer inside one of the snake pits. Wagner noticed a slight motion beneath her skirt: a coiled rattlesnake. He casually began to walk to the next pit, and the lady followed, unaware of what she had just missed. The story became part of the folklore of the first year. Who would have volunteered to take a knife to a female tourist and suction the venom from her naked rump?

As the weeks passed, the guides began to compete. Who could be more daring in their handling of the snakes? They held the snakes at mid-body and let them writhe around their arms. They let the snakes crawl inside their shirts. Gerry was among the most daring when he started letting small copperheads crawl inside the cavity of his mouth and out again.

The more comfortable the Reptile Gardens crew became, the more complacent they were. One day when the men were grabbing snakes to feed them, Gerry Wagner lost his grip and was bitten on the finger. Earl used a razor to cut an incision in the fang marks and wrapped a tourniquet around his arm. Gerry lay down and let his blood drain into a dishpan of warm water, but by night his arm was black to the shoulder. "His hand was so swollen that it looked like the skin would burst," Earl remembered. "His palm was about six inches thick, and when I made an incision, I could cut in a half-inch deep and all that would come out was a little blood as thick as Jell-O. The pain was terrible—Gerry prayed that he could die."

Through the whole experience, Gerry refused to go to the hospital. Reta Mae feared he wouldn't make it. For two weeks, she and Maude cared for him. Finally, he was able to get out of bed and come down the hill to town.

After such an experience, other men might have considered abandoning the whole concept of the Gardens or at least taking much greater precautions. For Earl, the lesson was much simpler: keep a supply of morphine on hand at all times and never hire a guide who was more interested in showing off than staying alive.

END OF THE SEASON

Economically, the first season at Reptile Gardens was a rollercoaster. Tourists from the east loved the death-defying snake handlers but grumbled about the primitive outhouses. Earl encouraged his staff, over and over, to emphasize service. Treat the tourists to a great experience, he implored the staff, and they would come back. Better yet, they would tell their friends.

In the second half of the 1937 season, gate receipts routinely surpassed $25 a day. But after Labor Day, receipts plunged to six dollars a day. Nevertheless, as the first season came to a close, Earl felt he had proven something to the local cynics who snickered about the "snake farm" south of town. Reptile Gardens had been a hit.

Most important, the future seemed full of promise. After the tourist season ended and the last families headed home to start school somewhere in the east, nearly 5,000 people, most of them local, traveled Highway 16 to witness the dedication of Abraham Lincoln's face at Mount Rushmore. This tangible sign of continued progress provided financiers and dreamers with good reason to hope that the Black Hills would draw more and more summer vacationers to the region. A few days later, at the end of September, Earl shuttered the windows, tilled the flowers into the soil and shut down for winter.

SUCCESS

In each of its first five years, Reptile Gardens grew, drafting its success off of the increased traffic to Mount Rushmore. When the opportunity arose, Earl tried new venues. He took his show on the road to the annual 4th of July Belle Fourche Roundup, which was 55 miles north of Rapid City. Godfrey Broken Rope painted a large canvas sign, "Den of Death," and for four days the snake boys tempted fate by free-handling the snakes, tossing them to one another and storing them casually in bags at night. The crew netted $60 from the "Den of Death," five percent of their seasonal profit. With the capital debt paid off in 1937 and the Gardens' reputation spreading, profit margins rose. The summer season of 1938 netted the partners $1,132 ($19,258 in 2015 dollars).

After two years, this kind of success didn't look like it would make anyone rich or even cover the cost of living through the long winter. Earl closed the Gardens in September, and he and the crew faced the grim chore of finding winter work. Gerry Wagner and Marvin Basham threw in the towel. Wagner took a job with a travelling carnival. Basham went to work for the Coast to Coast hardware store for $12.50 a week. In later years, Earl swore that he "bought out" his two partners. Wagner and Basham remembered differently. They never received a dime and probably never expected to. Despite two seasons in the black, Reptile Gardens simply wasn't worth anything yet.

Earl dropped out of the School of Mines and went back to making rock art. He also took a job selling automobiles for the local Oldsmobile-Cadillac-LaSalle dealership. He was a top-notch salesman, but he had gotten used to being his own boss. He grated against the hierarchy of the dealership and quit after a few months.

It was in the winter months that Earl's obsession with entrepreneurial gambles began to reveal itself. Sometimes it seemed that there was no get-rich-quick scheme he wouldn't try. When he discovered an advertisement for a new popcorn machine in the back of *Billboard*, he hopped a train to Chicago. With no capital to speak of, he ordered 100 units at a cost $12,000. When he went to the bank, Roy Dean turned him down flat. The bank had no interest in untested popcorn machines that did nothing to build the regional tourism economy. Earl regrouped and bought one machine rather than 100. He placed it in the Seventh Avenue Bar in downtown Rapid City and dubbed himself "The Popcorn King of the Middle West."

The sparkling white enamel popcorn machine with a glass front stood just under six feet tall. Insert a dime, and the popcorn popped in hot oil before your eyes, bag after bag of uniform, hot, buttery perfection. There was only one problem. The hot oil caked the machinery with a thick varnish. Twice a day, Earl had to break the machine down, scrub the parts and put it back together. His patience soon wore thin. He sold the machine to the bar owner for a $50 profit and moved on without the slightest reflection on what might have happened if he had actually purchased 100 machines.

Nothing seemed to shake his certainty that the next sure thing was just around the corner. Given his entrepreneurial nature, he knew he would continue to bet on new ideas at the margin, but increasingly he realized he was going to place his biggest bet on Reptile Gardens.

For the 1939 tourist season, Earl expanded the staff to ten. He set up a small zoo that included coyotes, eagles and a big black bear that posed for cameras drinking a bottle of soda pop. He bought old broken-down cars and parked them in the parking lot to make the Gardens look busy. He made small cardboard bumper stickers that could be tied with string to the front bumpers of visitors' automobiles.

He saved money and heightened the exotic character of the Gardens by cooking the meat of rattlesnakes and snapping turtles that died on the job for staff dinners. The snakes "tasted like tough chicken," according to Earl, but the turtles were delicious. "It was a tough job cutting up a big snapper, but worth the effort. We would also remove the heart, place it in a drinking glass of water and watch it beat for twenty-four hours. The favorite of all reptile eatables was snake liver; all snakes have a large liver and it tastes like velvet feels."

THE TRIUMPH OF MOUNT RUSHMORE

By the summer of 1939, Gutzon Borglum had been working on Mount Rushmore for close to 15 years, and with the dedication of Theodore Roosevelt's spectacled bust in July, the project was finally near completion. From the beginning, Borglum had imagined his sculpture as a monument to the nation's 'manifest destiny.' He bristled at the less-than-sublime culture of tourism that developed along the road leading to the mountain. In fact, the tension between Borglum and the local business community was palpable.

Historian John Taliaferro describes the unraveling of Borglum's relationship with local boosters in his definitive history of the Mount Rushmore project. "He was building the new Acropolis, not a Coney Island spectacle."

Borglum warned local boosters, "'I did not and don't intend that [Rushmore] shall be just a big thing, a three days' tourist wonder," and he accused these "nickel chasers" of conspiring to "degrade the standards of what I am doing...and cover the hills with hot dog stands.'"

To the architect Frank Lloyd Wright, who was no shrinking ego himself, Borglum complained, "[E]ighty percent of the [Black Hills] population, including their best, belong to the unburied dead, and that part of them that is alive...is concerned only with the most ordinary of material things.... My biggest fight in the Black Hills has not been with the granite, but [with] the stupid people."

Despite Borglum's outsized ego, his openly racist admiration of the Ku Klux Klan, his authoritarian condescension to anyone who challenged him and his open disdain for South Dakotans, the spectacle of his accomplishment tamed all envy and resentment. On July 2, thousands of people came to the mountain to dedicate the face of Theodore Roosevelt. The celebration overlapped with the 50th anniversary of South Dakota statehood. "Bud" Duhamel presided and the Choir of 100 sang the lyrics of Irving Berlin's new patriotic anthem, "God Bless America." Chief Red Cloud and Chief Standing Bear performed with a delegation of Lakotas from the Sioux Indian Pageant. Borglum's speech reflected his vision and his values. In his mind, his service to his generation was to "divine accurately what lies at the heart and soul of my race and record as nearly as possible the truth of our race's sacred and secret dreaming."

Speaking for South Dakotans, Governor Harlan Bushfield used the opportunity to champion the "epic achievements of South Dakota's pioneers." He told the throng of approving citizens that South Dakota's early gold miners and homesteaders "neither asked nor expected help." He then proceeded to attack his political critics, New Dealers, who had described South

Dakota as a "dust bowl state." The entire event was broadcast over CBS radio.

Where was Earl during this epic gathering? Where was the crew from Reptile Gardens? Did they grasp the magnitude of what was being created at Mount Rushmore? Did they reflect on the relationship between the monument and their snake garden? Earl left no record of whether he attended the celebration and dedication. In fact, there had been five huge gatherings at Mount Rushmore to mark its development, but Earl—who left extensive, detailed and eloquent journal entries about the badlands and snakes, the Sioux Indian Pageant and his own personal development—did not record a single comment about the significance of Mount Rushmore or its impact on Reptile Gardens and the regional economy.

Nonetheless, there is a hint. On July 3, the *Rapid City Daily Journal* covered the dedication of Roosevelt's face with a sprawling banner headline on the front page: "12,000 Attend Fete at Rushmore." The story was so long that it jumped to page eight. Next to a report on Governor Bushfield's speech, a brief three-inch human interest story ran under the headline, "Local Men Gulp Live Goldfish."

Goldfish swallowing had become a national fad in the spring, when a Harvard College student, running for freshman class president, swallowed a goldfish on a dare from his friends. The fad swept the nation's campuses and arrived in Rapid City on July 2. According to the *Journal*, "Earl Brockelsby and [G]erry Wagner happened to stop and admire the goldfish at the Ben Franklin store." The assistant store manager dared the two to swallow a goldfish. Brockelsby "reached in, selected one of the fattest of the tails, and gulped it down. Not to be outdone, Wagner also dipped out a goldfish and followed suit, to the amazement of [the manager] and several onlookers. After dashing out to a drugstore for a 'coke,' both goldfish gulpers agreed that, after all, there were a great many other delicacies they liked better."

Despite Earl's apparent indifference to the celebrations at Mount Rushmore, he was surrounded by reminders that Reptile Gardens' fate depended on the monument's success. Seventeen hundred automobiles a day brought three hundred thousand people to Mount Rushmore in the summer of 1939. Borglum claimed that tourists spent $25 million in the region and purchased 415 million gallons of gasoline, paying $4.1 million in federal gas taxes. While only a portion of this crowd stopped to pay a quarter and press their faces to the rattlesnake cages, it was easy to see that the potential market was enormous.

As the Gardens grew, Earl was haunted by one seemingly intractable problem. His workers kept getting bitten by rattlesnakes. Don Pederson was an engineering student at the School of Mines. A tall, handsome cowboy with a streak of casual bravado, he had a habit of reaching into the rattlesnake cage and stirring piles of snakes that had collected in the corners overnight. The tourists loved the hissing and rattling as the snakes separated and slithered to different corners of the enclosure. Earl admonished him to stop, but Don paid no attention—until he was bitten.

Pierre Stone suffered snakebites three days in a row: first by a small prairie rattler, then by a water moccasin and, on the third day, by a Pacific rattler. Earl dutifully cut through the fang marks and applied suction as he had done with other snakebites. But for the first time, Earl decided to take Stone to the doctor. The decision unleashed a vicious debate about whether to use anti-venom made from horse serum, risking an allergic reaction, or monitor Stone, treat the symptoms of the bite and wait out the pain. The doctor prevailed. Stone was injected with anti-venom and immediately broke out in hives. He almost died. It took Stone six weeks and a long process of skin grafting to recover.

Once again, Earl drew a simple lesson from these incidents: "Never hire a man who feels a great need to show off for the girls and thus to take too many chances."

Despite this new caution, dangerous accidents persisted. One day, both Jack Gentzler and Ed Westin were bitten by the same western diamondback rattler after laying their hands on the screen that enclosed its cage. Several years later, Bob Armstrong was giving a lecture about snake behavior and reassuring the crowd that if a snake handler stood perfectly still in the face of an agitated snake, the snake would not bite. The rattlesnake at his feet proceeded to bite him directly in the foot. Armstrong's foot swelled to more than twice its size over the next few days.

Earl was ambivalent about the bites. He tried to enforce more cautious and disciplined behavior among the guides, but he also promoted daring bravado and showmanship. Getting bitten was both an act of recklessness and a badge of courage that created a certain "bad boy" status among the crew. In the early days, it was painfully clear that Reptile Gardens was no garden at all. It could be fraught with danger, and the price of bravado was death-defying pain.

MARRIAGE

While the hired men at Reptile Gardens took foolish risks to impress the girls, Earl's own life took a turn toward domesticity. After four years of dating, he and Maude Wagner were married on July 21, 1940 at the Presbyterian church in Rapid City before a small group of friends and family. Posing for the photographer, Earl stood almost a head taller than Maude and squinted into the sun. He looked uncomfortable in a double-breasted suit. Beside him, Maude wore a pink sheer dress and clutched a bouquet of red roses.

Even on their wedding day, Maude and Earl evidenced the work ethic of the Dakota prairie. The Gardens opened at five a.m. that day, and the ceremony followed two hours later. The bride and groom then took a drive through the Black Hills and went back to work.

After the wedding, Maude quit her job at Woolworth's. The couple rented an apartment over the J. C. Penney store for $12.50 a month. Maude turned her energies toward making rock art souvenirs that could be sold at Reptile Gardens and other tourist shops. These souvenirs earned the couple $600 a year—not enough to make them rich, but enough to open a savings account for a down payment on a home. Their one extravagance was a three-month honeymoon trip through the Southwest and into Earl's beloved Mexico.

A SPECTACULAR DARE

— Chapter 5 —

The year that Reptile Gardens opened, Japan invaded China. The Spanish Civil War raged on the Iberian Peninsula. Two years later, just after the 1939 tourist season ended in the Black Hills, Germany invaded Poland. And before the first tourist lined up to purchase a ticket in 1940, Germany invaded France.

World war was imminent and the impact of war on Earl's friends and coworkers was the subject of daily conversation at the Gardens. Through the summers of 1939 and 1940, they followed the debate about American neutrality and whether Congress would, for the first time in U.S. history, institute a peacetime draft.

Maude's brother Gerald Wagner was the first to enlist. He joined the Army Medical Corps in 1939 and was deployed to the Philippines. Joe Garrett was next. He became a pilot and was stationed at the Naval Air Station in Pensacola, Florida. When he sold his quarter interest in the Gardens to Earl, he became the last of Earl's three original partners to leave, and Earl became the sole owner of Reptile Gardens.

Earl increasingly turned to a new a circle of friends. The group included Ed Westin, Bob Bigelow, Don Gross and Jack Gentzler. Each had come to Reptile Gardens between 1939 and 1940. They were all of draft age. Ed was painfully shy. He had started as a cook and general laborer, and it had taken months of effort by Earl to get him to open up and begin to guide. The others were college students, gregarious and opinionated. They challenged Earl intellectually and had strong opinions about the coming war. "[We] would sit around for hours at night philosophizing about life, our personal ambitions and the war in Europe," Earl remembered.

The conversations echoed a deep Midwestern streak of isolationism. Earl feared that President Roosevelt would stage a catastrophic event to force the nation into battle. "We all knew that the United States would be in the war. It was only a matter of time…Bob and Don made a pact that once we entered the war, they would get a mountain hide-a-way, fill it with books to study, and sit out the war." For Earl the threat of war was particularly unsettling. He had two close friends in harm's way, and yet he had doubts about his own ability to fight. He was not a conscientious objector. He was not deeply religious. He had never lacked for courage, but he was convinced that he could never take another man's life, even the life of an enemy.

Despite his inner turmoil, Earl caught a break. Maude was pregnant with their first child. Being a father bumped Earl down the draft list so far that in 1940 he thought the war might be over before the draft got to him.

From Pensacola, Joe Garrett wrote often to "Brock" and the boys at the "snake farm." With his eye focused on the end of the Depression rather than the impending war, he assured Earl that the upcoming tourist season would be successful. "Vacations are the offspring of extra money rather than extra time, and I believe times are much better this year than before." Instead of retreating into the Black Hills to wait out the war, Joe had a plan to control his own destiny: enlist in the Navy early, become a pilot and land a permanent assignment in Hawaii training the young pilots who would fight the war in the Pacific. "The Hawaiian Islands would be OK with me for a couple years," he signed off one letter to Earl. Joe got his wish. He was transferred to Hickam Field on the island of Oahu not far from the naval base at Pearl Harbor.

THE BIG BET

All over the country, war fever tempted young men into actions of bravado that they might normally have resisted. For a group of young snake handlers already living on the extreme edge of risk, it would take an act of incredible boldness to match the excitement of their everyday lives. That's just what Earl and Jack Gentzler dreamed up in October of 1941.

In a brief column on September 29, buried on page two of the *Journal,* the Junior Chamber of Commerce announced its plans to raise money for a new hospital by sponsoring an effort by daredevil parachutist George Hopkins to break the record of 25 parachute jumps in a single day. Hopkins claimed he could make 50 jumps. While it was never clear why anyone would need to make 50 parachute jumps in a day or why the public would want to watch, the sheer bravado, and perhaps the one-in-fifty chance of a disaster, tickled the imagination of the leaders of the Junior Chamber. It was just the kind of risk taking that young men who spent their summers with rattlesnakes crawling inside their shirts could appreciate, and Earl eagerly signed on to promote the event.

Small, lean and handsome, George Hopkins was straight out of central casting. In fact, he had recently been a stuntman at MGM Studios in Los Angeles. Originally from Watertown, South Dakota, Hopkins had run away to join a barnstorming flying circus at the age of 12. He had been a wing-walker at county fairs and air shows, and he had successfully made over 2,300 jumps at a time when the public still looked upon parachute jumping as a death wish. His most spectacular feat had been a record breaking "free fall," in which he bailed out of a plane and dropped 20,000 feet before opening his parachute.

Hopkins had trained Chiang Kai-shek's pilots to fight the Japanese. He had been a civilian instructor for the British Royal Air Force. With war approaching, his clean good looks and daredevil exploits had made him into a high-flying recruiting poster for the Armed Forces. And, as circumstance would have it, Hopkins was scheduled to vacation with his aunt, Mrs. Hugo Jenson of Sorum, South Dakota, at the exact moment that the Junior Chamber of Commerce was launching its campaign to raise money for a new hospital.

The parachute extravaganza at the Rapid City airport was risky enough, but the way Earl looked at it, Hopkins needed publicity to gather the biggest crowd possible. What better way to generate publicity than to have him undertake a stunt that was so spectacular in its own right that it would generate coast-to-coast free headlines? Earl invited Hopkins to lunch with Robert Dean, the owner of KOBH radio, and Boyd Leedom, the president of the Junior Chamber of Commerce. The group hatched a bold but reckless plan. As the front man for the group, Earl publicly bet Hopkins $50 that he could not parachute onto the top of Devils Tower and then climb down in a day.

The *Journal*, echoing the stereotypes of the day, described Devils Tower as "an object of superstitious awe to the Sioux, who once roamed the area." The 867-foot obelisk rose starkly out of the Wyoming plains, and its power was substantially more than a superstition to the Lakotas. Americans had given it the name Devils Tower, and Theodore Roosevelt had protected it as a national monument in 1906. To the Lakotas and the dozens of Northern Plains tribes for whom the unique geological formation was a sacred cultural landmark, it had always been known as *Mato Tipila* ("Bear Lodge").

For centuries, it had been the site of vision quests and summer sun dances. No one knows if Indians ever climbed to the top, but the first ascent by a white man took place in the late 1890s when local mountain climbers hammered and wedged wooden steps into the crevices and slowly crawled to the top. Over 50 years, there had been 45 known ascents. But no one had ever tried to jump out of an airplane and land on top.

From the prairie, the top of *Mato Tipila* seemed like a flat area just a little smaller than a football field—no problem for an experienced parachutist. After Hopkins landed, the plan was to drop an old truck axle that he could wedge into the rock and 1,000 feet of coiled rope that he could tie off and use to rappel down to the ground.

At the time, the monument was maintained by Newell F. Joyner, a local custodian from the National Park Service. He had heard rumors of a landing for days but reasoned that it was impossible because there would be no way for a single parachutist to get down. Updraft winds battered against the monument all day, even when the weather was calm on the ground. The top was a boulder field full of crevices, jagged edges and ledges. Any parachutist in his right mind would take one look at the landing zone and think, "Broken leg."

To keep from being blown off his target by the stiff winds, Hopkins planned to jump out of the plane only 600 feet above the landing zone. It would be a short jump onto a small, rocky landing zone in a stiff wind, with no room for error.

On September 30, he and his pilot circled the monument, but high winds proved impossible to navigate and they chose caution over recklessness. The next day, at 8:11 a.m., Hopkins tried again. Leaping from the plane at exactly the right moment, he opened his parachute. Landing squarely in the middle of the boulder field, he rolled his ankle and felt a twinge of pain but thought it was nothing to worry about.

At the base of the monument, Newell Joyner walked out of his office to investigate the commotion. A crowd of onlookers, including Earl and his co-conspirators, had gathered to watch the jump. Seeing Hopkins peering over the edge, Joyner was furious. Earl and his friends had not applied for a permit or notified him. They had no backup plan or emergency services on standby. As it turned out, Hopkins had no training in mountain climbing or rappelling. With the Park Service budget cut to bare bones, Joyner had no staff to help. And now, he worried, these young knuckleheads would blame the Park Service if anything went wrong.

In an attempt to keep a lid on the story, Joyner confronted Robert Dean from KOBH radio, but it was too late. A news release had already gone out to 400 radio stations, some as far away as New York.

Earl did not share Joyner's seething panic. The drop had happened just as he and Hopkins had planned. Low in the sky, pilot Joe Quinn circled above Hopkins as Jack Gentzler pushed the coiled rope and the axle out of the plane. "At this pace," Earl thought to himself, "Hopkins would be down in time for lunch." With the free publicity, people would line up to buy tickets to watch him break the jump record back in Rapid City.

Unfortunately, the rope bounced hard off the boulders, unraveled and fell deep into a crevice on a ledge 100 feet below Hopkins's reach. Within minutes, a reporter for the *Journal* filed a story that ran in the afternoon edition under a banner headline: "Parachutist Stranded on 867 Foot Devil's Tower: Hopkins Lands Safely, But Rope is Lost."

Hoping to try again, Earl switched pilots from Joe Quinn to Clyde Ice. If anyone could navigate the winds of *Mato Tipila* it would be Ice. He was widely known as the best pilot in the region. He had earned his reputation by taking off in the middle of blizzards to fly medical supplies and food to stranded ranch families. Earl had first met Ice in Kadoka, where he would land his biplane in a field east of town and dazzle the few local citizens brave enough to pay $2.50 for a 15-minute flight.

Late in the afternoon, Ice circled the monument and dropped a second rope and a grappling hook to retrieve the first rope. Food, whiskey, long underwear and blankets followed. With these provisions and darkness approaching, Hopkins settled between the rocks for the unanticipated challenge of surviving a freezing cold and windy night.

When morning arrived, the top of the Tower was cloaked in thick fog. Crowds began to gather and the press arrived. Local ranchers came to watch the spectacle and challenge Hopkins's bravery. "If he wanted to climb down, he could," one rancher confidently told a reporter. Fierce debates broke out about how steep the angle of descent would be and whether Hopkins could simply throw his rope over the edge and rappel down. With each twist in the conversation, it became clear how poorly planned the whole event had been and how steep the price of bad planning might be.

Joyner, increasingly nervous about losing control of the rescue, told Earl and other supporters that a second night on the Tower might result in Hopkins's death due to exposure. Joyner worried about the expense of the rescue. Earl quietly slipped him a note: "This is to say that I promise to see all expenses paid in connection with the rescue of Charles George Hopkins from the top of Devil's Tower, saving the Government from all such obligations." If Earl had any trepidation about this bold promise, he didn't express them.

By the end of the second day, Hopkins's rescue had pushed both the war and the Yankees-Dodgers World Series below the fold in the *Journal*. "Clyde Ice Flies to Rescue of Trapped Parachutist," blared the two-inch, all-caps headline.

Hopkins threw notes to Earl insisting that he was doing fine, but it was hard for the crowd at base camp to appreciate the havoc that relentless winds were causing on top of the Tower. They raged through the second night at 40 and 50 miles an hour. Intermittent rain pelted Hopkins, and even when it eased, the fog was thick and cold. By the third day, he was complaining that his arms were weak from the exposure. The moisture from the fog froze the fibers in the rope, and when he tried to uncoil the woven Manila hemp, it felt like rigid steel cable. Out of desperation, Hopkins briefly considered leaping off the steepest corner of the Tower with his parachute, hoping to catch an updraft that would carry him safely to the bottom.

Buffeted by the unpredictable wind currents, Clyde Ice continued his airdrops, sometimes letting go of his cargo only six feet above Hopkins's head: hot soup, a fur-lined aviator suit, a pup tent. Containers of water burst upon hitting the boulder field.

As the crowds grew and the debates raged, the press nicknamed Hopkins "Devil's Tower George." The event shifted between comedy and tragedy. On top of the monument, Hopkins found himself surrounded by chipmunks and mice that had never come into contact with humans. Joyner shouted suggestions that Hopkins use traps to capture the strange rodents. Hopkins laughed off the idea. He didn't need traps; he could feed them out of his hands. Meanwhile, Earl and Newell Joyner jousted for control of the rescue strategy from the ground below.

Completely unaware of the ferocious winds, the *Omaha World-Herald* offered to pay for a Goodyear blimp to hover over the monument with a rope ladder. Earl complained that it would take five days for the blimp to arrive, and the weather was getting worse. A team of mountaineers from Rocky Mountain National Park arrived and promised that they would have Hopkins safely down within the day. These were men who had climbed K2 in the Himalayas. They were experienced at just such dangerous mountain rescues, but they faltered on slippery rocks only an hour into their ascent and returned to the base.

By October 4, the tone of press reports had shifted. Hopkins was described as "marooned" on the mountain. Both Joyner and Earl made separate phone calls to Jack Durrance, a New Hampshire mountain climber and leader of the Dartmouth College mountaineering club. Durrance had climbed Devils Tower in 1938 and was confident that he could retrace his route up the monument. With his partner, Merrill McLane, Durrance flew to Denver on the morning of October 4, but their plane from Denver to Cheyenne, Wyoming, was grounded by a snowstorm. They resolved to drive from Denver to Devils Tower. Flanked by a police escort, they drove through fog, sleet and snow at a snail's pace.

On the morning of October 6, a crowd of 3,500 gathered. One columnist for the *Journal* framed the consequences of one more day on the mountain in bold relief. "The first six days of the Devil's Tower show have had a strong touch of farce and comedy," he wrote. "Prolonged stormy weather may turn the performance into stark tragedy."

With almost no sleep and faced with the same fog and slippery rocks that had turned back the first team of climbers, Durrance and McLane began their climb at 7:30 in the morning. They met Hopkins at the top eight hours later. After an hour of rest, desperate to take advantage of every second of daylight, they began their descent. As night fell, local radio stations flooded the mountainside with searchlights. After almost four hours, the weary rescue team and the even more exhausted George Hopkins slid down a rope into the beam of a searchlight, to the cheers of the crowd huddled around several roaring bonfires.

Hopkins shrugged off the risks he had taken. "Boy, I'll never grow whiskers," he joked with reporters. "This six-day beard is terrible." He had weighed 118 pounds on the day he jumped onto Devils Tower, but after six days of air drops, he had gained six pounds. "There was little to do but eat and Clyde Ice brought me plenty of food," he quipped. "I shared it with the rats, field mice, and chipmunks who kept me company."

Few reporters paid attention to Earl, who embraced Hopkins and then retreated from the spotlights. Hopkins might have been nursing a twisted ankle, wind-burned skin, dehydration and a bruised ego, but Earl had lost a small fortune. Over the course of six days, he had taken dozens of receipts, small and large, and shoved them into his pockets, dreading a final accounting. All the money that he and Maude had put away for a down payment on the home had been lost. "This started as a publicity stunt, but it backfired, then wildfired," Earl told the press, choosing a word that every prairie reporter understood. True to his word, Earl paid every bill.

Subtly, in the days after the descent, the press recalibrated their coverage of Hopkins. Instead of a reckless daredevil, a subject of ridicule, a lost man on a mountaintop, Hopkins was described as the "hero of Devil's Tower." A cowgirl poet from Wyoming wrote a song in his honor:

He's a bold bad man, he's a hot potato
Just from Rapid City, South Dakota
He flies around like a big tornado
And every time he lands, he gives a WARHOOP!

Two thousand people showed up at the Rapid City airport a week later to watch Hopkins try to break the record for parachute jumps in a single day. The event was a disaster. The winds were howling and he did not make his first attempt until after noon. He had only one parachute and no support team. Maude and Reta Mae volunteered to pack his parachutes, but when he crash-landed on the third jump after his parachute did not open properly, they were terrified that their volunteer efforts might have killed the star of the show. Hopkins did not complain, but he fractured the ankle that he had twisted on Devils Tower. After 13 jumps, his doctor implored him to give up. Hundreds of cars were turned back at the gate before they saw even one jump. The next day, the headlines from the Eastern Front recaptured the front page of the *Journal*: "Reds Claim Bitter Resistance As Nazi's Boast of More Gains."

WAR AT THE DOORSTEP

Earl's costly investment in Hopkins's daredevil stunt couldn't have come at a worse time. Eight weeks after the rescue, on Sunday, December 7, 1941, the Japanese attacked Pearl Harbor, drawing the United States into World War II and changing the lives of virtually every American and the future of Reptile Gardens.

On the morning after the attack, the *Journal* reported "Black Hills Has Men in Far East War Zone." No other information on specific service members was available because military censorship prevented soldiers from telling their parents what they had been doing during the attack, or even if they were in the Hawaiian Islands. It would be a week before Joe Garrett's family learned that he was "safe" in Hawaii.

On December 27, Joe wrote a long letter to Earl and Maude. He offered a cryptic bit of personal advice that he hoped would guide his friends through the war. "[F]rom my view-point I hope you will always consider 'no word' as 'good word.'...I wish there was some means of keeping my folks and friends assured that all is well and that I'm not nearly as concerned about my own well-being as most other people are."

"No word" was not a "good word" from Maude's brother, Gerald. Barely ten hours after the attack on Pearl Harbor, the Japanese bombed Manila, and two weeks later, they invaded the Philippines. After the evacuation of his hospital, Gerald's medical detachment fled to Bataan. Events unfolded very rapidly. On

March 12, General Douglas MacArthur fled Corregidor. U.S. Marines valiantly defended the island fortress until May 6, when U.S. defenses collapsed and American forces surrendered.

From December to the end of May, Gerald's unit tried its best to manage patients, both American and Filipino, through the shifting tides of battle and occupation. Their hospitals were often surrounded by Japanese artillery. When Corregidor fell, the Japanese moved Gerald's unit and other prisoners by train to Cabanatuan. Then they marched to the infamous Cabanatuan prison camp 20 miles deep into the Philippine jungle.

It is hard to imagine the intense emotion and anguish that must have engulfed Maude's family and the boys at Reptile Gardens. They knew that Gerald had been stationed in the Philippines. He had written his parents on February 5, in the middle of the invasion, from "a very friendly sort of jungle somewhere in the Philippines," asking his mother to send him "a chocolate malt—very thick—from Vic's Drug…. Then everything will be perfect." From subsequent news reports, they knew that General MacArthur had fled, and the Marines were in a pitched battle for Corregidor. But they knew nothing specific about Gerald's fate. His trail had gone dark, totally dark, and would remain so for over a year. On May 22, the War Department sent Maude's mother, Alice, a form letter notifying her that her son was "Missing in Action." The letter was blunt in its conclusion: "I deeply regret that it is impossible for me to give you more information than is contained in this letter," General J.A. Ulio wrote. "In the last days before the surrender of Bataan there were casualties which were not reported to the War Department. Conceivably the same is true of the surrender of Corregidor." It was not until ten months later, on March 3, 1943, that Alice received a cable from Washington telling her that Gerald was alive and a prisoner of war.

Earl and the new crew at the Gardens watched the war unfold against the very personal backdrop of their friends' travail.

Hundreds of tightknit South Dakota communities experienced similar grief and uncertainty. At the time of the Japanese attack on Pearl Harbor and the invasion of the Philippines, 5,725 South Dakota men were already in the Army reserves or National Guard. Another 4,000 were in the regular Army and Navy.

According to the Selective Service, 75,308 men were registered and available to be drafted, including Earl and all of his fellow workers. Ed Westin went first. Don Gross, Bob Bigelow and Jack Gentzler enlisted. Earl's fate was delayed by the birth of his first child, Judee, which came on June 15, 1942.

Earl hired nine employees that summer. It was a ragtag group that included Tommy Red Tomahawk and Jerre Campbell, a young woman from Yankton College. Earl was hesitant to hire a woman as a guide. A shy literature student who had no experience with the natural sciences, no passion for the outdoors and had never handled snakes, Campbell turned out to be a fearless tomboy. On her first day, Earl dressed her in a cowboy hat, blue jeans and a Reptile Gardens blouse with a coiled rattlesnake emblazoned across her back. He wrapped a half dozen non-poisonous snakes—indigos, bull snakes and a python—around her neck, and called the *Journal* for a promotional photograph that he quickly turned into a tourist postcard.

"I wasn't scared at all," Campbell remembered years later. "But after a few days I started having nightmares of rattlesnakes crawling up my leg."

Earl quickly learned that Campbell and Red Tomahawk were the most popular guides. An innocent young woman and an Indian warrior told better stories than glib, brash college boys. Earl pushed the guides to "put on a performance," and Campbell eagerly embraced the challenge. When she took a group to the steep-walled open pit where the poisonous snakes were kept, she jumped inside. Snakes hissed and coiled all around her. The tourists rushed to the edge of the wall and gaped as she delivered her lecture while gently prodding snakes that came too close with her hooked snake stick. To keep the crowd on edge, she waved her cowboy hat at snakes and teased them into striking at the felt brim.

Earl's decision to hire a full crew for the 1942 season was a bad misjudgment. As the U.S. organized for all-out war, factories were converted to produce military equipment and rationing was implemented to conserve food and gasoline for the military. Leisure travel plummeted. Visits to Mount Rushmore fell from 393,000 tourists in 1941 to 139,694, a decline of 65 percent in one year. All the tourist attractions that lived in the shadow of Mount Rushmore suffered similar collapses. "There were just no tourists," Campbell remembered. "We would spend most of the day sitting in the shade. One person would guide a small group, then try to sell them souvenirs. Then another person would take a group out. But we were never working all at the same time."

Earl would have done better if he had limited the staff to himself, Reta Mae and Maude, but true to his promises, he paid all of his employees until the end of summer. On their last day together, he handed each staff member a silver dollar and told them, "We're broke, that's all we made this year." Ever the showman, he then encouraged them all to stand at the edge of the cliff across the road from the Gardens and throw the silver dollars into the canyon below.

Headed into the winter, Earl was unsure how to support his wife and daughter or how long he could avoid the draft, so he did what he had always done: he began a manic scramble for new ventures.

MANIC ENERGY AND NEW INVESTMENTS

Earl was broke, but he had great credit. He had paid off every debt he had accumulated: to the lumberyard and the bank, for the land lease of Reptile Gardens and even for the unexpected expenses from the George Hopkins catastrophe on Devils Tower. As grim as his personal situation seemed, he was also a beneficiary of the uncertainty that surrounded the war. While hundreds of thousands of young men in his generation were drafted, Earl was a low priority. Even though he was 26 and in good health, he was married and had a child. Every day, the *Journal* reported news of the local boys at war: who had been killed in action, who had sent a letter home to mother, who was on leave, who had been given a medal for heroic service and who was MIA. Earl was one of the few men in their 20s in the Black Hills who remained a part of the local economy, able to invest in Rapid City enterprises, and he did so with a gambler's zeal.

Across the country, as the federal government mobilized the nation for war, it feverishly accelerated efforts to build munitions factories and military bases. East of town, the newly constructed $8.5 million Rapid City Army Air Base provided training to B-17 bomber pilots and bombardiers who flew over the desolate badlands of the Pine Ridge Indian Reservation. The Air Base brought the war closer to the Black Hills. It also created a new market of soldiers, who were bored and far from home. That's where Earl made his move.

Earl was no more passionate about coin-operated games and jukeboxes than he had been about automated popcorn machines, but he understood the power of scale. When Juleus Koers, a local businessman, approached him about buying a collection of poorly maintained coin-operated games, visions of baked-on popcorn oil may well have flashed through his head. But Koers assured Earl that the machines could generate $200 a month. Under the circumstances, Earl had nothing but time to work on the machines, so he agreed to pay Koers $1,800 in monthly installments.

The first week, the machines generated only $25—half of what he had expected, but unlike the popcorn machines, the problem was marketing, not mechanics. Earl cleaned and painted the machines. Most importantly, he changed their locations, experimenting with new sites rather than letting low-producing machines gather dust because it was easier to leave them than move them. In the new locations, Earl began to make money, and soon he was bringing in $300 a month.

When Earl asked Mort Wilkens for a job at the Casino Bowling Alley, Wilkens turned the table on him. He could not afford to hire Earl, but he offered to sell him the whole business. Art Dahl at the Rapid City National Bank loaned him the $8,000 down payment, and Earl immediately filled the lobby with coin-operated games.

For an additional $1,000, Earl bought another 100 used pinball machines, cannibalized 25 to repair the rest and placed 75 cleaned-up machines throughout the community. His quick expansion brought him into partnership with Harold Gregory, who controlled the game franchise at the new Rapid City Army Air Base, where young fliers and mechanics eagerly pumped nickels into machines to stave off the boredom between training flights.

To meet the demands of the air base, Earl returned to Art Dahl and borrowed another $10,000 to purchase $40,000 in new games and jukeboxes. With this capital, he expanded his base of operations to a radius of 300 miles around Rapid City. Recognizing the potential to sell Black Hills souvenirs to airmen from different parts of the country, he began to place his rock art in the Air Base post exchanges.

Earl may not have fulfilled his dream of becoming the popcorn king of the Midwest, but he was earning $1,400 a month from his pinball partnerships and more income from rock souvenirs, the bowling alley and other investments, almost all of it in small change that left no accounting trail. Suddenly, he was fast on his way to becoming rich. By the end of 1943, his monthly income was equal to just over $35,000 a month in 2015 dollars.

Owning one pinball machine or jukebox would never make a man rich, but Earl's genius had been to recognize that he could scale up coin-operated machines in a way that he could never scale up a one-of-a-kind, stand-alone tourist destination like Reptile Gardens. The trick was never to own one machine, but to own a thousand.

If he could sustain his profits, if the war took a turn toward victory and he could avoid being drafted, even if he could transfer the daily operations to competent management while he was in the Army, he might be able to build a gaming empire that would solve the problem of what to do during the winter months when Reptile Gardens closed. Earl had developed a golden touch by combining a manic work ethic with access to capital from Art Dahl and a nose for marketing and management. He also had no competition willing to work as hard.

Earl's business tastes were eclectic. He had not given up on Reptile Gardens, but he had learned the hard way that tourism was dead for the duration of the war. His new investments, including the Palace Meat Market in downtown Rapid City, could be managed by surrogates if he was drafted and still generate enough income to keep Maude and Judee comfortable until the war ended. "By working day and night, I had made four businesses profitable and also paid for in less than nine months," he wrote years later.

THE MENTALITY OF WAR

— Chapter 6 —

Everything about his impending draft into the Army rubbed against Earl's personality. "Yes, sir." "No, sir." Stand in line. March in line. It just wasn't the way Earl and the boys had operated at Reptile Gardens. From childhood, Earl had displayed a brash indifference to authority, including that of his parents, his teachers and school principals, as well as bankers and city leaders. He trusted his own compass. He thrived when he was able to work relentlessly toward a goal and when he was in control. But since he had not volunteered, he had lost the ability to control his participation in the war effort. As a draftee, he would be a cog in a huge, impersonal machine that did not care a wit about his entrepreneurial skills, his management success or his business creativity.

One brutal lesson in the Army way came from his friend John Vucurevich, who, like Joe Garrett, had tried to plan his way through the war, but his efforts backfired. Vucurevich was married. He had enlisted in officer training and was commissioned a second lieutenant. When the Army decided it had too many young officers, Vucurevich and thousands of others were released, only to be drafted six months later.

Earl's reluctance to go to war grew as friends who were already in the armed services sent home reports colored with cynicism and resignation. Jack Gentzler, for example, almost always addressed his letters to both Earl and Maude. But on August 6, 1943, he wrote only to Earl. His thoughts were for male eyes only. Jack had been stationed in North Africa as a fighter pilot, and his squadron had hopped the Mediterranean to Sicily in early July 1943 to fly cover for the invasion of Italy. In the letter, he criticized British arrogance, French colonialism in North Africa and the political nature of the war. He saved his harshest judgment for American GI's and disparaged press reports that described noble, patriotic American soldiers. "Everybody over here steals anything they can lay their hands on. Back in Africa it was the same way too…I have seen GI's at a place about 500 yards up the road standing around waiting their turn to come once for a dime in an old whore that hasn't anything for a bed but a flea-ridden stack of straw in the corner, and if it isn't that, then their main idea is to find some wine and get dead drunk as fast as they can and as cheap as they can."

Earl's friend Don Gross had landed a job as a military policeman on troop trains moving back and forth from Minneapolis to Butte, Montana. "I'd give my right arm to be working in the snake gardens right now," he wrote on October 6. His description of the troops under his charge was as cynical as Gentzler's. "How do you stand with the Army, Earl? If they keep horsing around with this drafting fathers they may get you yet. Stay out as long as you possibly can. I am ready to throw in the towel…Everyone on my train seems to be good. All they ever do is gamble—play dice in the vestibule, and get stinkin' drunk."

Earl's draft notice finally arrived in early November 1943. He was given only one week to report for his physical. Anticipating the call for months, he had regularly asked his contacts at the draft board to let him have two weeks to get his business affairs in order when his number came up. After all, even with Reptile Gardens closed for the duration, he was running four active businesses and he was an important member of the Rapid City business community. The answer came back: "No way." An Army colonel told him that if he was a farmer with a cow that was going to calve, he could wait a few days, "but bowling alleys, slot machines, and juke boxes absolutely weren't needed for the war effort."

On one of his last visits to the Rapid City National Bank, Earl bumped into Harry Devereaux, chairman of the board. Devereaux was part of the old guard in the city's business community. The two men had served together on Chamber of Commerce committees. Earl reassured the banker that his businesses would be in good hands during his absence and would make it through the war. Devereaux was skeptical. Perhaps he recognized that the key to Earl's success had been his obsessive management style, his attention to the daily details, his work ethic. Perhaps he believed that no businesses could escape the war unscathed. Earl reassured his banker: "I thanked him and explained I had honest men of ability running each of my four businesses and felt things would go just great while I was gone."

A MASS OF MEN

The train to Fort Crook, Nebraska, was crowded with misfits. As the *Journal* reported, the passengers represented "the largest group of selective service prospects to leave in a single day since the draft began, including a number of fathers and family heads for the first time." Several moderately successful entrepreneurs were also on board, including Earl, his Reptile Gardens partner

Marvin Basham and the young banker John Vucurevich, along with 50 others, including a large number of Lakota men from the Pine Ridge Indian Reservation.

"We were composed of bartenders, gamblers, and others with similar occupations," Earl remembered. "The draft board knew that we were not only non-essential to the war effort but perhaps society would be better off without us anyway. Whiskey bottles were passed up and down the aisles and soon the coach was filled with drunks, cursing and singing."

Army doctors in Omaha noted that Earl had "a history of moderate frontal headaches…occasionally incapacitating." He had mild scoliosis and average eyesight. Otherwise, they pronounced him fit to be a soldier. Earl bristled at the humiliation of the physical and the not-so-subtle questions that doctors asked to expose homosexuals. "The Army has a way of stripping a man of all individuality and leaving him completely without dignity," he wrote later. "There is just no way that five hundred men can look respectable once they have removed every stitch of clothing and then trudged slowly, hour after hour, in long lines from one doctor to another."

He watched doctors manipulate the results of their own tests. He heard his fellow draftees lie about their ailments. He saw officers from the Army and Navy fight over who would get which draftee. "As the day wore on, I became more and more disgusted with my fellow man. It made me sick to see [the draftees] crawl so unashamedly before the doctors, before their fellow draftees, and most of all before themselves."

Marv Basham was inducted into the Navy, Earl into the Army. On November 17, 1943, he was given a week to return home, pack his bags and report to Fort Leavenworth, Kansas, for classification. The induction process made no sense, he wrote, "where a professional truck driver is put in the Ski Corps, a good old Southern boy is slated for service in Alaska, and the village idiot is offered a chance for Officer's training."

Earl proved hard to classify. He was older than most draftees and married with a child. He had business and leadership experience, and after a decade of Depression, it was no small feat to be modestly wealthy. All of these qualities baffled officers and fellow draftees. And then there were the snakes. On his "Enlistment Record" his occupation was listed as "reptile keeper." What was the Army going to do with a man who was so comfortable under stress that he roamed through town with poisonous snakes under his hat? How could a snake expert be of use to the Army? At Fort Leavenworth, Earl resigned himself to the boring daily drudgery of waiting for someone, anyone, to tell him what to do next.

BASIC TRAINING

After a week without a formal classification or any hint about where he might be assigned, Earl was ordered to board a train for the Infantry Replacement Training Center at Camp Fannin near Tyler, Texas. The Army had determined that the best job for a man of his skills would be as an infantry scout with training in intelligence and reconnaissance.

Earl's affinities lay with the draftees, and he became a barracks favorite for his ability to challenge and undercut young college-educated officers. He relished his ability to catch an officer in a mistake and embarrass authority. A pattern emerged. He was too intelligent and articulate to remain a private, but he was too anti-authority to be a good officer.

The ambiguity surrounding Earl's place in the Army intensified around the question of whether Maude and Judee should come to Texas and rent a house while Earl was in training. "After the first month I hated the Army life so much and was so lonesome that I wrote to Maudie and asked her to come to Texas as soon as I found a house to live in."

Ordinarily, privates didn't have the resources for such luxury. When Earl placed an advertisement in the Tyler newspaper searching for a furnished house to rent for his family, he was called before his company commander and dressed down for setting himself above both draftees and officers. Earl's response was matter-of-fact: "I told him I was sorry for the officers but thought that I had as much right as they did to have my family with me."

Earl languished in Texas for almost five months, stealing away from camp every weekend to spend precious time with Maude and Judee. In May 1944, he was given a week to return home to organize his business affairs and report to the 106th Infantry Division near Columbus, Indiana, to work in Intelligence.

The 106th Infantry Division of the United States Army was not shrouded in glory. Its soldiers had not fought at Bull Run or in the trenches of Château-Thierry. In fact, before 1943, the 106th had no history at all. It had been organized as a "replacement division," where surplus clerks, musicians, cooks and misfits waited to be assigned to combat divisions whose ranks had been decimated on the battlefield. Back home, when the ranks of the 106th thinned, they were filled by a steady flow of newly trained conscripts—fresh-faced 18-year-olds and the last of the older, married men.

As he had done in Texas, Earl found a new home for Maude and Judee in Columbus. He had no idea how long he would be in Indiana, but he signed a five-month lease. He spent one night in the new house and then the entire 106th was sent on training maneuvers. Maude and Judee were left to fend for themselves. Even though Earl was only a few miles away, he might as well have been overseas.

Maude hoped that the rhythm of Texas could be repeated in Indiana. Earl would train all week, then come "home" on weekend leave. But life in the 106th was more intense. Maude wrote to Earl every day, sometimes twice a day. The tone and spirit of her letters mixed matter-of-fact business with intimate expressions of love and longing. She called him "Dearest Hubby." "So far all I have done since you left is wash and iron, but I manage to keep fairly busy and the days don't go too slowly. I'll be so glad tho, when I can see you. I do miss you a lot darling." She reported on family affairs and the little news she could gather from friends about the war effort. She reported on Judee's temperamental loneliness. "Judee was talking a lot about you today. I gave her a spanking and you should have heard her scream for you. You know, she is used to Daddy's sympathy at those times." Two-year old Judee scribbled her signature at the end of each letter.

Maude worried about what was ahead. "I have just been thinking of how lonely it will be when you are gone next time and I am here alone. I wish we could find someone nice to stay with us, but I imagine that's impossible. If you get acquainted with any fellows whose wife is here, maybe I could get them to stay with me while you are on bivouac." Earl wrote as often as he could, and Maude saved his letters with tender care.

Meanwhile, Earl marched 20 miles with a 60-pound pack into a remote wooded area. He and his fellow soldiers spent a week experiencing simulated battlefield conditions and then trudged 20 miles back to camp. Marching in the Indiana countryside kept the men busy and conditioned, but the exercises hardly simulated combat. For Earl, it was all make-work and needlessly risky. In the raging heat of an Indiana summer, wearing full combat dress, new boots and helmets that boiled their brains, men began to fall out of line like bowling pins. On the march back to camp one day, Earl counted 400 men by the side of the road waiting for ambulances.

The drills came to an end after June 6, 1944, when the Allied armies invaded Europe. Within 72 hours of the first landings on Omaha Beach, Earl was on a train to Baltimore and staged for deployment to Europe. Maude and Judee followed and set up camp in a Baltimore hotel, even though Earl was confined to base awaiting the imminent order to ship out. Earl promptly went AWOL, caught a bus to the hotel and spent his evenings with Maude.

"We would have dinner, even go to the movies, and then after talking a bit I would catch a bus back to camp, arriving just in time to crawl into a bunk for an hour and then get up for reveille." Each night, he looked at Judee asleep in her crib. "I tried to remember every little detail about her appearance, even how her cheek felt in my hand. Each time I felt that this might be the last time I would see her."

His motives were sentimental and romantic, but the behavior was yet another signal of Earl's anti-authoritarian impulse and his growing conviction that the rules of the Army were so strict and arbitrary that they existed to be broken. What's more, even if they might be necessary for some soldiers, they certainly didn't apply to him.

After a week in Baltimore, without notice, without time to race back to the hotel and kiss Maude goodbye, Earl was shipped to Boston by train and then to Wales on a converted luxury steamer. He was surrounded by strangers who slept in bunkbeds stacked four-high from floor to ceiling. The compartment smelled of sweat, the brine of the latrines and seasickness and echoed the light snores of men who slept only in fits and starts. "I don't know how many thousand men were on the boat," Earl later reflected, "but enough so that I didn't see one familiar face."

After arriving in Wales, Earl wrote, "We marched through the villages on narrow roads, beside stone fences covered with green ivy, and passed houses with their window boxes filled with red geraniums, carefully tended gardens, and windows that sparkled in the sunlight. Not only were the windows polished, but the poor grade of glass used in them added to their beauty as the waves in the glass caught the light and threw it back to us with varying lights and shadows. Some of the cottages had thatched roofs, which made them even more picturesque. They reminded me of colorful calendar paintings I had seen when a little boy."

As his company waited anxiously for their next orders, Earl saw something he had never seen before: African-American soldiers strolling through the countryside arm in arm with their English dates. Growing up in South Dakota, he had known only one African-American girl in his entire high school. He had employed only one black man at the bowling alley and counted him a good employee. But that was the extent of his firsthand acquaintance with African Americans. During basic training in Texas, southern conscripts had called him a "nigger lover" when he challenged their abusive language. But in Wales, he found himself caught off guard by the openness of interracial dating. "Now, to see the violent reaction of some of my fellow soldiers made me start to think of what I really felt about Negroes, and especially the races mixing on dates. I wasn't sure I approved of the latter but I couldn't think of any reason why."

The bucolic experience of Wales lasted one week. At the last minute, Earl was reclassified from Intelligence to infantry scout with the 235th Forward Replacement Company of the First Army. Back in Texas, Earl had been told that being classified as a scout was a death sentence. Weighed down with a heavy pack, including gas mask and two changes of gas-impregnable fatigues, he and a "replacement packet" of 300 men spent a half-day crossing the English Channel and contemplating their fate.

IN THE WAKE OF BATTLE

Landing on Omaha Beach a month after the D-Day invasion, the 300 soldiers of the 235th faced no German resistance. They were surrounded by the wreckage of sunken ships and landing craft and the carcasses of tanks and heavy artillery blown to bits and abandoned on the beach. The German guns had long since been silenced or redeployed inland. After Earl and his comrades waded through the shallow tide and scaled the bluffs, they came across the body of a single dead American soldier lying by the side of the road. It was not the death that startled Earl but the silent indifference of those who passed.

After a five-mile march, Earl's unit dug in for the night at Carentan, a village in the hedgerow district of Normandy that had been the scene of intense fighting between the Germans and the 101st Airborne Division on D-Day. He shared a foxhole with a young recruit from Texas whom he had never met before. The first night was more dream than reality. "Our foxhole had the odor of freshly-plowed fields. Memories of planting my garden each spring filled my mind. Could this really be war! Someone was playing taps, not with the harsh sound of a bugle but on a trumpet. The notes filled the night air and each note was as perfectly played as the song of a meadowlark after a spring rain."

The trumpet solo had hardly stopped when German planes flew over. "They dropped phosphorus flares which seemed to light up the night until it was brighter than the noonday sun. Soon we heard bombers and then the dull booms of bombs…Our 'ach ach' guns started firing, then the machine guns with their tracer bullets." To the north, the British searchlights probed the sky. As Earl later wrote, this was the most exciting 4th of July that anyone could possibly imagine. Scared and exhausted, far from home, Earl and the boy from Texas slept a fitful night.

The second night, Earl and his new buddy were so tired that they threw their bedrolls on the ground without digging a foxhole. As soon as Earl fell asleep, the German bombers appeared. When a nearby ammunition depot was hit, the exploding ordinance lit up the sky, sending shrapnel screaming through the night. Earl scrambled into a nearby hedgerow ditch and found himself cheek to cheek with a terrified teenage soldier.

"I could see that I was next to an 18-year old boy, only he looked more like he was sixteen. He was shaking all over with terror and was unable to say a word. His stark terror made me sick to think that the human animal was so stupid he would let wars happen; wars that would drive a young man out of his mind. I made a sincere pledge at that moment that should there ever be an opportunity to do or say anything that might help prevent the horror of war being fostered on the boys of America, I would do or say it."

For several days, Earl wrestled with his fears and his conscience. He kept thinking about the sergeant in Texas who had warned him that the only future for a scout in a frontline unit was to be wounded or killed in action. Was he a pacifist? If his pacifism did not spring from religious conviction, then where did it come from? He began to pray and then checked himself. "Why should I seek out God now, through fear for my future?" He told himself: "If I wanted to talk to God I should do it when all was well and not use Him as a last resort because I was afraid of my future."

As the days wore on, Earl's confidence returned. A voice inside assured him that he would make it through the war. Rather than being assigned to the dangerous job of scout, he volunteered to manage the company's payroll. He read news from *Stars and Stripes* to men who craved the smallest tidbits from the front or news from home. He considered these small acts of purpose in an otherwise aimless routine of marching, trench digging, mess and waiting.

On July 25, Earl watched as the sky filled with heavy bombers—the opening act of Operation Cobra, General Omar Bradley's campaign to break out of the hedgerow countryside, where Bradley's First Army tanks had been trapped for a month. The Americans hoped to capture the town of Saint-Lô and then sprint toward Germany. As wave after wave of bombers dropped their bombs, clouds of drifting dust obscured the battlefield. Had any of these young pilots and bombardiers trained over the badlands in South Dakota? Were these the young bombardiers who had spent aimless hours playing Earl's pinball machines?

New waves of aircraft dropped their ordinance on the dust clouds of earlier waves, and as the haze and debris drifted over the trenches, American infantry found themselves under bombardment from their own air force. Friendly fire killed 111 soldiers, including Bradley's close friend General Lesley McNair, and 490 soldiers were wounded. Years later, Bradley remembered the bombing in his memoir, *A General's Life*. "The ground belched, shook and spewed dirt to the sky. Scores of our troops were hit, their bodies flung from slit trenches. Doughboys were dazed and frightened....A bomb landed squarely on McNair in a slit trench and threw his body sixty feet and mangled it beyond recognition except for the three stars on his collar." For Earl, the spectacle was further confirmation that war was madness writ large.

Shortly after the bombing stopped, the purpose of the 235th Forward Replacement Company became clear. As soldiers from frontline companies were killed and wounded, Earl's troops were dispatched to fill the voids. Under the conditions of combat, there were no "buddies" in the replacement units, no "band of brothers," just a constant stream of anonymous young recruits passing through.

Curiously, Earl thought to himself, everyone else in his packet eventually ended up assigned to a frontline unit except him. Soon enough, an officer explained the way that the Army worked in combat. Rules, regulations, chains of command were fine back home, but in the real stress of war, practical solutions to practical problems took over. Earl had proven himself valuable to his commanding officers. He was a jack-of-all-trades. He commanded the respect of younger troops even though he himself was only a private. He could scout forward positions, check bombed-out buildings for booby traps and mines and then return to the office, keep the payroll and read *Stars and Stripes* to the men.

Besides, the officer explained, the replacement company desperately needed staff. They had been organized to handle 300 to 500 men at a time. Now they were handling 1,500. Earl represented a solution to their problem. If he received orders to join a forward unit, he was told, "disappear for a few days" until his orders got lost in the shuffle.

Earl fell into a routine. He followed the frontline troops, and his replacement company followed him. He scouted abandoned buildings and homes for German stragglers. He interacted with terrified French civilians whose homes were half blown apart and booby-trapped by retreating Germans. He looked for good places for his company to camp, where trees were thick enough to protect the troops and the soil soft enough to dig a good foxhole.

One day, returning from a forward scout, Earl came upon a group of soldiers standing in a circle watching a company cook rape an elderly French woman. "The woman was terrified," Earl remembered. "Her screams and pleading seemed to make no difference. Just as we arrived on the scene our sergeant-of-the-guard came up, leveled his rifle at our cook and told him if he didn't get up immediately he would blow his head off. The cook looked up and said, 'Shoot and be damned.'"

More often, sexual coercion did not require physical violence. Cooks came into villages with truckloads of food. Among a starving populace, food gave the cooks privileges. "Frequently, we wouldn't be in a new area for an hour and our cooks would already have their 'shack jobs,' often with the permission of the woman's husband. Hunger certainly destroys pride and builds strange relationships," Earl concluded. As American units pushed deeper and deeper into France, the most absurd sight for a prudish married man from South Dakota was to see soldiers and their "dates" settling into foxholes together for the night.

Over the first two months, Earl proved himself enough to get a battlefield promotion to sergeant. He was given command of 300 men. He detested rules and orders and enforced only a casual discipline among his troops. He allowed them to hike rather than march. He explained as much as he could about what their objectives were, where they were going and what he expected of them, but he rarely gave an explicit order. He made no claims of superiority. He wore no stripes. He waited last in line for mess and was first in line as the troops approached danger.

"I found that rank had very little to do with getting any job done," he wrote. "Most of the men hated to be treated as though they were numbers. If you worked with them and for them they would reciprocate…Yelling and screaming at men never helped get the job done. Everyone wanted to be treated with human dignity and, war or no war, every man was entitled to as much personal consideration as possible."

Every day, in the hustle to keep up with a moving battlefield, Earl came across the bodies of American soldiers, booby-trapped foxholes where German soldiers had slept only a day before, constant small arms fire and at night, bands of French farmers armed with pitchforks, antique shotguns, a few modern rifles and a vigilante approach to justice, prowling the darkness for German stragglers.

His unit was not in combat—they were a day behind the front lines—but the least inattention to detail could end in disaster or humiliation. One night, sound asleep in his foxhole, Earl was startled awake thinking he was being beaten in his chest by a German soldier. He screamed in terror that the unit was under attack, only to discover that a fellow GI from a nearby foxhole had awakened to take a piss and accidently stumbled into Earl's foxhole, his boots landing squarely on Earl's chest and face. On other nights, soldiers would go to bed exhausted only to awake in three inches of water that had seeped up from the ground. One night, Earl woke to discover a mouse gently tugging at his scalp, trying to capture the fine strands of hair to line her nest.

By late August, Earl's unit could see Paris on the horizon. The troops had marched 180 miles in six weeks. True to his personality, Earl and a fellow sergeant went AWOL and hitched a ride to the "City of Light" in the back of a farmer's truck. They spent the night exploring Paris. Befriended by Free French soldiers who were rushing through the city mopping up rogue German units, they dined with a French family, slept in a Parisian hotel and crept back into camp before anyone knew that they had been gone.

Finally, after two months of dodging orders that never arrived, his officers decided to make Earl's position official as a scout for the 235th. They drafted a letter requesting his permanent assignment to the unit and sent him back to depot headquarters, 40 miles to the rear, for an official stamp of approval.

To everyone's surprise, the clerk could not find Earl's original orders. Searching the Army's records, he could not find Earl at all. Officially, he wasn't in France. He wasn't even in the Army. Despite the mud on his boots and the stink in his uniform, he did not exist. "I could have gone home and no one would have missed me because on paper I didn't exist," Earl remembered. The chaos did clarify one thing. Since shipping out from Boston, Earl had never been paid. Soon enough, the Army created new paperwork. He was reenlisted and back in France.

WAR BEHIND THE LINES

— Chapter 7 —

If one day Earl found himself climbing over maggot-infested bodies and cautiously scouting bombed out homes, the next day he was touched by sentimental songs from home or acts of generous kindness from strangers. On one occasion, he walked his troops six miles to the rear to listen to Bing Crosby sing "I'll be home for Christmas." He bawled like a baby, and when he turned around to wipe his eyes, he discovered a thousand men laying on a grassy hillside amphitheater crying with him.

On a scouting mission to Huy, Belgium, near the Meuse River, Earl discovered just how confusing and fluid the lines of battle could be. Hidden in a forest several miles from his company, he passed a unit of infantry fighting German stragglers. After digging in for the night, he went in search of intelligence from local citizens and met a man walking down the road. When Earl confronted the stranger, he discovered that the man was an American pilot from Chicago who had been shot down, parachuted to safety and was then turned over to a Madame Paquot, leader of the local underground. He had been in her care for three weeks, wandering the countryside in search of forward American units.

The airman directed Earl and his fellow scouts to Madame Paquot's home and kept on walking. "A touch of the knocker brought her to the door," Earl remembered. Her welcome was warm but reserved. "She had the calm, competent manner of the professional nurse. Her blue-gray eyes would almost close when she smiled and her dark hair was hardly touched with gray. She had a strong face, yet it was filled with compassion." Paquot had been the assistant to a doctor who had led the local underground. After he was captured by the Germans and killed, she had taken the dangerous job of coordinating the underground activities."

As they waited for their company to catch up, Earl and his partners hid in their foxholes by day and then basked in the civility of Madame Paquot's home at night. They played Hearts by candlelight with the sound of gunfire all around them. They dined with a local duke and duchess who owned the game preserve where Earl had set up camp. They ate sumptuous pies that Madame Paquot baked by day. They slept on her floor. And for the first time in weeks, they bathed in hot water.

In Huy, Earl developed a severe case of trench foot. Each afternoon, sitting in his foxhole, he would sterilize a razor with a match and drain the pockets of puss that had blistered. Then he would put on his wet socks, tie his boots tight and hobble into town for evening festivities. He read an article in *Stars and Stripes* encouraging soldiers to avoid trench foot by alternating between wet socks and dry socks. "Brilliant idea," the GI's laughed—no one had a second pair of socks.

Earl allowed himself to believe that the war was winding down. During his scouting activities in the countryside, he saw the telltale signs of an army in retreat, more and more bodies of German soldiers, dead and abandoned by their comrades on the side of the road. Near the town of Trier, he took a bicycle ride into the country beyond camp. He passed an amphitheater built by the Romans. He sat on an ancient stone wall and watched small groups of German soldiers only 150 yards away moving through abandoned farms. He saw the Germans. They saw him. No one bothered to shoot.

Like his comrades, Earl took wine and champagne wherever he found it and spent many nights drinking the boredom away. But for the most part, he resisted the temptation to pillage the countryside of Belgium. Scouts traveled light. He had no place to store war booty. But one night, when he camped at an abandoned castle, he found a pair of leather-bound editions of *Aesop's Fables* in the library, printed in the 1600s. He put them into his backpack. Weeks later, in Bonn, he pilfered small meteorite specimens from the university geology department to bring home to the School of Mines.

By late October, the fast-moving Allied invasion crossed from Belgium into Germany. The first city to be liberated was Aachen. The siege lasted five weeks. When Earl finally entered the city, he found a ghost town reduced to rubble. The only building that had not been destroyed was the cathedral in the center of town. All day, they searched the bombed-out buildings and could not find the slightest hint of life. Then, without warning, they spotted a young woman walking directly toward them. She wore high heels and silk stockings. A wide-brimmed hat cast a shadow across her face. She carried a woven basket of freshly cut flowers. She did not look at the American soldiers. She did not look to her left or her right. "We were in awe and speechless," Earl remembered. "She turned the next corner and was soon out of sight."

As the weeks rolled by, and Earl became more confident of his responsibilities, he embraced the role of the field sergeant and disdained the culture of the officer corps. Sergeants were the backbone of the Army, the men who solved practical problems without ego or entitlement. Sergeants won the respect of their men by hard work and meaningful discipline, when discipline really mattered. Earl's direct supervisor, Sergeant Nicke, typified the citizen soldier that Earl idealized. He had been active in civic and church groups at home, and he "looked and acted like an industrious civilian who had put on his uniform to masquerade as a soldier."

On several occasions in his wartime journal, Earl celebrated the "citizen soldier," the informality of the battlefield, and the ability of sergeants to distinguish between the need for real discipline in dangerous situations and the phony discipline of a rearguard officer trying to assert his authority.

Officers, in his view, had outsized egos, an inflated sense of self-importance often disconnected from war experience. Too often, they demanded attention to arbitrary rules that had no meaning on the front lines. Officers slept on cots, ate fresh eggs for breakfast and traveled by Jeep. Sergeants walked. Earl was chastised more than once by officers for "unsoldierly behavior," like calling the troops "fellas" rather than "men." In particular, Earl bristled at officers who tried to enforce racial segregation in the foxholes.

On one occasion, standing in line for a meal, Earl was talking with an African-American soldier about a library project they were working on together. A Southern soldier grew irate, demanding that the black soldier stand behind him. It was a sergeant who came to the rescue—a Southern sergeant. "A young soldier...swore at my librarian and told him, 'no damned nigger' could step in line in front of him. My friend was about to retreat when (Sgt.) Shaw picked the soldier up, carried him back down the line, and told him that this man could get in line any place that he wanted to. Here was Sgt. Shaw, a North Carolina Negro-hater, recognizing a man's ability and not caring what the color of his skin might be."

THE FINAL MONTHS

As the war began to wind down, with the lines holding firm and German defensive positions falling into retreat, whole units were given leave. Earl used his opportunities to explore Belgium and France. He spent a week in Paris. The view of red-tile roofs from the top of the Eiffel Tower reminded him of the red rock strata of the badlands at home. While thousands of soldiers spent their time getting drunk and chasing Parisian girls, Earl got lost in the underground wall of skulls in the Paris catacombs. He spent two days in the Louvre and watched in tears on the day that the *Winged Victory of Samothrace* was restored to its pedestal. The priceless second-century marble sculpture of Nike, the Greek goddess of victory, had been removed from the museum in 1939 and hidden in a bunker outside Paris to protect it from bombing and Nazi theft. He counted only one other American soldier at the Louvre during his two days.

Earl had trouble synthesizing his experiences and beliefs into a holistic view of the war. He was a pacifist, but he was not religious. He had seen men heroically fight for their brothers, and he had seen American soldiers rape women. He had little respect for officers and even less respect for politicians back in Washington. On the first Tuesday of November, he assembled the troops of the 235th to vote in the presidential election. President Roosevelt was running for a fourth term. Thomas Dewey was the Republican challenger. Norman Thomas had campaigned as a Socialist. Of 300 men, only 3 voted. Earl voted for the Socialist. "[Thomas] was the most intelligent of the three," Earl reasoned, "so I placed my 'X' by his name, feeling as the rest of our company—that it made no difference to us who was elected."

On the 1st of December 1944, Earl and the 235th moved into the Belgium village of Malmedy, almost 40 miles south and east of Liege. An old cathedral dominated the center of the picturesque town, nestled into one of a hundred slender mountain valleys that flowed out of Germany onto the flatlands of Belgium. The steep mountains were Malmedy's best defense against war. The valley was impassable, secure—a perfect European village in which to celebrate Christmas. Earl and his unit settled into an abandoned newsprint factory. They chopped down a ten-foot Christmas tree, set it inside the factory warehouse, scavenged light bulbs and used fingernail polish to paint the bulbs red. The highlight of his first week was to slip back to Liege for a day to purchase a gray and white rabbit coat for Judee.

The only sign of war that broke the peacefulness of Liege and Malmedy was a persistent bombardment by German V-1 and V-2 rockets. The city's bridges over the Meuse River and its narrow roads were a chokepoint for troops and supply trains of the First Army marching into Germany. In an attempt to slow the movement of troops, rockets rained down on the city in 15-minute intervals. Earl likened the "putt putting" sound of the pulsating jet engines of the rockets to "a truck motor which was missing on two cylinders." The rockets seemed like an act of desperation. They terrorized the villages and killed civilians but could not hold back the inevitable advance of American troops into Germany.

One night, after a day of roaming the streets of Liege and an evening of drinking in a bar near their hotel, Earl and his friend Ray Sobotka were shaken by a V-1 rocket. "We were almost asleep when we heard one come in, the motor stop, and then, instead of the usual distant explosion, we heard the whistle of air past its wings, as it hurdled toward the ground. We both, almost by instinct, rolled out of our beds and lay face down on the floor. In a second there was a great explosion and the windows were blown across our room!" The V-1 had hit the nightclub where they had been drinking only an hour earlier. Bloodied victims stumbled onto the street. Earl and Sergeant Sobotka ran to the screams and carried bodies from the rubble, including a soldier in uniform whose face had been blown away, leaving only a gaping hole breathing in and out where his mouth had been.

They were the only soldiers at the scene. They had no tools, no shovels, no bulldozers—only their bare hands. As soon as civilian authorities showed up, the two men returned to their hotel, swept the glass from their beds and spent a night tossing in their sleep in the intervals between the "putt-putts" of more V-1 engines.

The bombardment of Liege was a powerful expression of the contradictions in Earl's life. He was not in combat. Practically speaking, he was a company clerk for a non-combat unit behind the front lines. But he was also a scout, and too often the rear could become the front in a split second. His days often flipped from calm to terror: go to Liege to buy a rabbit coat for his daughter; spend the night digging dead bodies out of a rubble pile. He had few deep friendships. He was lonely. He was too repressed to take up with the Belgian and French girls he met, as many of his friends were doing. After the Liege incident, he confessed to Sobotka that, for the first time since he had landed on Normandy Beach, he was demoralized and scared.

In dozens of small villages on an arc that ran from Echternach to Monschau—south to north through the Ardennes Forest—American soldiers were spread in a thin line waiting out the winter. If they were lucky, the war would be over by spring. The winter would be bone-chillingly cold, but at least they were safe, protected by the thick forest and narrow mountainous valleys. Among the units spread across the frontier was Earl's old division, the 106th from Camp Fannin, Texas. The 106th had never seen combat. It had not been organized as a combat unit. A wide stretch of the front was being held by clerks, typists and men who had just completed basic training. Earl judged them as "discarded misfits." A veteran of seven months in Europe, Earl seemed to forget that he had recently been a "discarded misfit" himself.

On the morning of December 17, he awoke to the sound of canons. At first, he thought that the Americans had moved heavy artillery into position during the night and were pounding the Germans, but then a three-story stone house nearby exploded into a pile of dust and rubble. He was confused and wondered why American artillery would be shelling Malmedy.

In reality, the German Army was not retreating as everyone had assumed. Behind an all-out assault of Panzer tank divisions, the Germans were attacking, sweeping across the entire Allied front. Under Adolf Hitler's personal command, the Germans had launched a massive surprise attack. The Battle of the Bulge was underway. Earl's unit was isolated, and the 106th bore the brunt of the assault.

By the afternoon of the 17th, all the units in Malmedy except Earl's had moved out of the village, some towards the rear, some into the breach. Small arms fire from German paratroopers who had dropped into the field at night cut into the boom of the artillery. Malmedy was surrounded on three sides. It was still not clear what was going on, and communications had been cut. The 235th was blind. Three-man teams of scouts were sent out to gather intelligence. Standing on the roof of the paper factory, Earl could hear the staccato rattle of machine guns close by. When one of the scout teams returned with injured soldiers from the 285th Field Artillery Observation Battalion, the terrifying reality of the battle became clear.

The 1st Panzer Division had swallowed the 285th whole. Eighty-four American prisoners from the fast-moving battle were herded into an open field and shot. Those who were not killed by the machine guns were shot in the head by German officers. A few who feigned death survived. After the war, the Malmedy massacre would lead to war crimes trials of the German officers involved, but in the weeks after the incident, the informal word spread among some American troops to take no German SS officers prisoner: execute them on the spot.

Quickly, the Battle of the Bulge devolved into ruthless slaughter. Years later, Earl claimed to be surprised by the headlines in American newspapers charging that the Germans had committed "murder" and a "massacre." The German blitz strategy had left their forward commanders with no rearguard capacity to take prisoners and hold them. Earl believed that the Germans had done exactly what American soldiers had done in similar situations. "This wasn't a calculated, pre-meditated decision," he argued, "but a necessary result of a gigantic plan of military action. When American troops had no facilities for handling prisoners, as sometimes happened in paratroop action, they, too, marched any would-be prisoners back a few yards and shot them dead. The soldiers I talked with never thought of this action as a massacre and were surprised that American newspapers played it up as such."

The war had no doubt made Earl callous, but he was searching for a deeper meaning behind the slaughter. He was not defending the German massacre. The whole idea of war was madness. War made men into murderers, and it was wrong, he thought, to single out the behavior of a handful of Germans for prosecution when soldiers on all sides had committed atrocities.

With only their winter overcoats, weapons and ammunition, the 235th fled along the railroad toward Stavelot. They were the last Americans to escape Malmedy. Earl had just received a Christmas package of salted peanuts from Maude's sister, Blanche. He stuffed them into his pocket and retreated. For two days, he rationed himself three peanuts for every meal until they ran out.

Some of the men had been rousted from bars only minutes before the retreat. It was a ragtag march. When they arrived at a precarious bridge over a deep ravine, slick with fog and light rain, drunks carried drunks on their shoulders. Some soldiers simply gave up and returned to Malmedy, hoping to hide out in basements until the German offensive passed.

After an eight-mile march through the night, they found Stavelot abandoned, with German units entering the town from the opposite direction. Huddled around a kerosene lamp, the officers determined to keep moving toward Verviers and Liege. When they staggered into Verviers, they had no ability to communicate with battalion headquarters and no knowledge of where the Germans were or how far the offensive had progressed.

The exhausted men fell asleep in a brick shoe factory, only to be wakened moments later when a German mortar blew out the windows and collapsed a wall of the factory onto the sleeping soldiers. Their eyes were filled with dirt, and the clouds of plaster were suffocating. The men scrambled onto the cobblestone street below. Earl had lost track of only one man during the retreat: a young redheaded soldier who was a veteran of North Africa. He had recovered from a wound and was waiting with the 235th for assignment to a new unit. Earl had recognized that the soldier was not fit for duty. His nerves were shot. He had hidden in a corner of the newspaper factory in Malmedy when the German shelling began. When the mortar exploded, he ran to a blown-out window and jumped. No one ever saw him again. "Multiply this boy by many thousands," Earl remembered years later, "and you have enough terror to fill your sleep with nightmares all the rest of your life."

Standing in the street, the dazed soldiers were hit again and again by mortars. One exploded an electric powerline, sending the wires whipping back and forth across the street like a Chinese dragon and showering the soldiers with sparks. Earl dove to the ground, face down on the cobblestones. When he gathered himself to stand up, he discovered that he was bleeding from his hand, his lip and the top of his scalp. He squeezed bits of rubble from his hand and scalp and moved on.

Earl's unit spent the night huddled against a nearby building trying to keep warm. When he discovered an officer's Jeep parked near a local restaurant, he stole a blanket from the back seat and slept in the cobblestone alley.

While the 235th was in retreat during the first days of the Battle of the Bulge, Earl's old unit, the 106th Division, was being cut to shreds. The division had been spread too thin when it moved into position in early December and was asked to defend 26 miles of mountainous front. When the German blitz struck, the line collapsed. Two of three regiments of the 106th were encircled and forced to surrender. Over 6,000 men were taken prisoner. It was one of the largest mass surrenders in the history of the US Army. Another 417 were killed in action and 1,278 were wounded. When they were finally able to regroup, the remnants of the 106th fought valiantly at St. Vith, holding off the German advance long enough to stall the offensive's timetable and wreck the march toward Antwerp.

By the thousands, American soldiers were thrown into the breach, no matter what their training. Administrative units arrived from Britain; newly trained units came straight from the United States. Even the staff of the 235th was called to the front. Earl and several other sergeants were sent to battalion headquarters to be given last-minute medical examinations to clear them for assignment to frontline units.

As he had been told by commanding officers several times before, Earl was to give the doctors any excuse he could think of that would send him back to the 235th instead of the front. He told the doctors that he had been diagnosed with a bad heart as a child. He claimed that doctors had discovered high blood pressure during his induction physical and ordered limited duty. But his official induction physical at Fort Crook had given his heart a clean bill of health. His heart was normal in every way. The record was muddy, and that's just what his officers at the 235th wanted. But soon enough it became clear that he was not going back to the 235th. The minor conspiracy to save Earl had backfired. He was sent to the General Hospital in Liege to have his heart examined.

Earl roamed the grounds of the giant tent city. An entire ward had been set aside for victims of "shell shock." Trench foot cases filled cots by the thousands. Earl felt fine, but his electrocardiogram showed that he did have a serious heart murmur. Electrocardiograms were notoriously inaccurate, with high rates of false positives. The doctor in charge wanted to send Earl to a desk job in the rear. They compromised on a diagnosis of asthma as the reason for his mild wheezing, and Earl hitchhiked back to the 235th the next morning, promising the doctor that he would have his heart checked every two weeks.

The Battle of the Bulge ended in late January. The last major offensive of the Third Reich was exhausted. For most of March and April, as the 235th moved from Belgium into Germany, talk turned to the end of the European war and the inevitable transfer of troops to the Pacific theater. Earl's company stopped sending men into frontline units and converted to the task of preparing them to be sent home for reprocessing before shipping out for the war against Japan. It was a torturous process to deal with men who had survived the war in Europe and the Battle of the Bulge only to face the prospect of more combat in Asia.

Under the strain, Earl lost his taste for food. He began to vomit at the odor of the chow line. He reached a point where he could not swallow food. His urine was the weak brown color of Army coffee. When he turned his head, he would wretch and dry-heave. Whatever his ailment, it appeared so rapidly and so forcefully that he could not believe it was psychosomatic. The battalion doctor took one look and ordered Earl onto a flight to the hospital in Nancy, France, where doctors diagnosed an advanced case of infectious hepatitis (known today as hepatitis A).

Earl was put into isolation with another soldier who had hepatitis. During the night, his tent-mate died. When the orderly appeared at Earl's bedside the next morning, the only advice he could give in advance of the doctor's visit was to warn Earl to "lie at attention" when the doctor entered. The orderly's advice confirmed everything that Earl hated about the Army. "This was unbelievable," he wrote later. "My roommate was dead, I was so ill that every movement brought violent vomiting, and I was supposed to lie at attention! As lousy as I felt, I gave a word of thanks that I was not in a rear unit like this where one had to put up with such crap."

For days, Earl lay in excruciating pain, eating nothing and drinking only fruit juice and water until the sickness passed. When he was finally strong enough to walk around the hospital grounds, he came upon a group of drunken soldiers who were pushing and wrestling with a middle-aged woman. "Will you or won't you?", one of the men yelled. "The woman was terrified," Earl remembered. "Both she and the paratrooper lying on her were surrounded by a couple dozen of his friends, all cheering, shouting and encouraging the rape. Here I was, so weak that I could barely stand, and I wanted so badly to stop this but knew exactly what would happen. I would be beaten to a pulp by the cheering drunks. I slowly walked back to the hospital, ashamed of my uniform and ashamed of myself."

Upon his release from the hospital, Earl was reassigned to a new unit. He promptly went AWOL and hitchhiked to the only home he knew, back to the 235th.

After Germany surrendered on May 8, 1945, the 235th was stationed in Marburg, Germany. The rage of defeat often overwhelmed the local populace. Young women who dated GI's had their heads shaved by German vigilantes. Bodies of American soldiers were occasionally found floating in the Lahn River. One morning, when he went to the door of the recreation center to begin the day, Earl found a "blob of meat" nailed to the door. It was a human tongue. Why? He never knew. Whose tongue? He never knew. Who was the message intended for? He never knew.

MADAME RETROUT SCHULTZ-BASKEN, PH.D.

Earl had handled the trauma of war by turning inward. He was lonely, but he counted it a small price to pay for emotional security. He claimed that he had learned the art of emotional withdrawal from his relationships with his mother and father as a child in Kadoka, where he depended only on himself and held others at a distance.

He wrote Maude every day and corresponded with his friends from Reptile Gardens as often as the war allowed. He took it hard when he learned that Bob Bigelow had been shot down over the remote Ploieşti oil fields of Romania. Bob had been one of the Reptile Gardens gang who had plotted to sit out the war in a cabin deep in the Black Hills, studying philosophy. He had ended up as a navigator on a bomber crew. Alive after his plane crashed, Bob had been carried away on a litter, but then he disappeared completely. He was never listed as a patient in any hospital nor were his dog tags saved. Earl mourned the news of his friend's death for many years. "He, his smile, his laughter had vanished forever," Earl wrote. "This was true of thousands of others. No one ever knew what became of them and they were part of that great mass of unknown soldiers."

In every town the 235th entered, Earl found some comfort in the children. Perhaps they reminded him of Judee or his sister Reta Mae when she was a child. Perhaps he was drawn to their innocence and vulnerability. A powerful, anxious protective instinct swept over him. In village after village, he adopted a waif and then passed on to the next village and the next waif. Children were scattered everywhere across Europe like artillery shell casings—the refuse of so much violence. It wasn't until he reached

Marburg that he allowed himself to feel again. He would never admit it, even later in life, but in a way unique to himself, Earl met a woman in Marburg and fell in love.

Retrout Schultz-Basken was a red-haired, green-eyed philosopher. A part-time journalist and author of several books, she spoke English, French and Italian in addition to her native German. She was also an unapologetic Nazi. Her husband was a German soldier on the Russian front. She had no knowledge of where he was or even whether he was alive. She was disdainful of the German women who had supported the Nazis, sent their husbands and brothers off to war and then, after the surrender, fell into overnight romances with American soldiers in exchange for food, safety or the remote possibility of marriage. She had no intention of starting a romance with Earl.

For his part, Earl had soberly avoided sexual conquests, though the opportunity presented itself many times. By his own admission, he was sexually repressed. His comrades had jokingly given him the nickname "The Virgin of the ETO (European Theater of Operations)." Earl had met Shultz-Basken at the Army Post Exchange in Marburg, where she moonlighted as a salesgirl. Neither was looking for sex, but both were looking for someone to talk to. He asked to walk her home, and she cautiously agreed.

For weeks, Earl spent his evenings with Retrout and her friends. The stimulation was similar to the late-night debating society that had developed around campfires at Reptile Gardens, with one substantial difference. Retrout was not a pretentious innocent. She was a serious scholar. The boys at Reptile Gardens had been strong on opinion and conviction. Retrout and her friends were educated. In long conversations about how Nietzsche's philosophy had influenced Hitler and how Arthur Schopenhauer's atheism and asceticism held the potential for individual enlightenment in a world driven by self-interest, Retrout and her friends pushed Earl to come to terms with his own philosophical outlook.

Earl sensed that he belonged in this intellectual community, which he could never find at home. Every night, he braved the uncertain conditions of an occupied German town to visit Retrout and her colleagues. "[We] would spend the evening discussing whatever might come to mind, from Russian politics to Plato's 'Ideal Republic,' and the morality of war to speculation on man's inhumanity to man."

Finally, Shultz-Basken broached the idea of the two becoming lovers. Lost in the emotional intensity of the moment, Earl was unsure whether to embrace passion and intimacy or push it away. In the end, he pushed it away. Years later, he rationalized his modesty by claiming that he was afraid of losing a friendship and the intellectual stimulation that he valued more than sexual conquest. But it is also true that he was passionately in love with Maude. He had written her every day that he had been in Europe, and the end of the war meant that he would be going home soon. Earl remained close friends with Retrout Schultz-Basken for the rest of their lives. They corresponded regularly, and she visited Rapid City and Reptile Gardens several times.

As the months dragged on between the end of the fighting and Earl's return home, he continued to explore Europe. From Marburg, Germany, where the 235th was camped, he took trips to Paris, Bonn and the French Riviera. But like thousands of veterans, the end of war in Europe cast Earl into a state of high anxiety and anticipation. Because he had been among the last drafted, and because he had been relatively unscathed by combat, it stood to reason that Earl would be high on the list of GI's scheduled for transfer to the Pacific theater. Soldiers from the European front who had experienced the D-Day invasion dreaded the prospect of invading Japan. Gathered around their cook fires, they debated how many men it would take: 200,000, 500,000, a million? Would they face chemical weapons? Kamikaze bombers? An enraged and terrified citizenry called to defend the empire? The potential casualties were too ghastly to imagine. And then, on August 6, the world changed in the time it took to split the atom. Within days of the bombing of Hiroshima and Nagasaki, the Japanese surrendered. All was devastation and silence and relief.

The next several months wore hardest on Maude, who waited and waited and waited for her husband to come home. In mid-September, she wrote: "I want you to come so badly it's nearly a physical pain. I know as soon as I know you are coming I'll feel like a new woman. Not that I'm sick, but I just feel lifeless so much of the time. As soon as you come, life will have meaning."

In her letters, Maude reported on the poor financial condition of the Palace Meat Market. She wrote about her antipathy to labor strikes coursing through the nation. "It seems people don't want to work for their money any more." She became more and more morose about their separation and impending money problems. "Don't worry, dear," she wrote, "we will always have enough money to live on, and that is all that is necessary. We will probably all be killed in an atomic bomb war in 25 years anyway, and money or material possessions won't help then."

By the end of September, Maude was convinced that Earl's return was imminent. "Things are looking more and more favorable for your speedy return," she wrote. "I just don't dare let myself think about it…I will never be able to contain myself when I know you are on the way." In the meantime, she busied herself with small acts of domesticity. "I am going to get out all of your clothes and air them and have them pressed."

Earl's letters included a steady stream of ideas for the rebuilding of Reptile Gardens. Maude was supportive but cautious. "Your new ideas for the Reptile Gardens sound great to me. I hope you won't do so much when you get home that you will never be home, but I will try to be broad minded and not care too much if I only see you a couple of hours a day…I will try to be cooperative. Anything but bars, gambling devices and the coin machine."

As September turned to October, with no more clarity about when Earl would come home, Maude's letters became more impassioned. "Gee, I am so lonesome, and so anxious for you to come home," she wrote on October 12. "I love you so much darling, I can hardly wait. I am thinking more and more in terms of things you and I will do. It will truly be grand, darling."

Finally, Earl was discharged on November 26, 1945, at Camp McCoy, Wisconsin, and caught a train home. On his induction papers, Earl had been described as a "reptile keeper." On his release, they called him a "herpetologist." He was moving up in the world.

HOME IS
WHERE THE WORK IS

— Chapter 8 —

As weary GI's returned to the Black Hills, they brought personal traumas that their loved ones could never grasp. Arriving alone or in small groups at train stations with barely a day's notice, they were greeted by wives whose lives had also been transformed by the war. Maude and three-year-old Judee, wearing the rabbit coat that he had sent home from Germany, met Earl at the train station in Rapid City with a gaggle of friends and relatives. Judee burst into tears when the strange man stepped off the train and embraced her. It was a scene played out a million times as soldiers came home to children they had only known as babies or not known at all.

As the GI's tried to put their war experiences behind them, they measured their survival against the tragedies of others. Among Earl's friends, Ken Scissons, Ed Westin, Boyd Leedom and John Vucurevich all came home, but the snake boys of Reptile Gardens were hit hard by the war. Bob Bigelow had died after his plane was shot down over Romania. When Jack Gentzler's plane was shot up during a mission over Europe, he was forced to bail out. His parachute failed to open and he died on impact. All through the war, Maude's family worried about what had become of her brother Gerald. Almost three years after the Japanese invasion, Allied forces liberated the Philippines and their infamous jungle prison camps. Remarkably, Maude's brother, Gerald, had survived the death marches and the prison camp as a medic. After he came home to Rapid City, violent memories of beatings, malnutrition, torture and Japanese firing squads haunted him for the rest of his life.

By some postwar accounts, one in four casualties in World War II were from "battle fatigue"—what we now call post-traumatic stress disorder (PTSD). Some soldiers were overcome by single traumatic incidents, while others were broken by prolonged, unrelenting exposure to battle and death. Earl had seen tents full of "shell shocked" soldiers at the General Hospital in Liege. Some, like Gerald Wagner, were overwhelmed by imprisonment. Others came home numb and quiet and collapsed years later.

In private moments or with Maude, Earl expressed a sense of guilt that he had survived, but otherwise he showed no symptoms of post-traumatic stress. He counted himself among the lucky. Like other GI's, he coped by coming home and going to work. "I returned from the Army one night in December, 1945," Earl wrote years later. "[I] took a two-hour vacation the next morning and started back to work."

POSTWAR BUSINESS

The American economy had been turned upside down by the war. Oversized headlines in the *Rapid City Journal* reported myriad strikes roiling the nation as GI's struggled to integrate themselves into a labor force whose wages had been held down to support the war effort. Workers expected a "peace dividend," but returning GI's flooded the labor market, dampening wages even further. The unions rebelled. Textile workers, steel workers, coal and oil workers, autoworkers, longshoremen, Hollywood actors and crews, and Bell telephone workers all went on strikes or threatened to strike. Many soldiers, especially Midwesterners, had little patience for the union fight. They had had enough of conflict. When Earl's ship docked in New York, the soldiers were greeted by cheering longshoremen, who had a history of striking for higher wages. The soldiers responded with boos.

The battle between big labor and big industry stuck in Maude's throat. Echoing a popular sentiment of the conservative Plains states, she had written to Earl often in the closing days of the war to express her opposition to the militant labor movement. In the Black Hills, these struggles were largely irrelevant. Small businesses were not unionized, and the largest companies generally employed fewer than 20 workers. The emerging tourist sector, of which Reptile Gardens would become an important part, was a seasonal economy, built on the summer labor of teenagers and part-time workers.

Roadside entrepreneurs like Earl waited desperately for gas rationing to end and for middle-class Americans to travel again. Finally, in September, consumers were allowed to buy as much fuel as they could afford, and returning soldiers and their families eagerly planned last-minute, local vacations before winter set in. Even in the dog days of late summer, tourism at local cabins and trailer parks exploded. Mount Rushmore reported a 200 percent increase in visitors from the last two weeks of August to the first two weeks of September. Cabin rentals rose 85 percent in the same period. The Evans Plunge waterpark in Hot Springs reported one car a day in July but 25 cars a day after gas rationing was lifted. At the Hotel Alex Johnson, occupancy rates rose 100 percent from July to August. "Travel Bug Bites Millions," syndicated columnist Rosellen Callahan reported. "Many of today's tourists had never traveled farther than the next county before the war," she reported, but now, "for the first time, they have been able to save enough for a vacation trip."

Nationally, the American Automobile Association (AAA) surveyed late-season tourists and offered an encouraging report for tourism operators. Eighty-five to ninety percent of those surveyed favored tourism by automobile. Forty-three percent expected to vacation in the "Far West," compared to only twenty-four percent in Florida and the Gulf region.

For Earl and Reptile Gardens, however, the challenges were conspicuous. The tourist economy was still seasonal and regional. The Black Hills was not even mentioned on the list of national tourist locations in the AAA survey. Tourists most likely to visit the Black Hills were not rich East Coast families but middle-class families from the industrial Midwest. Many were union workers whose ability to vacation was directly linked to the higher wages and paid vacations that came with union jobs. The culture of the Northern Plains may have been hostile to the union movement, but an important percentage of the tourists on whom the economy depended earned their vacation income from union jobs.

Despite the uptick in vacation rentals and late-season tourists, boosters of the Black Hills economy had reason to be concerned about the future. During the war, the economy had adapted to the stimulation of the Army airbase, but soon after the Japanese surrender, the War Department announced that the base would close on September 21. Overnight, it seemed, 500 people would be laid off, with more and more GI's coming home every day and few local job options on the horizon.

How could a seasonal tourism economy be transformed into a year-round economy? It took a half-day to swing off the highway, visit Mount Rushmore and be back on the road. How could tourists be enticed to stay a second day, a third, a week? Most important of all, how could tourism enterprises overcome the debilitating effect of winter?

BID TO BECOME AN INTERNATIONAL CENTER

The imagination and boosterism that had led to the creation of Mount Rushmore continued to flourish in the postwar era. The patrons of Black Hills tourism, led by Earl's mentor Paul Bellamy and encouraged by the state's political leadership, hatched an extravagant plan—naive as it was bold—to promote the Black Hills as the site for the future home of the United Nations.

While the nations of the world gathered in San Francisco to explore the organization of a new world order, the competition for a United Nations headquarters was stiff. New York was the obvious American choice. The city was accessible to Europe and was the most diverse in the nation. But real estate in New York was too precious and too expensive to support such an expansive complex. In the moment of hesitation, almost 300 American communities—from Niagara Falls to the Kiamichi Mountains of Oklahoma—formed booster organizations to promote their virtues before the United Nations.

Paul Bellamy was the chief advocate of the Black Hills. He had the personality and bravado of a circus barker, but his inspiration was much more personal. His son, a bomber pilot, had been killed over England. In his grief, Bellamy dedicated himself to international peace. An indefatigable lobbyist, he argued that the Black Hills were unique. No place else had Mount Rushmore or was called "The Shrine of Democracy." "[The Black Hills] has an equable, energizing climate with no extremes of heat, cold, wind, rain or dust," Bellamy proclaimed in one of the first invitations to the nations of the world to consider the Black Hills, signed by the governors of Wyoming, Nebraska and South Dakota.

Bellamy's nuanced political analysis was calculated to appeal to small countries who were worried that their voice and sovereignty would be marginalized by larger nations. South Dakota, he argued, was a small state that held its own within the federal system of the United States. Although he mangled the text and history of the Constitution and the nation, he confidently proclaimed: "The United States of America have demonstrated by nearly four hundred years of history that a federation of sovereign states can exist successfully with each state retaining its sovereign identity and control of local matters and yet delegating some of its sovereignty to the national federation."

Bellamy was off by 240 years. He dismissed the Civil War, the impact of the New Deal and World War II on the consolidation of federal power, and the association of states' rights with segregation and racial discrimination, but his perspective was true to the spirit of South Dakota's political culture. As often happened with Black Hills tourism boosters, Bellamy was writing for an international audience, but his message was written to reinforce local values.

Bellamy also promoted the practical attributes of establishing the world headquarters of the United Nations in western South Dakota. "It is within brief travel distance from the great cities of Chicago, Detroit, Minneapolis, St. Paul, Cheyenne, Billings, Great Falls, Lincoln, Denver, Omaha, Kansas City, St. Louis and numerous others constituting the inner circle of industrial, agricultural and cultural America." European leaders, heirs to the cultural riches of London, Paris, Berlin, New York and Moscow, may have considered Chicago a world-class city. Minneapolis-Saint Paul would have been barely known to the leaders of emerging Asia and Latin America. But promoting the Black Hills as a brief travel distance from the "great cities" of Cheyenne, Billings and Great Falls was booster hyperbole at its best.

"Hills World Capital Bid Gains Publicity," the *Journal* reported on September 13, sharing the details of Bellamy's newest 16-page illustrated brochure. Despite the fact that Rapid City's airport was small and had virtually no commercial traffic, Bellamy pronounced that the Black Hills were equally convenient by air travel from all nations. "No racial, religious or nationalistic controversies exist," he promised, expressing a casual indifference to the region's tormented history with its native Lakota population. Bellamy's most powerful argument, which gained him modest traction with the emerging Arab nations of the Middle East, was that the Black Hills were far from the vice and temptation of alcohol, prostitution, gambling and other sins of New York and the large European cities.

South Dakota congressman Karl Mundt joined the effort by campaigning for the Black Hills during a trip to the Soviet Union. Writing home to local newspapers, he reported that the idea had been well received by the Stalinists. Bellamy suggested a variety of sites to the selection committee, but he favored the gentle valley of Spring Creek, ten miles south of Rapid City. Local architect Luvine Berg sketched an elaborate headquarters complex with all the trappings and grandeur of a world's fair complex or the Champs-Élysées in Paris.

On November 14, as Bellamy was presenting his case to the UN Selection Committee in San Francisco, the *Rapid City Journal* reported that shortly before the president's death, Bellamy had apparently won the support of Franklin D. Roosevelt. The endorsement derived from a dinner table conversation that had been relayed to Black Hills boosters by a third party, but the veracity of this report was soon called into question. For security and climate reasons, FDR had actually favored the Azores, a chain of islands 850 miles west of Portugal in the North Atlantic Ocean. When asked to comment on Nebraska, FDR suggested that it was too isolated and too boring. As for the Black Hills, he seemed to have shrugged and admitted that a Black Hills site near Mount Rushmore was worthy of consideration. From this thin thread, Bellamy wove a tapestry of presidential endorsement.

Hope for the Black Hills' bid faded in late November. When Bellamy returned from his presentation in San Francisco, he confessed that he had received a "mixed reaction." A week later, he offered an alternative argument to promote the Black Hills as a center for world trade. "Under Bellamy's scheme," the *Journal* reported, "each nation would set up a pavilion with a permanent display of products, curios, customs and costumes." Bellamy imagined "a continual stream of tourists coming to visit this new 'world capital' of trade, all of them standing in line to buy mementoes."

Before the end of the year, Bellamy ran out of steam and ideas. On December 22, as a blizzard shrouded the Black Hills holiday season in snow, the *Journal* reported that South Dakota was no longer being considered for the UN headquarters. In New York, the Rockefeller family had negotiated an incredible land swap to make space available along the East River in Manhattan.

A MORE MODEST VISION

While Paul Bellamy promoted a grand vision for the future of the Black Hills, Earl was quietly engaged in the more modest task of sketching his plans for Reptile Gardens. He left no indication in his private memoirs or his correspondence that he was even remotely aware of Bellamy's efforts, yet the UN campaign raised issues that would be critically important to the future of Reptile Gardens.

Earl had shut down the Gardens when he boarded his troop train, and no one had bothered to care for the building. When he walked in the door on his second day home, he found a vandalized wreck. The windows were broken. The roof leaked, and the floor was burned where hobos had built fires. He spent the day cleaning up human feces from the corners of rooms.

As Earl began to rebuild Reptile Gardens in the winter of 1946, he was no longer the skinny, flamboyant man-child who had hidden rattlesnakes under his hat and posed for postcards grinning and chomping on the fat belly of a rattlesnake. War had etched the first wrinkles into his face. In photographs taken after the war, he appeared more serious and mature. As a youthful entrepreneur, he dressed like a brash cowboy cleaned up for a dance. If he wasn't sporting a bolo tie, he wore a garish, wide necktie that clashed with the plaid patterns of his shirts. In those late Depression years, his clothes hung loose over his skinny frame and his dirty, limp blue jeans were rolled at the cuff. After the war, Earl's clothes were tailored and included stylish Western shirts with elaborate embroidery set off with a red scarf. He wore cavalry jodhpurs with knee-high laced boots, especially when he was working with snakes. An oversized Stetson rode with a confident tilt across his forehead. Out on the town, he liked decorative Western shirts with gabardine slacks tucked into ornate cowboy boots.

Like many men, he had smoked before the war, but military service made him a nicotine addict. At Reptile Gardens, he spent his days with a cigarette in one hand and a writhing snake in the other. The nicotine stimulated him to work long hours. Earl attributed his energy to a Midwestern work ethic, but Maude suspected otherwise. She had seen the cycle of manic creativity and exhausted depression coming. She had pleaded in her wartime letters for him to spend more time at home. But his mind raced with ideas, and he could not, or would not, throttle down.

By May, Earl's new building was ready for opening day. The new façade with its brightly colored bricks glittered in the morning sun—an ode to the geological wonders of the Black Hills. Inside the Gardens, Earl had built several roofed pavilions where the guides could handle snakes and give their lectures. A new inventory of reptiles included exotic snakes that Earl had ordered from around the world. Nearby, he obtained a new home in the shape of a giant log for the Petrified Woods and scattered extra petrified wood on the hillside to make the tour more interesting.

To promote the Gardens, Earl hired an airplane to drag a banner a hundred miles from Rapid City to Kadoka and back in the morning hours when the highest number of cars were on the road. He crafted roadside billboards and nailed them to fence posts. The signs were so successful that he negotiated deals with local ranchers and built even bigger signs, some as large as 20 by 60 feet, and set them in roadside pastures. He printed thousands of nickel-sized stickers with a picture of a coiled rattlesnake and adhered them to real nickels. These tokens became one of his most popular advertising stunts, until his archrival, Helen Duhamel, complained to the FBI that Earl was defacing coins. When two grim-faced agents appeared at his door and threatened him with prosecution, Earl burst out laughing. He was a war veteran. FBI agents didn't intimidate. Still, he agreed to never deface coins again.

Earl's plans could barely contain his imagination. There was no road map to success. There was no clear vision of what tourists wanted after they had visited Mount Rushmore. There was only instinct and experience, and Earl drew heavily on his own life experiences. Tourists wanted to be amazed, to come close to danger without being in danger. They wanted to experience the thrill that he had felt as a child when the circus came to town. Most of all, they wanted an experience that was unique—something they could not find back home.

Much of what Earl understood about the psychology of tourist families was a product of the middle class automobile revolution. Before the war, railroads had catered to an elite clientele who traveled to the frontier West for intellectual stimulation. These were people who might visit Paris or London one year, and travel by luxury train to Yellowstone or the Grand Canyon the next year. They engaged the American West as armchair archeologists, amateur anthropologists of Indian culture or art collectors. They came to appreciate fossils and geology. They came for spiritual renewal, or, in the case of Mount Rushmore, they traveled thousands of miles to celebrate their patriotism. But by the late 1940s, almost no one traveled to the Black Hills by railroad or purchased a ticket for Paul Bellamy's luxury guided tours. The freedom of the automobile allowed families to go where they wanted on their own schedule and created a new kind of tourist psychology. Automobile tourists wanted freedom from the monotony and drudgery of industrial or office jobs in crowded cities. They wanted to have fun. They wanted to escape. It was for this new generation of automobile tourists that Earl built the new Reptile Gardens at the confluence of entertainment, service, nature and aesthetics.

Well-cultivated gardens communicated a sense of order. The design of the new façade celebrated a sense of place. The staff wore rawhide-trimmed cowboy hats and Western shirts with "Reptile Gardens" embroidered across the back of a coiled, hissing rattlesnake. The image evoked the sense of adventure and danger that was a cornerstone of the mythology of the American West. Every small detail mattered to Earl.

American families hit the road in unprecedented numbers in the summer of 1946. Mount Rushmore hosted 53,000 people in the first 18 days of July—seven times more than 1945. On the single day of July 2, almost 4,000 people visited the Shrine of Democracy. The *Journal* reported that an "army of tourists" was on the march. "It has been estimated that 60,000,000 persons will take to the highways of the USA this year. Most of them, from the looks of things, are already in the Black Hills of South Dakota." A *Journal* editorial warned that local facilities were being "swamped by tourists," and as many as 200 people were sleeping in their cars every night because they could not find accommodations.

Reptile Gardens flourished. Before the war, Earl's informal count of cars passing on the road led him to conclude that one in three vehicles stopped at Reptile Gardens. After the war, the number slipped to one in five, but there were far more cars on the road. Most of the tourist families came from the Midwest, arriving in the Black Hills after a long day's automobile ride from home on ever improving roads. To accommodate farm families used to rising at daybreak, Earl opened the doors at five a.m. By 10:30 in the morning, half the daily traffic had passed through the front gate.

The Pawley family from Auburn, Michigan, was typical of the flood of tourists who took to the road in the first years after the war. Lynn, Alice and their two boys, including a precocious twelve-year-old son, Ray, piled into the family car in the spring of 1948 for the four-day drive to Yellowstone National Park. It was a sign of the American Century that a blue-collar worker who had spent the war helping to develop Saran Wrap at the Dow Chemical plant in Midland, Michigan, could climb behind the wheel of his own automobile, throw off the constraints of wartime rationing and take his family on a vacation to the American West.

A visit to the Black Hills was a one-day stopover, but it changed young Ray's life. "No one came to the Black Hills back then unless they were coming to see the Four Faces," Ray remembered years later. "But all along the highway we kept seeing roadside billboards that advertised the Black Hills Reptile Gardens."

Among the foundational principles that Earl built into the marketing of Reptile Gardens was his belief that mothers made the decisions about where to go and what to do on family vacations. Mothers controlled the money. Fathers did what they were told. If a roadside attraction wanted to succeed, it had to entice the mother of the family, and the quickest way to convince a mother to stop and spend a day at Reptile Gardens was to excite the children in the backseat. The children convinced mother. Mother convinced father. And that's just the way it happened for the Pawleys.

Young Ray had been an "incorrigible animal lover" for as long as he could remember. "The wild kind, not domestic animals," he pointed out.

Ray was smart in an outdoor way and active in the Boy Scouts, but he was an outsider at school, and by his own admission, he just didn't fit in. On the morning that the Pawleys arrived at Reptile Gardens, Ray had no particular interest in snakes, but that quickly changed when one of the guides walked among the tourists with a large bull snake gently wrapped around his neck so that the children could move close and touch. Ray reached out and ran his hand across the smooth scales, relishing the touch. "It changed my life forever," he remembered.

Four years later, as a 16-year-old, Ray returned to Reptile Gardens as a guide and assistant curator. The boy who had described himself as "out of sync" with his classmates back in Saginaw suddenly found himself surrounded by people just like himself. "I remember thinking that Heaven couldn't be any better than this."

NEW LEADERSHIP

Before the war, Earl had managed a crew that was largely his own age and generally his equal. He supervised friends who expected to go off on their own careers and adventures and for whom Reptile Gardens was a summer job in the middle of the Great Depression. After the war, he was the undisputed owner and boss, and with Maude's encouragement, he began to look upon Reptile Gardens as a business rather than an adventure.

Many GI's came home to jobs in factories that mimicked and reinforced the regimentation that they had grown accustomed to in the Army. But Army life had taught Earl different lessons. In Germany, in command of hundreds of young soldiers near the front lines, he had rejected what he considered the phony regimentation of the Army in favor of a more relaxed discipline that relied on self-motivation. At Reptile Gardens, Earl was convinced that this was the only way to manage creative young people. According to his nephew, Joe Maierhauser Jr., "[Earl] created a place where each person was free to be who they were. Being a free spirit himself, he surrounded himself with other free spirits and outcasts, and let them roll."

For the veterans at Reptile Gardens like Ed Westin and Gerald Wagner, the war cast an ever-present shadow, and the Gardens became a refuge. Gerry struggled to recover from the emotional strain of his imprisonment. Reta Mae grieved that "he was never the same again." Though they remained close, their prewar adolescent romance was over. She was also changing.

After graduating from high school in 1938, in the years before the war when Earl was taking adventures to the West Coast and dreaming of ways to get rich, Reta Mae had enrolled in accounting and clerical courses at the business college in Rapid City. During the winters, she worked as a clerk at the J.J. Newberry Co. variety store downtown. She was later a secretary in an accounting firm. She worked at Sears, Roebuck & Company as a clerk and then as assistant manager in the order office before moving on to become a bookkeeper for the South Dakota State Highway Department.

Just 21 years old when the war started, Reta Mae had been a hard-luck romantic who dated a steady stream of soldiers passing through the Army airbase. She fell in love with a dashing Italian-American pilot. When he was killed in combat, she withdrew from her dreams and focused on the practical opportunities in front of her, including the task of keeping her brother's businesses profitable. She kept the accounts of his various enterprises and paid the bills. She made difficult personnel decisions in Earl's name as the businesses declined into debt. When she was not tending to Earl's interests, she worked at a local collections agency, where she developed a thick skin and a blunt, no-nonsense ability to confront people and settle problems. Through all of these ordeals, she and Maude grew closer. By the end of the war, Reta Mae was no longer the kid sister or the butt of Earl's pranks. Over the next few years, she became his essential partner, his confidante, the keeper of dreams and secrets. Together, she and Maude gave structure and focus to Earl's creative instincts and offered advice as he welcomed back veterans and new employees to the Gardens.

Like Maude and Reta Mae, Jerre Campbell, the Yankton College literature student turned snake handler, found other employment during the war. She worked in a steel factory in Indiana and hustled freelance assignments for the society page of her hometown newspaper in Iowa. She returned to the Gardens in the summer of 1946 but stayed only a year before taking a job as a feature reporter for the *Rapid City Journal*. Her greatest contribution was to introduce Earl to her brother Jim and his wife Lee.

Jim Campbell was an artist and philosophy student at the University of Iowa. He was brilliant, curious, an intellectual sponge. He had no training in zoology or herpetology, but like Earl, he had the ability to critique abstract expressionist art in the morning and build a chicken coop in the afternoon.

Campbell and his wife came to the Gardens more by way of conspiracy than an interest in snakes. Despite Jim's parents' insistence that he remain single until he graduated from college, Jim and Lee had eloped in the winter of 1946. For the first months of their marriage, they lived apart, snatching moments of intimacy whenever or wherever they could while Jim tried to maintain the fiction of being single. But as the summer of '46 approached, the deception wore thin. Jerre offered a solution. Lee could move to Rapid City with her and take a job at Reptile Gardens. Jim would be free to make long visits with his sister and, 500 miles from home, sleep in the same bed with his wife. Over the next 20 years, Jim became Earl's stalwart partner and second-in-command, while Lee became Earl's secretary.

Joe Maierhauser rounded out the group of new employees who would lead Reptile Gardens into the future. Joe's parents were German immigrants who settled in Chicago and opened a butcher shop before moving to a small town near Yankton, South Dakota. At the height of the Depression, with his butcher shop struggling to survive, Joe's father burned the ledger that kept count of the outstanding credits he had given local farmers and ranchers. His wife was outraged, but he insisted that the old debts not be held over his neighbors. In the midst of this poverty, Joe was a golden boy: tall, handsome and muscular. He had enlisted in the Navy at the age of 17 but never served in combat or even left an American port. His only claim to wartime adventure had been to get into a fistfight with a Marine on shore leave. For years after the war, Joe proudly claimed to have "kicked the Marine's ass," but it was an incident of no consequence when stacked against the war experiences of Gerald, Ed Westin, Earl and even Joe's own brother, Francis, who had fought in the Battle of the Bulge.

After the war, Joe enrolled at the South Dakota School of Mines in Rapid City, but he showed no interest in becoming an engineer. Joe joined the staff at Reptile Gardens and quickly became sales manager and then general manager. Unlike Jim Campbell, he made no pretense of being intellectually curious. He was drawn to Earl's flash, his confidence and his desire to get rich. Above all, Joe was a player—a ladies' man. It was only a matter of time before Joe and Reta Mae began to date.

POLITICS
AND CIVIC LEADERSHIP

— *Chapter 9* —

The end of the war brought a generational shift in the political and civic life of Rapid City, and Earl was in the heart of it. He became a director of the Junior Chamber of Commerce. He chaired the Tourism Committee. By this time, the Black Hills economy had just begun to feel the potential of automobile tourism. As the nation poured its energies into highway construction, passenger travel on railroads declined to a trickle. For war veterans of Earl's generation, regular, affordable air service held the most promise for delivering tourists from the East Coast and Europe.

Paul Bellamy had been one of the first to see an opportunity in aviation. In 1946, he applied to federal regulators for permission to fly passengers between Great Falls, Montana (one of the "great cities of the world" in Bellamy's United Nations campaign), Rapid City and Chicago. Bellamy argued that the "Black Hills can never be adequately served by service other than air. The Missouri River constitutes a geographical barrier not readily overcome by surface transportation." As a member of the Rapid

City Chamber of Commerce Aviation Committee, Earl shared Bellamy's enthusiasm.

Community service brought Earl into the public eye. Only four months after his return home, he decided to run for the Rapid City Commission (the City Council) "as a representative of the city's younger businessmen and veterans." In many ways, his campaign reflected a national trend, as men who had tested their leadership skills in combat—including John F. Kennedy—came home and stood for political office as representatives of a generation who looked beyond the Depression and war to a new era of economic growth.

Boyd Leedom, Earl's boyhood friend from Kadoka and scion of one of western South Dakota's most politically connected families, managed Earl's campaign. Leedom understood that South Dakota was deeply Republican. The disdain of the state's leaders for Roosevelt and the New Deal could only be matched by the zeal with which they relied on federal programs to keep the state's economy afloat. But no irony was great enough to pierce the myth of the rugged individual or break the hold of the Republican Party on the state. By the 1940s, the radical progressivism of Peter Norbeck had been elbowed from the party's memory.

Despite his protest vote for Socialist Party candidate Norman Thomas in the 1944 presidential election, Earl understood this heritage. His father had been a Republican, and his father's father had been Republican. "If you were a businessman in South Dakota, you were a Republican. That's just who you were," Earl wrote in his memoir.

Earl also understood that civic politics in Rapid City consisted of Republican businessmen ruling over a tame political process. The *Journal* headline the day before the 1946 municipal election underscored this point: "Light Voting Probable—No Issues Involved." Election day surprised the paper and the candidate.

Earl's resounding victory four days later forced the *Journal* to reverse course. The headline—"Vote Interest High Here...WWII Veteran Tops in Three Wards"—signaled a generational shift. "Rapid City citizens Tuesday trooped to the polls in numbers more than double those of recent years to elect Earl Brockelsby and I.H. Chase as new city commissioners," the paper reported. "The heavy endorsement given Brockelsby was viewed by his campaign committee today as an expression of a wish to place a young man on the commission who is representative as well of the veterans of World War II." Earl was only 29 years old—the youngest man ever to serve on the City Commission.

THE FIGHT FOR HOUSING

One of the most crippling legacies of depression and war was the lack of housing in cities. For 20 years, the nation had been on the move—from farms to cities, from farm labor to industrial labor—and the nation's housing construction had not kept pace. Even though Rapid City was small, it faced the same problem, as homestead families and ranchers, especially veterans, moved from declining country towns into the city.

The 1945 state census revealed a dramatic 15.6 percent decline in the state's population over ten years. At the end of the war, there were 102,271 fewer people in South Dakota than there had been in 1935. Only three of South Dakota's 68 counties showed growth: Todd County, home to the Rosebud Sioux Tribe; the Sioux Falls metropolitan area of Minnehaha County; and Rapid City's Pennington County, which had added 3,117 newcomers, most of them from failing farms and ranches in adjacent counties.

Some of these newcomers to Rapid City were students at the School of Mines, which saw enrollment spike after the war. According to the school's administration, three to five veterans were enrolling at the college daily, and many of these nontraditional students could not find housing for their wives and children. In 1945, city officials had suggested that there was an immediate demand for 1,000 living units in Rapid City.

Veterans spearheaded the local movement to build more housing. In addition to electing Earl to the City Commission, they took over the Chamber of Commerce housing committee. They pressured Mayor Fred Dusek into creating a task force of city officials to study the problem and make recommendations. Soon after Earl's election, the mayor appointed him to the committee. On the national level, veterans pushed for passage of the GI Bill to provide easily accessible home loans for veterans.

The housing problem in Rapid City was exacerbated when the War Department reversed course and announced that the airbase would stay open after all as a training facility for a heavy bomber squadron—part of America's postwar strategic commitment to global security. It was one thing to provide housing for airmen in temporary barracks during wartime. It was quite another to provide permanent housing for the officer corps and their families, who would be stationed at the new airbase. Even in 1948, three years after the end of the war, city officials estimated that over 100 military families were still living in unheated tourist cabins.

Overzealous efforts to solve this situation created a new crisis. A group led by Paul Bellamy received a $100,000 grant from the Federal Public Housing Authority to build 36 new "emergency" rental units, where World War II veterans would receive priority. The project was so small it offered only a Band-Aid solution. Contractors shaved the top off a hill near the School of Mines, behind Rapid City High School, and began construction of the Hillcrest housing development. But they did not consider the hydrological consequences of flattening the hill. Rain that had previously run off the steep hillside instead soaked into the soil and gathered in the subterranean layer of bentonite clay. The hillside began to slide into the high school. A half-dozen homes were damaged at the base of the hill. Several of the newly constructed apartments were damaged. The project was a disaster.

With the project facing bankruptcy, Earl and a new group of investors bailed out Bellamy's group. They drilled wells into the hillside, and water that had saturated the soil was pumped out as quickly as it accumulated. It was a daredevil scheme, expensive and complicated, but it worked. Earl's intervention saved Paul Bellamy from an embarrassing bankruptcy.

The housing crisis illustrated the urgent need for infrastructure investment in sewers, roads and public services, but it also revealed an ideological tension deep in the character of western South Dakota. When Earl and other commissioners met with the business community to argue for more investment in housing and infrastructure, they were stonewalled. Businessmen complained that taxes were too high. Earl and other commissioners argued that businessmen were demanding that the city government support growth, but they were unwilling to pay the taxes to make expansion possible. Earl criticized the business community and even suggested that many businessmen were underreporting their inventories to keep their taxes low.

For Earl, this fundamental contradiction in Republican postwar ideology was frustrating. To him, city government should be about problem solving, not rigid ideological pronouncements. The city needed new infrastructure, which would help business. But the business community opposed the taxes needed to pay for the infrastructure.

Earl's peers on the City Commission and other civic leaders seemed to appreciate his willingness to speak his mind. In 1948, by a 6-3 vote, the city commissioners elected Earl mayor. The *Rapid City Journal* commended the commission's decision: "He has shown vigor and judgment in wrestling with the city's many problems, with which he has become very familiar, so that the selection of the commission seems an excellent one."

Earl relished the prestige that came with the office, but he quickly grew frustrated with the inability of government to accomplish even the most basic goals. He led a campaign to incorporate Rapid Valley within the city's borders but could not rally enough support from the business community to succeed. Once again, he believed, businessmen who failed to see the importance of city growth were their own worst enemies. Increasingly, Earl was trapped between wanting the celebrity status of a community leader and wanting to retreat from the pettiness of government to Reptile Gardens, where he was in total control.

RATTLESNAKE HUNTING

When civic affairs became frustrating, Earl often drove out to the badlands, where south-facing hillsides were thick with rattlesnake dens. Each summer, he would take a gaggle of teenage workers from Reptile Gardens into the prairie with him. They stalked the dangerous terrain in tennis shoes and shorts with poking sticks and more bravado than skill. After a long day in the hot sun, the crew might return home with 20, even 30, snakes and a lifetime of tall tales.

One day, in the summer of 1948, Earl got a call from his boyhood friend Kenny Scissons, and the two badlands boys went rattlesnake hunting near Maude's hometown of Wood. Like many Lakotas with a deeply rooted warrior identity, Kenny had enlisted early in the war effort. He wanted to be an Army Ranger, but when the Army discovered that he had a wife and child, they rejected his appeal. He transferred to a British commando unit and was trained in Scotland, then delivered to the German lines in North Africa. He was a sniper and saboteur, attacking German camps at night and killing sentries when the rest of the camp was asleep. Twice he disappeared for so long behind enemy lines that the Army sent notices to his wife that he was "missing in action." Earl spent almost 24 months in the Army. Kenny spent 39.

After the war, Kenny took a job as a game warden for the state and was assigned to the old Norbeck wildlife preserve, which had been renamed Custer State Park. He spent two years culling the buffalo, elk and deer herds that had gone unattended during the war. In 1948, he was reassigned to his old home territory east of Rosebud. Among his many duties, he tracked down rattlesnake dens.

Kenny had already set out a series of box-like snake traps at the openings of suspected snake dens when Earl arrived. When they went to check the traps, they discovered hundreds of snakes, twisted into writhing balls of energy. The traps were full. The snakes were piled up on each other trying to escape. Using a hooked snake stick, Kenny pulled the snakes apart and moved them gently away from the holes toward Earl. Earl pinned the snakes to the ground, picked them up behind their jaws and tossed them into a burlap sack.

All day long, they went about their work. "The big thrill was to bend over, pick up the rattler, and not get bitten by the snakes that were all around me," Earl remembered years later. At the end of the day, they had captured 465 rattlesnakes. It was as far away from the drudgery of city government as Earl could get. Forty years later, he could remember every detail. It was "one of the most exciting days of my life."

THE BREAKDOWN

— Chapter 10 —

In the years after the war, Earl's energy was boundless. He became the true patriarch of an extended family that included people drawn to him by both blood and sweat. He doled out jobs and favors, money and advice, to loved ones and strangers. He won awards for his service to the community. Soon after Maude delivered the couple's second daughter, Janet, in September 1947, Earl brought his father, who was suffering from emphysema, to live in his home. Earl's mother lived down the street. By 1948, Brockelsby was no longer the brash young entrepreneur sitting outside the banker's office hoping to get a loan. He arrived at the Gardens at sunrise, worked through lunch and went home after dark. He spent his nights being mayor, caught up in endless meetings, often two or three a night. Endless complaints. Endless problems. Few solutions. He joined every civic club in town: the Chamber of Commerce, the Cosmopolitan Club, the Mariners Club, the Presbyterian Church Men's Club. He was even director of the

American Red Cross. No one, least of all Earl, seemed to notice that he was exhausted.

Then the migraines returned. It had been years since he experienced the painful headaches of his youth. But he had become a chain smoker in the Army, and when he tried to sleep, his mind wandered across the fitful landscape of fanciful dreams of the future and the unsolvable problems of the here and now.

SEARCHING FOR A CURATOR

After the end of the tourist season in 1949, Earl and Maude traveled to New York. Earl wanted a vacation, but he also had two other interests. He was looking to purchase a printing press for his souvenir business. But more importantly, he needed a fulltime curator for the reptile collection.

The Gardens had grown exponentially since the end of the war, and become one of the largest private collections of snakes in the world, including 17 varieties of rattlesnakes and exotic snakes like the Russell's Viper from India. It was home to 1,700 reptiles in all, including a rare 120-year-old giant land tortoise from the Aldabra islands in the Indian Ocean off the eastern coast of Africa. Earl had nicknamed the tortoise "Methuselah." He was so connected to the 375-pound giant that he described it as "a mystical personal symbol linking man and reptile."

The tortoise was a public relations coup. Almost a hundred pounds heavier and 50 years older than the only other *Testudo gigantea* in the country, which was exhibited at the New York Zoological Society, Methuselah was just the kind of spectacle that Earl believed could cement the reputation of a place like Reptile Gardens and make it more than a half-day excursion sideshow on the way to Mount Rushmore. He could imagine the way that Methuselah's slow, gentle gait might entice tourist families. It was not quite like being lifted onto the back of a circus elephant's

▲ *Earl Brockelsby in 1946.*

▲ Earl, aged nine, at home in Kadoka, South Dakota, 1925.

▼ Earl (front row, left) and Kenny Scissons (top row left) with seventh grade championship basketball team.

◄ Fifteen-year-old Earl with sister Reta Mae and brother Bill on the steps of the family home in Rapid City, South Dakota, 1931.

▲ Earl with his parents, John Earl and Sara "Emma" (Kingsbury) Brockelsby, on the eve of World War II.

◄ Earl and Maude Wagner married in the early morning of July 21, 1940. After a half-day honeymoon, they returned to work in the afternoon.

▶ *Earl clowning around with snake guides Bob Biglow and Don Gross, 1941.*

▼ *Reptile Gardens, 1940.*

◀ Reta Mae and Earl promoted rattlesnake sandwiches at a county fair. This image became a popular postcard in 1940.

▼ "Man Bites Rattlesnake" was one of the most popular postcards from Reptile Gardens in the late 1930s.

▲ Earl (right) with his high school friend and first partner, Joe Garrett, handling rattlesnakes at the Petrified Woods a year before Reptile Gardens opened, 1936.

▶ Snakes galore! Earl with nephew Gaynor Wild.

▶ Parachutist George Hopkins, the day before his daredevil jump onto Devils Tower, 1941.

▼ Earl and Dave Clark hunting rattlesnakes at Thompson's Butte, South Dakota, 1943.

▲ The all-American family, 1960: (left to right) Jeff, Johnny, Earl, Maude, Judee and Janet.

▶ Maude and Judee Brockelsby during World War II.

▲ *Earl's younger sister, Reta Mae, became his closest confidante and a beloved matriarch for hundreds of young workers who spent their summers working at Reptile Gardens.*

◀ Jerre Campbell was the first female snake guide hired by Earl in 1942. Later, she became a reporter for the Rapid City Journal.

▶ Snake guide Francis Red Tomahawk, 1949.

▲ Earl carried his heavy Hasselblad camera everywhere he travelled, but his first love was to photograph the badlands of South Dakota.

◀ Reptile Gardens Curator Earl Chace milking the venom from a rattlesnake.

▲ Building the new Reptile Gardens dome, 1964.

◀ The stalwarts: John Evans, Francine Armstrong, and Marshall Young on the road in the badlands, 1962.

▲ Nick Hall wrestling an alligator, 1967.

▶ Jim Campbell feeding a Gila monster and beaded lizard, 1950.

▼ Ray Pawley lecturing from inside the "snake pit."

▼ *Earl with villagers in Papua New Guinea.*

▶ *Brenda Adam, 1971. Earl married Brenda in 1973. The couple divorced in 1986.*

▶ Earl's grandson Jon-Jon Oldham with Shirley Tyler on Methuselah, the tortoise, 1966.

▲ Earl (cowboy hat upper left) and Reptile Gardens crew unloading African crocodiles, 1956.

◀ Nephew Joe Maierhauser, Jr. succeeded Earl as CEO of Reptile Gardens.

▼ Earl and Korczak Ziolkowski, sculptor of Crazy Horse Memorial, 1982.

trunk, but the image of riding an ancient tortoise was the type of experience that would last a lifetime in the memory of a child.

Investing in animals like Methuselah posed an enormous risk. It had already been shipped halfway around the world to Miami and then to New York when Earl purchased it. He shipped it by express rail to Reptile Gardens, but when Methuselah arrived with a mild case of pneumonia, it would not eat, and Earl could not figure out why. He ordered the crew to sterilize the feeding dishes and wash Methuselah's food, but nothing seemed to work. The desperate situation confirmed what Earl had already come to understand: with more exotic reptiles came more exotic problems.

Most Black Hills tourist enterprises were comfortable in their small, seasonal niches. They did not pretend to the national stage. But the purchase of Methuselah signaled Earl's desire to make the Gardens into a world-class destination, where tourists could expect the highest levels of service, entertainment and education. He obsessed about how to create the spectacle: African crocodiles, gigantic anacondas, Indian hooded cobras, African monitor lizards, Gila monsters from the Sonoran Desert and a herd of giant tortoises. His vision went far beyond his expertise. He needed a curator with broad experience who could develop relationships with public zoos and universities, someone with credibility who could write about and popularize the exhibitions at the Gardens.

While on his trip to New York, Earl began to ask at the reptile house of the world-famous Bronx Zoo how to treat Methuselah's sickness. One of the staff offered a simple diagnosis and prescription. Methuselah needed more bacteria in his gut, not less. "Stop washing his food, and put some dirt in the feeding bowls."

Earl Chace was a self-taught herpetologist who had spent most of the war in India as part of a public health team combating malaria. Like many scientists who grew up in the 1930s,

Chace was trained in nature more than a classroom. Like Earl Brockelsby, he was the kid who skipped school to hunt for snakes and play with lizards. Before the war, experience mattered. A man who knew his subject from a life in nature could rise to the top of any public zoo. After the war, public zoos and universities were more demanding and more stultifying than he cared for. Suddenly, academic credentials mattered. No matter how much experience Chace had, he didn't have a Ph.D. in biology and didn't want one. When he returned to his job at the Bronx Zoo, he discovered that he was a man without a future.

The very qualities that put a ceiling on his career in New York endeared him to Earl Brockelsby. He didn't have an advanced degree. No one at Reptile Gardens had an advanced degree. And the way Earl understood tourism, nobody wanted a guide who was a scientific snob. Besides, Chace was a brilliant storyteller. He could mesmerize a crowd. He could lead staff. When Earl invited him to become curator at Reptile Gardens, Chace packed his family and moved to the American West.

MENTAL BREAKDOWN

Earl tried to enjoy the rest of his vacation. He walked the avenues of Manhattan with Maude, dined out and, for once in his life, made an effort to relax. But it didn't work.

The migraine headaches pounded like prairie thunder. Daylight triggered a sharp pain that scratched relentlessly at his optic nerves. He retreated into the hotel closet for the relief of darkness. He could not breathe. An elephant sat on his chest, and each breath seemed like it would lead to a heart attack. The man who boasted that he could walk all day through the rugged badlands was so weak that he could not walk a Manhattan block. Rather than embracing the crowds of New York as an adventure, he was terrified. "I was in a continual state of terror…

sleep wouldn't come. A ride in an automobile was an exercise in terror." He contemplated suicide.

Maude brought him home to Rapid City by train. No one at Reptile Gardens, except Reta Mae, understood his condition. Since the breakdown happened immediately after the tourist season, Earl's absence from the office was hardly noticed. His term as mayor expired without incident or comment. He forced himself to exercise, but he could not gain weight. He lay in bed like a disjointed skeleton. He tried to quit smoking, but he could not muster the motivation. He studied mental illness, piling books by the side of his bed and reading late into the night. The only refuge he could find was three miles west of downtown. Along Rapid Creek, he and Maude had purchased creekside property where he planned to design and build his dream home.

He had spent so much of his young life inside his own imagination, and now he imagined a home along the creek with the children playing hip-deep in the water, a garden of exotic flowers and vegetables and a small prairie of daffodils and wildflowers. For a while, he seemed to recover. But then, in early December 1949, after his father died, grief sent Earl into a new round of anxiety and depression. "I didn't have the strength to read or listen to music. I couldn't go to church or the movies as crowds terrified me." For years, he had managed the manic highs, the creativity, the ability to work all day and through the night, with the low-grade depression that always followed. But at the end of 1949, it was all depression.

The stigma of mental illness in America in the late 1940s was powerful. Earlier generations had removed afflicted relatives from society, warehousing them in insane asylums or locking them up at home. Sigmund Freud's ideas had swept the country in the years before the war. After the war, psychoanalytic terms like ego and id entered mainstream conversations, but doctors and pharmacists had only clumsy tools for treating depression.

Everyone understood that a successful businessman, a man of the American work ethic, could become so exhausted, so drained of "nervous energy," that he might collapse. The euphemisms that surrounded Earl's diagnosis always led back to a form of nervous exhaustion. To be "drained of nervous energy," to work so hard that you "use up" your reserves of strength, was in its own twisted way a badge of honor, the only way that mental illness could be understood without stigma. A man who worked himself to exhaustion" wasn't mentally ill. He was an American hero who had left the battlefield on his shield.

Earl knew differently. He knew that something more complicated was going on. In desperation, and with the growing realization that he could not will himself to recovery, he wrapped up his father's affairs and made final arrangements for the burial. Then he turned to Dr. Franklin Ebaugh, the preeminent psychiatrist in Denver, with the expectation that he would be institutionalized.

Ebaugh was a pioneer in the development of psychopathic hospitals, institutions where psychiatric patients could be segregated from the general populations of public hospitals and treated by experts in psychiatry. He had been director of the Department of Neuropsychiatric Medicine at Philadelphia General Hospital in the 1920s, before moving to the University of Colorado, where he became director of the Colorado Psychopathic Hospital. Ebaugh counseled Earl against institutionalization, sent him home to Rapid City, advised rest and prescribed a regime of tranquilizers, including America's first antianxiety drug—Miltown.

Earl was hardly alone in dealing with his problems. Miltown quickly became one of the most popular drugs in the United States. By 1957, it accounted for a third of all prescriptions written that year. Recreational users called it a "dehydrated martini." In a

2009 retrospective, *Newsweek* suggested that the drug launched the age of psychiatric "cure-alls," with the widespread side effect of creating psychological dependence.

The momentum of the booming postwar economy compensated for the absence of Earl's creativity and management, and Reptile Gardens ran smoothly through the tourist seasons of 1950 and '51 under the leadership of Reta Mae and Joe Maierhauser, Jim and Lee Campbell, and Earl Chace.

By his own admission, Earl spent the first years after his breakdown "more or less a bum, spending my time and energy as I please. Which means I spend little time with my businesses." He worked on plans for the new house. In the spring, he celebrated the explosion of golden daffodils along the creek and refused to cut the knee-high grass until the last flowers had gone to seed. He thrust his hands deep in the warming soil and planted a riotous garden of roses, bright purple dahlias and amaryllis, vegetables and even strawberries. He tended the garden with a maniac's zeal all summer long.

He made a ritual of the nightly dog races. As one of the founders and a major investor in the track, he sat in a box above the grandstand and held court with his friends. Maude and the children enjoyed summer evenings at the track, but she disdained his heavy betting, his preoccupation with the smallest details of the racing sheet and his pretentious claims that he had the inside dope on the performance history of dogs that no one else had ever heard of. He won boastfully and lost quietly.

He spent his weekends hiking in the badlands, where he found the solitude of ancient fossils and eroded buttes his best therapy. He hiked from Sylvan Lake to Harney Peak, camped at the summit and woke with the sunrise. He kept up an extensive correspondence with anyone who wrote to him. Maude took care of the girls, as well as their newborn, Johnny, and she enforced Earl's daily regime of quiet and relaxation.

PRANKS

Solitude and contemplation also unleashed a wicked side of Earl's humor. As a young man, he had gleefully played pranks on Reta Mae and his young partners. The pranks were innocent (like pouring tadpoles in a pitcher of lemonade that Reta Mae had prepared for the crew). They became part of the folklore of the early days at Reptile Gardens—the kind of practical jokes that enlivened a boring day when no tourists came through the gate.

With time to contemplate his mischief during his recovery, the practical jokes grew more elaborate. When the editor of the *Rapid City Journal* hosted a cocktail party for community leaders, Earl hauled a dead alligator to the editor's door, propped its mouth open, neatly placed the Sunday edition of the newspaper in the alligator's mouth and rang the doorbell. After a moment of terror and a good laugh, Earl proceeded to cut off the alligator's tail and roast alligator steaks. On another occasion, Earl switched the keys on a colleague's typewriter, creating a brain spasm when every typed word was misspelled for no apparent reason. Then there was the time when Earl sneaked over to Joe Maierhauser's home and taped black tarpaper over every window. When Joe woke in the dark and was late to work, Earl proceeded to chastise him for his bad work habits.

Not to be outdone, Earl's victims fought back. When he and Maude moved into their new home along the creek, friends rented a bulldozer and placed a three-ton limestone boulder in the driveway. The original plan had been to dump the boulder onto the driveway when the new cement was still wet, but the common sense of wives thwarted the escapade. Earl loved the prank so much that he moved the boulder only a few feet into the yard, where it stayed until the house was torn down many years later. It was then moved to Reptile Gardens, where it took a place of honor along one of the pathways.

As the pranks became more elaborate and potentially destructive, Maude grew increasingly uneasy. The moment of truth came when Earl Chace decided to take a vacation after several years on the job. Earl plotted to have Chace's home jacked onto blocks and towed to a nearby vacant lot. Maude thought this was going too far. After nearly a decade of escalating tit for tat, she intervened and put a stop to the mischief.

RETURN TO BUSINESS

— Chapter 11 —

Earl's manic creativity eventually brought him back to the Gardens. Even though he was heavily sedated by increasing doses of Milltown and barbiturates, he could not calm his imagination or his obsession with expanding his business investments. He purchased the lease to operate the public park at Colossal Cave near Tucson, Arizona, and dispatched Joe Maierhauser to run it. He opened Fairyland Zoo in Custer, South Dakota, and asked Jim Campbell to be in charge. On paper, Maierhauser and Campbell were partners, but their stake was small, and it was Earl's money (and his access to credit) that kept the start-up enterprises afloat. Meanwhile, he paid attention to every detail of what souvenirs were put on the display shelves and how they were priced. He oversaw the purchase and maintenance of the growing menagerie of animals. He calculated how much it would cost to pave the entrance roads and fretted over the effectiveness of the highway and bumper signs. He authorized every purchase that Earl Chace made to enhance the reptile collection and often found himself financially vulnerable to his own impulse to go big and bold.

It was one thing to purchase snakes from ranch boys who knocked on the backdoor or to spend a day catching snakes in the badlands, but to keep up with the high mortality rates, Reptile Gardens needed thousands of snakes every summer. The commercial snake trade was increasingly competitive and, for the most part, lawless.

Rattlesnakes, which still sparked the fascination of tourists, were a commodity business for Earl. He bought them by the ton because many didn't live very long. In some parts of the country in the early spring, hunters pumped gasoline into rattlesnake dens. The fumes burned the lungs and respiratory systems of the snakes. As they emerged from their dens for air, they were easily captured. By the time these snakes arrived at Reptile Gardens, even by express rail, many were already dead or half-dead. Earl had the dead snakes skinned and transformed into dozens of souvenirs: boots, belts and cowboy hatbands. The heads were pickled and lacquered into menacing poses. Fangs and rattles were used to make earrings. If the snakes died at Reptile Gardens, the meat was frozen and sold as a gourmet oddity. Throughout the summer, Earl placed orders for live snakes just to stay ahead of the daily death toll. Snakes that survived the summer were simply disposed of. It was too expensive to heat and feed snakes whose respiratory systems were so compromised that they could not make it through the winter anyway, especially since new snakes could be ordered every spring.

Earl kept an eye out for opportunities to acquire snakes cheaply. In Okeene, Oklahoma, for example, locals had engaged in an annual rattlesnake roundup since 1939. Other towns followed suit, including Waynoka, which began an annual hunt in 1946. Locals delighted in serving the deep-fried white meat of the rattlesnake at these events, but every year the number of snakes killed or captured far exceeded the demand of adventurous diners. In 1959, Earl contracted with the Junior Chamber of Commerce in Okeene and the Saddle Club in Waynoka to purchase all the rattlesnakes from their annual "roundups."

When Earl agreed to the Oklahoma contracts, he expected to pay $1,200 for a ton of snakes. But instead of capturing a ton, the roundup sponsors captured six tons—12,000 pounds of rattlesnakes.

When the snakes arrived, Earl dumped them into outdoor alligator pens, where they piled up four feet deep in the corners, the snakes on top crushing the snakes on the bottom, the snakes on the bottom struggling against the dark and weight in a vain effort to reach daylight. The *Journal* and local television and radio covered the arrival of the snakes, but behind the scenes, chaos reigned.

Every morning for two weeks, Earl Chace climbed into the alligator pits with a hooked staff, pulled out the dead and injured and tossed them to Earl. After weeks of futile effort, a spring snowstorm hit Rapid City and dumped ten inches of snow on Reptile Gardens. The snakes died by the thousands. Earl hustled. He sold a half-ton to a restaurant in Minneapolis and promised to save another frozen ton for the summer menu. Weeks passed after the first delivery. The restaurant never called back.

Always inventive, with an eye for headlines, Earl filled the trunk of his car with several hundred dead, frozen rattlesnakes and took off on a business trip to Arizona. He stopped in Greeley, Colorado, to have dinner with a young woman who had worked the summer at Reptile Gardens. After dinner, as the snow began to fall in large flakes across the campus, the two hatched a devious prank. They salted the campus with 200 dead rattlesnakes and watched them become covered with snow. A few days later, when the snow melted, students were terrified by the discovery that their campus had been invaded by rattlesnakes. The local newspaper speculated that the snakes had come out of the mountains during a warm spell and become trapped outside sorority houses by the snowstorm. It was a stretch, but under the circumstances, it was the best explanation anyone could come up with.

The same ruthless quality that governed local snake round-ups also ruled the international market in large reptiles, such as alligators, crocodiles and giant lizards. The reptile trade was concentrated in the Southern United States from Florida, through Louisiana, to the Texas-Mexico border, to Arizona and Southern California. Isolated on the Northern Plains, at least a thousand miles from places like Miami, El Paso and Slidell, Louisiana, Reptile Gardens was, by any measure, an outlier, despite the fact that it held the largest, most diverse private collection of reptiles in the world.

Public zoos and university biology departments combed the small advertisements in the back pages of *Billboard* magazine with the same ruthless competitiveness as private zoos and breeding farms. Along the border, Mexican police and federal agents turned a blind eye for a $20 handshake. On one occasion, when 13 boxes of reptiles from Mexico proved too large to smuggle across the border in the trunk of a car, Earl's contacts arranged for the El Paso Police Department to supply a paddy wagon and the boxes "sailed over the bridge with no questions asked."

Operating on the margins of weak national laws and few international trade restrictions, reptile traders adhered strictly to one principle: "Catch me if you can." Most poor nations didn't have the law enforcement capability or the desire. The scale of the trade was enormous and profitable. Arthur Jones, a trader in Slidell, Louisiana, willing to take big risks for big profits, once illegally exported 80,000 baby caimans in a three-month period from Barranquilla, Colombia, into the United States for four cents an animal. He sold them into the American market as "baby alligators" at huge markups.

Like most collectors, Earl made deals by mail, sent money wires to people he had never met and got hustled as often as he hit the jackpot. He worked with dozens of dealers from Papua New Guinea to Florida, but no matter how trustworthy the relationships, the hustle was always the same. Twelve-foot alligators turned out to be eight feet. Twenty-foot anacondas turned out to be eleven feet. Too often, a ten-foot diamondback rattler from North Carolina passed through a broker in Florida and turned out to be a six-foot snake when it arrived in South Dakota. Everyone was driven by the same two demands: the rarest species and the biggest specimens. In the trade of alligators and crocodiles, size mattered.

By 1956, Earl had a steady flow of alligators into Reptile Gardens. Some of the largest he kept for "alligator wrestling" exhibitions. Others he sold. Many were small. Many died. In 1956 alone, he purchased several hundred alligators. Years later, he bought an entire alligator farm in Denver, Colorado, and trucked 400 gators to Rapid City. Most died within a few weeks and were buried in a bone yard behind the Gardens.

Arthur Jones was one of Earl's main suppliers. He operated by a simple principle: no individual specimen was valuable because the supply was infinite. Tourists didn't come to a zoo to see one snake in a cage or one monkey in a tree or one alligator in a concrete pond. They came to see hundreds, slithering over each other and fighting. If the reptiles died from stress or poisoning or starvation, they just captured more. If snakes died by the hundreds, new ones could be purchased by the hundreds. Reptiles were a volume business.

"In spite of the huge quantity of Diamondbacks we got this spring. They are all dead now," Earl wrote to Ray Olive at Reptile Jungle in Slidell, Louisiana. Halfway through the 1959 tourist season, Earl acknowledged, "I can use any rattlesnakes you might have on hand." Earl asked for the pound price and a rush order.

There were no Humane Society campaigns to save snakes. Almost nothing was so exotic that it had real value—except crocodiles.

SEARCH FOR A GIANT CROCODILE

A giant crocodile on the Northern Plains—now that would be a spectacle. Earl had reached out to traders from Australia to New Guinea to Africa but had never been able to close a deal for a single giant croc. Every inquiry he made about a twelve-foot specimen came back with the same reply: "Will an eight foot croc be okay?"

The inability to find large crocodiles was a direct result of the orgy of overhunting in Australia and the island nations of Southeast Asia and the Pacific. In the first decades of the twentieth century, crocodiles had been hunted by the millions, skinned and shipped to Europe, where their hides were turned into upscale ladies' handbags, suitcases, shoes, belts, hatbands and any other accessory that needed an exotic story to inflate its price. As fast as a primordial lake or river was discovered in the interior of New Guinea, the crocs were wiped out. By 1955, all the hunters had stories about the 20-foot crocodile. Everyone had seen one, many hunters claimed to have shot one, but no one could find one.

The hunt for giant crocodiles was inflamed by bestselling adventure books like Brian Dempster's *River of Eyes* and Frank Buck's *Wild Cargo*. The most famous crocodile hunter in New Guinea was George Craig. According to legend, he had killed thousands of crocodiles for the hide market, then turned against hunting and captured the largest crocodiles in the world, which he kept at an isolated jungle refuge on an island in the Fly River Delta of Papua New Guinea.

By the 1950s, there was only one place that had not been overhunted, one place that still remained largely unknown to European and American explorers, one place where the ecosystem had not yet been colonized—the remote wilds of the Okavango Delta and the headwaters of the Zambezi River known as the Caprivi Strip in Southern Africa. To conquer the Caprivi Strip, capture giant crocodiles and transport them down the Zambezi to Livingstone, then by rail to the port of Beira on the Mozambique coast and then by ship to New Orleans would take an open checkbook, fearless courage, the ability to improvise on the fly and a massive ego. Earl knew only one man who combined those qualities: Arthur Jones.

Jones was not an easy man to like. Although Earl did a steady business with Jones, he described him as "the most disliked man I have ever known." Small in stature, Jones was an avid bodybuilder. He casually carried a .44 caliber pistol in his belt. Like most swashbuckling adventurers, his outsized personality operated in the shadows between truth and absurdity. In a profile for *NBC News* later in his life, the correspondent described Jones as "too powerful, too rich and too aggressive to be called eccentric. But whose tough talk about his projects, his passions, his philosophy of life, can sometimes offend the faint of heart."

Jones described himself politically as "miles to the right of Attila the Hun." He was an outspoken white supremacist. "Younger women, faster airplanes, and bigger crocodiles," was his motto. When asked to describe his attitude toward women, Jones, seated next to his fifth wife, unabashedly observed, "Women are wonderful. Every man should own several." He became host of a popular television adventure show called *Wild Cargo* that promised to "bring man-size adventure into your living room." He claimed to have killed 73 men and 600 elephants during the course of his African adventures. According to Jones, every story he told about himself was true. Every story that others told about him was a bald-faced lie.

All of Jones's boasting later in life began with the amazing tale of the six months he hunted the world's largest crocodiles in the Caprivi Strip.

The story began in the summer of 1956, when Jones approached Earl with a proposal. "Hell, I'm the only man who can catch those big crocs," he insisted. "Send me $5,000 and I'll take off for Africa." That's the way things were done in the reptile trade: a handshake, a wire transfer and a big adventure, at the end of which partners almost always ended up hating each other and feeling cheated.

Jones invited Earl to come with him to Africa, but for all his fearlessness, Earl was a businessman first and an adventurer second. He had several businesses to run. He was stretched thin financially from purchasing the lease to operate the Colossal Cave, and he was pouring profits from Reptile Gardens into the money pit of Fairyland Zoo in Custer, where Jim Campbell couldn't turn a profit to save his life. Increased prescriptions for Miltown kept Earl sedated, but the memories of the breakdown were never far away. A year in the most remote and dangerous corner of Africa was too much. Besides, when Earl reflected on the project, he realized that even though Arthur Jones probably was the only man for the job, he didn't want to spend a long day, much less half a year, with Jones.

The deal seemed straightforward on the surface. Earl would provide the capital. Jones would provide the temerity and the muscle. If Jones could capture 50 or 100 crocodiles and get them back to the United States, the partners would sell the ones they didn't need and split the profits.

With only a backpack and Earl's cash in his wallet, Jones took off for the Belgian Congo in August. He quickly discovered that crocodiles had been hunted out in the Congo River, so he headed for the Caprivi Strip. South African authorities did not allow Europeans into the area. They suspected that Jones was a fortune hunter in search of gold or diamonds. They had regularly refused to give permits to crocodile hunters, and the region was so remote that there was no threat from poachers. But the idea of capturing giant crocodiles and shipping them to the United States seemed so absurd on its face that they granted Jones a permit to try.

To get to the Caprivi Strip, Jones and his small crew traveled 50 miles up the Zambezi River from Livingstone, then another 50 miles by Jeep on a narrow dirt trail. With all their gear, they walked 12 miles through the swamps and bush to the lake, where they pitched camp and set their traps. There were no other Europeans. No game wardens. No police.

"In the Caprivi we could do anything we were big enough to do; and we did," Jones wrote in his autobiography. "By comparison to the things we did in the Caprivi Strip, the first trip to the moon would look like a few kids camping in their own back yard." Over the course of six months, Jones lost 80 pounds and struggled through three bouts of malaria, but he captured over 100 crocodiles, all over 12 feet in length, a few over 14 feet.

It was easy enough to bait and capture crocodiles along the shoreline, but his real challenge was keeping them alive until they could be shipped. He staked his first captures to the lakeshore but soon discovered that other crocodiles would cannibalize them. He constructed an elaborate fenced enclosure near the shore and fed the captured crocs chickens, donkeys and horses until he had wiped out the local market in domestic animals. He illegally poached local antelope. Despite all these efforts, he discovered that crocodiles under stress would just stop eating and starve themselves to death. He finally loaded the healthiest into steel tanks for shipment and prayed that they could make the passage to New Orleans without eating.

Throughout the year, as Jones encountered one obstacle after another, he wired Earl for more money. "I am still paying out to Arthur Jones in Africa in his attempt to capture crocodiles," Earl complained to Joe Maierhauser in late October 1956. "I feel I am in one of those positions where I am pouring money down a rat hole and all I expect to get out of it is a mouse."

By the time Jones was ready to ship the first 48 crocs back to the United States, Earl had invested $21,000 in the project—$16,000 more than his original pledge. Reptile Gardens needed only five crocodiles for exhibition. Earl expected to recover his investment when Jones sold the remaining 40. But the deal with Jones had been vague, full of bluster and an accounting nightmare. Jones never accounted for the money Earl sent to him in Africa, and when crocodiles arrived in their steel cages at the dock in New Orleans, the shipping company refused to release the animals until the shipping bill was paid.

A bitter argument followed. Jones insisted that Earl pay the shipping bill. Earl insisted on an accounting of the money he had already provided. Jones said that he had never received money from Earl and described Earl's version of the story as, "an outright lie...nothing short of an outright attempt on Earl's part to cheat me on the deal, so I told him to go to Hell."

From Earl's perspective, the argument over money was the price of partnering with Arthur Jones. "He left Africa almost like any place he stays, a completely hated young man, who has taken all and given nothing in return," Earl complained to Maierhauser. After a few days, Earl dispatched Joe to New Orleans to resolve the dispute. Joe packed a .38 caliber pistol, just in case, but confessed that he didn't know what he would do with it if the situation became confrontational.

Maierhauser returned to Reptile Gardens with six crocodiles. The largest bull crocodile killed three younger males, but the three that remained lived at Reptile Gardens for the next 25 years.

Earl agonized over the remaining 40 crocodiles and his financial losses. Jones insisted that he was trying to sell the surviving crocodiles in Florida, but Earl never saw any money and concluded that Jones was all talk. In late May, frustrated and strapped for cash, he sent Earl Chace and Kenny Scissons to Louisiana to confront Jones. Both had done hard duty in the Army during the war. They were not the kind of men to be intimidated by Jones's bluster. When Chace arrived home with a second cargo of crocodiles, Earl promptly placed an advertisement in the back pages of *Billboard* offering the crocodiles for sale.

Earl never recovered his full investment. In the end, he estimated he had lost $14,000 on the adventure. Every time he confronted Jones about a full accounting, Jones proposed to make payment in snakes, monkeys, Galápagos tortoises and alligators—anything but the missing crocs. Eventually, Earl wrote off his losses and moved on.

Arthur Jones occasionally visited Reptile Gardens, always with new deals and new tales of adventure, including a widely publicized expedition to save a herd of baby elephants whose mothers had been killed by poachers. He continued to pursue his interest in bodybuilding. In 1970, his invention of a system of weight-lifting machines known as Nautilus made him a multimillionaire overnight, with his own fleet of commercial jets piloted by his wife. Jones had offered Earl a chance to be one of the first investors in the company, but Earl turned him down cold. Asked years later if he regretted losing the opportunity, Earl quietly reflected that no matter how big the fortune, he would never partner with Arthur Jones again.

MIXING FAMILY, FRIENDS AND BUSINESS

— Chapter 12 —

It was never in Earl Brockelsby's nature to focus on only one thing. Juggling complexity added to the adventure in his life, especially if new relationships or new enterprises contained an element of risk. Part of his genius, and his mental illness, was an ability to focus copious amounts of intellectual and manic energy on an increasing number of endeavors until he crashed. The Miltown prescription cut off the extreme highs and lows, but Earl had a gambler's personality and disdain for playing it safe.

At Hidden City, Earl said he had "complete faith" that he would never be bitten by the rattlesnake under his hat. Considering the blood flow around the skull and the extreme swelling and necrosis that accompanied all bites, a strike to the head might well have killed him. And yet, at Reptile Gardens, he handled rattlesnakes for half a century and was never seriously bitten.

For Earl, snakebites resulted from recklessness. No matter how dangerous his behavior looked to a tourist, behind the bravado he was a master of measured risk. His ability to calculate risk and to measure his own abilities and the abilities of others made him fearless. His hubris, his competitiveness and his compulsive desire to test the outer boundaries of life's experiences combined to create a personality suited to gambling. "He could bet $1 on a ping pong game," his son John remembered, "and be just as competitive as a $100,000 bet on wheat in the commodity market. No matter what the challenge, he believed he was smarter and better than those who bet against him."

Earl measured his intelligence by the risks he took. He bet on dog races, oil wells in Wyoming, treasure hunts on Cocos Island and real estate in the undeveloped suburbs of Rapid City. His calculations and sometimes even a sense of social responsibility kept him from disaster. When a fellow investor encouraged Earl to sell shares of a dog track in Montana to his friends in Rapid City, for example, Earl turned him down. "I don't mind seeing friends lose $1,000 here and there who can afford it," he wrote to his partner, "but if there is much risk involved, I don't want my name to be used to help persuade a retired couple, the working man or the school teacher to put money into such a cause."

Earl's compulsion to take risks led him to the high-stakes market for global commodities. Traditionally, South Dakota farmers and ranchers had taken modest stakes in commodity markets as a hedge against the volatility of wheat, corn, soybeans and cattle—agricultural products and markets that they understood. Earl preferred the more volatile commodities that local brokers called "exotics." These were products that a western South Dakota rancher had no experience with—pork bellies, coffee, cocoa, orange juice, silver and gold, which often came packaged in complex deals that few people understood.

To invest in commodities Earl did not need to be responsible for a staff of teenagers. He was not dependent on shady foreign reptile brokers or obscure conservation laws. He was not constrained by limits set by long winters or the fickle tastes of tourists. His only limits were his intelligence and his tolerance for risk. For Earl, investing in commodities was not a terrifying roller coaster ride where failure lurked at every margin call. It was a liberating expression of self-confidence.

From the mid 1950s until the end of his life Earl traded heavily in exotic commodities. He lost occasionally, like the time he was forced to actually take delivery of a large position in orange juice that was rotting in a railroad car in the Chicago freight yards. At other times he made huge profits that allowed him to pay off capital debts and the unforeseen disasters that seemed to regularly bedevil Reptile Gardens. But despite his gambler's boastfulness, the commodity markets did not make him a millionaire. It was the steady revenue from Reptile Gardens that funded his generosity to family and friends, allowed him to pay for the children's college educations and graduation trips to Europe and bankrolled his international travel. He bragged about his commodity profits, and he complained incessantly that Reptile Gardens was barely breaking even, but in the end it was the tortoise not the hare that created his wealth.

In the 1950s, flush with the profits from five solid years of growth after the war and confident that profits on the commodity market could backstop any missteps, Earl created a complex web of partnerships and new roadside tourism enterprises that he hoped would transform Reptile Gardens into a vertically integrated tourism empire. The expansion was a calculated gamble by a man who believed that by sheer force of personality he could control both the growth of his business and his personal relations.

FAIRYLAND ZOO

No one in Earl's inner circle was more dedicated than Jim Campbell, and no one worked harder, especially at jobs that he hated. Jim viewed adversity as a measuring stick of self-discipline and personal growth. He also had a unique personal relationship with

Reptile Gardens. He had lived at the Gardens through the winter of 1949-50, through blizzard and cold on the lonely hilltop, and the experience had left him with a "mystical feeling" that Reptile Gardens was "a friend to me." Its fate was his fate.

When Earl assigned him to work the front door for the 1950 tourist season, Jim had complied. He hated the job, but he accepted it as a personal challenge and did his best. At the end of summer, he borrowed money from Earl to return to college in Iowa. Earl had offered the loan without a second thought, but inside his own head, Jim agonized about the debt. He worried about the dependency it created on Earl's generosity and the suspicion of Maude and Reta Mae that he was taking advantage of Earl. He feared that Earl did not want him to return the next summer. He was completely wrong.

Jim had misinterpreted the assignment to work the front door and Earl's criticisms of his work habits. A good greeter was worth his weight in gold, Earl argued. A good doorman made families feel welcome, directed them to the most interesting exhibitions and steered them into the gift shop. In the years before the war, Earl and the old crew had learned how important it was to meet tourist families at the gate. Earl had even set his own desk at the front door and greeted new visitors himself. It was all a part of Earl's belief in superior service and customer relations. But Campbell was not comfortable at the door. No one could match Jim's work ethic. The staff admired him. But with strangers he could be awkward and lacked the jovial "come on in" personality that was so essential at the front door.

Earl's relationship with Jim was suspended somewhere between father, brother and boss. The boundaries were less than exact. Simple gestures like giving a loan for college or criticizing work habits became wrapped up in the personal relationship. Jim wanted more from his hard work and his relationship with Earl. He believed he had earned more. He wanted to be a partner.

Earl's solution was to expand and offer Jim a minority stake and a management role in the Fairyland Zoo, a new roadside enterprise that Earl had started in 1949 in the Black Hills town of Custer. But almost immediately, the project ran into trouble. Campbell had no passion for details, and the thin line between success and failure in roadside tourism was dictated by the smallest details: how many monkeys to buy, where to place roadside signs, how many rock souvenirs to put in display cases, how to price the postcards. No matter how successful Earl became, those details were the essence of his business day. They held little interest for Jim.

Earl looked upon the Zoo as an opportunity to give Jim space to be his own man and to have control over one of Earl's enterprises, but he grew frustrated when Jim refused to listen to his advice. Earl encouraged him to build the Zoo around a "Monkey Village." People adored monkeys. While Jim could spend hours studying the behavioral development of the family's pet chimpanzee, he was slow to grasp the importance of creating a spectacle of hundreds of monkeys swinging limb to limb in a fabricated monkey village. Earl tried to convince Jim to develop a small buffalo herd, but he resisted. If the buffalo charged a tourist or ran through a fence onto the highway, it could become a public relations nightmare. Despite his best efforts, Earl could not get Campbell to think like a tourist. After five years, Earl concluded: "Poor Jim seems to work so hard and get so little done."

Jim's management style was not the real problem. Earl had violated his own first principle of roadside tourism by putting the Zoo on the outskirts of Custer, away from the most well-traveled tourist routes. Tourists had to search for the Zoo, and that, by itself, was enough to kill the small profit margin. Meanwhile, Earl was bleeding money to Arthur Jones and the Africa crocodile expedition. By transferring profits from Reptile Gardens to keep the Zoo afloat, he was risking what he had labored so hard to build at the Gardens.

In the spring of 1956, Earl resolved to give it one more season. If Jim could not turn a profit, Earl would sell the Zoo and cut his losses. "I am going to apply every spare brain cell I have to make that damn zoo make some money this year," he confided to Joe Maierhauser. "If it isn't going good by August, believe me I will try to sell."

At the end of the season he put the Zoo on the market for $50,000, including all the animals and gift shop inventory. Privately, he thought if he got only $25,000, he would be "darned happy." But even at a fire sale price, he had no bidders. In the meantime, he struggled to manage a more distant operation.

COLOSSAL CAVE, TUCSON, ARIZONA

In 1956, Earl leased the management concession at Colossal Cave, 20 miles southeast of Tucson, Arizona. Stalactites and stalagmites formed by millions of years of slow seepage of groundwater through the limestone ceilings created a mysterious, otherworldly character, enhanced by layers of popular mythology and exploration. The cave had been used by local Native American tribes for at least a thousand years as shelter and as a food cache. In the late nineteenth century, bandits used the cave as a hideout from the law. At the beginning of the twentieth century, it had been mined for its supply of bat guano and then abandoned. By the 1930s, the cave was owned by the State of Arizona and recognized as a geological treasure. But it was not accessible to tourists until the Civilian Conservation Corps (CCC) rebuilt and expanded the cave's primitive infrastructure. CCC workers dynamited the cave entrance, developed a network of paved underground trails, including a lighting system, and constructed aboveground headquarters buildings from the native stone. By 1956, all the cave needed to become a national tourist attraction was a manager who understood tourism and had a strategy for publicity.

For Earl, it was the right project at the right time. Colossal Cave gave him a foot in the door in a region he loved. Unlike South Dakota, Arizona offered the potential to build a year-round attraction, but the Cave also presented Earl with a new set of challenges that he had never faced before.

The tension between education and entertainment, a key conflict in tourism in the American West, came into sharp relief at Colossal Cave. At Reptile Gardens, Earl felt a relentless pressure to develop entertainment programming. The Cave was organized more like a national park than a roadside attraction. The emphasis was on education, archeology, conservation and Indian culture—not on creating popular spectacles that could pull people through the turnstiles. As a result, the Cave suffered from low attendance.

To tackle the new challenges, Earl made Joe Maierhauser a partner and dispatched him to Arizona to manage the Cave. Joe had proved himself during Earl's recovery. By 1955, Earl had enough trust in Joe's work to promote him to general manager at Reptile Gardens. But the decision to send Joe to Arizona was not just about business.

After a yearlong romance, Joe had married Reta Mae in 1949. Five years later, she gave birth to Joe Jr. As employer and employee and as brothers-in-law, Earl and Joe struggled to define their relationship. Joe was family, and that was the rub.

If Jim Campbell appealed to Earl's philosophical and intellectual sensibilities, Joe appealed to Earl's dark side. Joe was devoted to Earl but cavalier about his responsibilities to Reta Mae and Joe Jr. Even after his marriage, he continued to chase women. He wanted to be in the family but not in his marriage. He did not want the responsibilities of fatherhood. His philandering made Reta Mae miserable and may have contributed to her depression. But in the 1950s, there was still a powerful stigma to divorce, and neither Joe nor Reta Mae were willing to end their marriage and walk away.

The situation was unsustainable, especially for Earl. Although his first allegiance was to his sister, he became Joe's enabler. Joe confessed his frustrations with the marriage to Earl, and Earl acknowledged that Reta Mae's mood swings and depression could be overwhelming. When Earl wanted to share something private with Joe, he scribbled cryptic handwritten notes at the bottom of business letters that had been typed by Reta Mae. It was an emotional high-wire act.

The move to Arizona allowed Joe to gain distance from Reta Mae and to pursue the lifestyle of a single man without rubbing it in her face. Earl hoped that Joe would eventually come to his senses, reconcile with Reta Mae and settle down. Time and again, he prodded Joe to pay attention to his wife, to write her a letter, to send her a gift, to make an effort at Christmas, to invite her to visit Arizona, to spend time with his young son. Over and over Joe resisted, leaving the burden on Earl to keep Joe's secrets, even as he tried to protect his sister.

The strain was evident in correspondence between the two men. "She has her good and bad days," Earl scolded Joe, "and says that the only thing that really keeps her going is when she receives a letter from you. So you better keep them coming."

Earl bought Reta Mae a wristwatch for Christmas in 1956 and signed the card from Joe. As he had since they were children, Earl obsessed over Reta Mae's security. "I dreamed about Reta Mae," he wrote to Joe. "Dreamed she was kidnapped along with her two children. I don't know where the second child came from! There was a long and exhausting search but we finally got her back safe and sound." Earl also assumed a greater role in Joe Jr.'s life, and along with Earl Chace and Jim Campbell, he became a surrogate father to the boy.

While he conspired to keep Joe and Reta Mae separate, but together, in a relationship that satisfied no one, Earl micromanaged and second-guessed every decision Joe made about the operation of Colossal Cave. The two men were partners, but it was Earl's money, strategy, experience and daily directions that made the business a success. Earl's intervention drove Joe to fits of exasperation and passive-aggressive denial. Earl would send a suggestion, and Joe would throw it in the trashcan. Earl would inquire about Joe's response, and Joe would refuse to answer. Earl would criticize the inaction. Joe would dig in. Time would pass, both men would apologize for overreacting and the process would begin all over again.

At times, Earl's interest in creating a spectacle that would bring tourists to the Cave generated crude proposals that blurred the line between circus sideshow and the more traditional education goals of the State of Arizona. Earl knew he was pressing the boundaries of propriety, but he could not resist. His creativity always moved toward the spectacle and only as an afterthought to education or scholarship. "This reeks of fraud, and perhaps, you are more principled than I," Earl explained as a preface to one proposal to Joe in 1957, "but the degree of one's principles are based so often on the percentage possibility of being caught! ...I can acquire some old Indian skulls for a fairly reasonable price [and] I could send them down to you or even fragments of an entire old skeleton and if possible, it would be best if they were discovered by someone other than yourself." The discovery of old Indian skulls would transform the Cave from a passive educational lesson in geology into a treasure hunt. The Cave would come alive with more mythology and more mystery.

Joe refused to pursue the scheme, but Earl gave one of the skulls to a local sculptor who made rubber castings that Earl used to frame the cage of a king cobra under the title "Mankiller." He mounted one of the skulls over a bucket of smoking dry ice and made it the table centerpiece at the family Halloween party.

Earl believed that if people were offended by salting Colossal Cave with old Indian skulls, he could dismiss it as an epic prank. All was fair in the pursuit of a tourist nickel. If it was fraudulent, at least it was entertaining. Moved by a good story that could be told again and again back home, no tourist would complain. In the 1930s, Earl had understood that it was the mystery that surrounded Hidden City that made it popular, not the fake archeology. Twenty years later, the same rules applied. It was the spectacle and entertainment that tourists were attracted to, not the faux archeology of Indian bones hidden in the back of a cave.

Joe's values were more in sync with the educational values of the state. He came early to an interest in conservation. He was cautious about the way the Cave was publicly represented. Earl was carefree and careless.

On one trip to Arizona, Earl traveled with a frozen 18-foot python in his trunk. At two a.m. one morning, he found himself resting at De Anza Park in Tucson with the nearly defrosted python, so he wrapped the stiff carcass around the trunk of a palm tree and left it hanging. The mysterious snake was discovered the next day, and the *Arizona Star* newspaper promptly reported the news. A long, thoughtful article offered sober reflections by local herpetologists about the consequences of raising pet pythons that might escape and be run over by a late-night driver unprepared to encounter an 18-foot snake in the middle of the road. Earl could not resist the temptation to gloat. He clipped the article from the newspaper and sent it to the *Rapid City Journal*, where the editors quickly reasoned that it was one of Earl's pranks. When the Arizona authorities discovered that the entire episode had been a practical joke by a man who described himself as the Snake King of South Dakota, they were none too happy that the prankster was also the proprietor of their Colossal Cave.

Joe and Earl carried on a daily correspondence. The distance between them mediated the stress of their personal relationship. Both men had fantasies of building a tourism conglomerate spread across several states that might rival Disneyland or Knott's Berry Farm.

Walt Disney had been among the first to grasp the transition from the old-style educational tourism of the railroad era to the entertainment tourism of the automobile age. If there was one place that the public embraced the freedom of automobile culture, it was Southern California. Walt Disney paved the way to a new vacation experience that celebrated fantasy escapism. But both Reptile Gardens and Colossal Cave were distant from large population centers. Their isolation was their Achilles heel, and Joe and Earl were timid about making the large, risky investments that would be necessary to create a Disneyland in the Northern Plains or the Arizona desert.

When Earl had the opportunity to turn the movie set town of Old Tucson into a regional theme park, he hesitated. Since 1939, the location had been the film site for various Hollywood westerns, including *Gunfight at the O.K. Corral*. Old Tucson was a small investment, but $250,000 for cleanup, a new restaurant, improved shops and children's rides was too big a gamble. "I have been used to thinking in terms of $20,000, $25,000 or even $50,000 as the place in the business world where I belong," Earl wrote to Joe in April 1959. "It just plain scares hell out of me when I think about going on the hook for very large amounts and thus being in debt for years and years to come."

Joe agreed. "In cold reality, Earl, our current attempts to make money in the tourist business are not good enough to create optimism in a new venture. Where in the world did our youthful optimism go? I imagine we would even take a new lover with a lack of enthusiasm!"

After a trip to Southern California, Earl concluded that the scale of the investment at Disneyland made him feel "insignificant" as a tourism operator. He needed capital, but he hated debt, and while he had no problem risking his own modest assets, he had a strong ethical antipathy to courting investment from friends who could not afford the risks.

Without capital to work with, Colossal Cave limped along. At one point, Earl complained to Joe that he was courting a fraud investigation by kiting checks at Colossal Cave, but on a grander, more informal scale, Earl was doing the same. One week he would send a check to Joe to cover an unexpected expense at the Cave. Then Joe would write a check to a vendor and hope that he could cover it by the time it arrived at the bank. A week later, Joe would write another check to Earl to cover an unseen expense at Reptile Gardens. Back and forth, they stayed one step ahead of the bank. In their imagination, they were always one good idea away from a breakthrough, and then the next week, they were one bounced check closer to bankruptcy.

As if to punctuate the feeling that they were running at top speed but not moving forward, Joe reported that Colossal Cave had brought in $63,140 in receipts in 1958, $51,523 in gross profit. After expenses were paid, the enterprise had netted only $705. For all his work, Earl's 80 percent share for the whole year was $564.38.

To Earl's amazement, Jim Campbell began to show a profit at Fairyland Zoo in 1958. His nose to the grindstone, relentless work ethic had finally paid off. On Jim's initiative, Earl purchased an ensemble of trained barnyard animal acts from a roadside attraction in Southern California known as Bewitched Village. The acts included trained chickens, pigs, cows and rabbits. They became a popular part of the Fairyland Zoo project. But rather than the new investments complementing each other in the creation of a tourism empire, Earl worried that he was building a giant, undercapitalized Rube Goldberg machine with lots of moving elements that never quite synchronized.

If any one investment symbolized the precarious ledge on which Earl was operating, it was the sure bet of selling 50 squirrel monkeys in the spring of 1959. Like so many of the oddball, get-rich-quick schemes that came across Earl's desk in the 1950s, this project involved the same Arthur Jones that Earl had sworn to never do business with again.

A MONKEY IN EVERY HOME

To Earl's everlasting frustration, Jones had never fully accounted for all the crocodiles he had captured in Africa. A year after the escapade, Earl figured that Jones still owed him more than $14,000. As if he was doing Earl a favor, Jones offered substitute snakes, alligators and monkeys at arbitrary and inflated prices. Earl found it difficult to understand how giving Jones more money for animals he did not want would resolve the issue. But such was the nature of deals with Arthur Jones.

In the spring of 1959, Jones made an offer that actually seemed like it might make money. He was looking to dump a shipment of Amazonian squirrel monkeys into the pet market. Earl thought he could sell the small monkeys as pets to families in Rapid City. He ordered 50 at ten dollars apiece and paid an additional two dollars each for express shipping. When they arrived, Earl intended to sell them for $15. For all his time and effort, Earl stood to make three dollars a monkey, a total of $150 on the first shipment. He judged it worth the effort. Selling pet monkeys to teenagers would generate great publicity and goodwill with the community. The project had all the public relations pizzazz of a parachute jump onto Devils Tower.

Earl kept one monkey as a pet for his family and gave it to 12-year-old Janet, who thanked her father but privately confessed that the monkey smelled and wreaked havoc on her room. He sold the others quickly, using Janet's attachment to her monkey as a testimonial. "The fad is catching," he wrote to a friend in New Mexico. "After one family got one, the next family wanted to get one too." He ordered 50 more for Rapid City and arranged for Jones to send a shipment of 50 to Joe in Arizona. It was exactly the kind of tone-deaf idea that did not fit with the identity of the Cave. "Rapid City has gone crazy over them," he told Joe, "and I am sure Tucson would too."

To move the second shipment, Earl changed the name of the monkeys to "Golden Monkeys" and raised the price. No one in Rapid City would know that his or her pets were a completely different species, and "golden monkey" had a regal ring to it. He advertised on radio and in the *Journal*: "For the sweetest pet you ever owned see the beautiful golden monkeys, no larger than a squirrel, for sale at the Reptile Gardens for only $16.95."

For unsuspecting parents, the cost and challenge of owning a monkey turned out to be substantially more than a goldfish or cat. Earl encouraged the parents to purchase a pair of heavy-duty leather gloves to handle the monkeys until they settled down. Then there was the need for a birdcage for the monkeys to live in. The digestive systems of the monkeys were delicate. Earl advised feeding them a teaspoon of hamburger every day, along with sliced apples, bananas and other assorted fruits. But the monkeys made a mess, smelled and required daily attention. Some monkeys "settled down," but many ransacked their new homes, biting children, soiling and scratching the furniture and refusing to retreat into their cages at night.

A few parents whose children had made extravagant promises about caring for their new pets and then abandoned their monkey to mother's care wanted their money back. That was bad enough. In Arizona, Joe was concerned that the monkeys carried worms and would require expensive antibiotic treatments or vaccinations. He worried that the monkeys couldn't pass inspection by local animal regulatory boards. Earl suggested that they say nothing about the health of the monkeys unless local officials asked. Weeks later, almost as an afterthought, Earl fired off a note to Arthur Jones. "I wonder what the danger of rabies is. One person was bitten by their monkey, which also frothed at the mouth before it died. Do these monkeys receive any shots or any quarantine before coming into the country?"

Other monkeys began to die. The Brockelsby family pet died first. "I think that had I started giving him vitamin supplements, he would have survived," Earl wrote. Vitamins! Leather gloves! Vaccinations! The monkeys were supposed to be easy to care for pets. By mid-summer, half the monkeys sold in Rapid City had died. Earl stopped calling them pets and started calling them "specimens."

Joe's experience at Colossal Cave was no better. When the first shipment of 50 arrived, one was already dead. Two more died the next day. "They arrived a little bloody from eating each other," Joe wrote to Earl. "We've been giving them hamburger in the hopes they will stop. Only a handful are clean enough to sell this weekend." Within six months, almost all of the monkeys were dead.

Earl had made a business out of controlling the interaction between humans and dangerous reptiles. He had made money by understanding the fascination that humans had for the exotic. He had been the first to warn people that snakes were not "pets." But when he tried to make a quick profit by obscuring the line between domestic and wild, he crashed—all for a few hundred dollars.

RETA MAE

Earl's effort to save the marriage between his sister and his business partner seemed hopeless. One day in the fall of 1960, Reta Mae handed Earl a lengthy letter to deliver to Joe. "When you read this I will be dead," she began. "And you will finally have your wish—you will be rid of me." For eight pages she alternated between a cool, dispassionate description of how she wanted Joe Jr. to be raised (by Earl) and raging outbursts about how much she loved Joe and felt betrayed by his move to Arizona. "I have thought so many times how I would welcome insanity or death, as then my mind would be free at last."

She never acted on her letter. Perhaps she never intended to. Perhaps it was a drastic, misguided attempt to keep hold of the one true love she had ever known. Regardless of her intent, the letter must have made Earl think about his mother's desperate threats to hang herself in the family closet. He let time pass, kept Reta Mae's secrets and never gave the suicide note to Joe. It was part of the unbearable burden of patriarchy to be in the middle of so much despair and to believe it was his responsibility to navigate the shallows of everyone's unhappiness, even when he could not manage his own.

Reta Mae joined an informal therapy group and rebounded from her depression. She rebuilt her life around her love for Joe Jr. and worked to reunite her family. "I have decided to take matters into my own hands and guide fate," she wrote to Joe about her new plans to move to Arizona. "I want the opportunity to try family life again and most of all I want Joey and I to be near you again." It was an impulsive idea that did not take into consideration Joe's lack of commitment to the marriage, and it met a predictable fate. Joe did not want to try again. He wanted a divorce.

"There seems to be no end to emotional problems," Joe wrote to Earl in January 1963. "You are right in assuming that I would like to run away for a few years—but I can't do it and neither could you—the fact remains that a divorce is the best all the way around. Her threats to kill herself and Joey cut pretty deep—a person knows better but they are paralyzing thoughts nonetheless."

Unable to hold his sister's marriage together, Earl began to look for ways to extricate himself from the business partnership with Joe and Colossal Cave. But this effort was pushed to the background as he suddenly faced a major threat to the future of Reptile Gardens.

MOVING THE HIGHWAY AND MOVING ON

— Chapter 13 —

By the late 1950s, Earl had been in the roadside tourism business for 20 years, and he had learned his lessons through hard experience. When entrepreneurs came to him with romantic ideas for new attractions, Earl always asked one question: "Where are you planning to build your attraction?" More important than the spectacle, more important than the advertising strategy, more important than the cost of operation, was the location. He had learned this lesson at Sioux Pageant, at the Petrified Forest and at Reptile Gardens. He had given his location much consideration and chosen perfectly. And when he acted against this first principle, as at Fairyland Zoo, for example, he had paid the consequences. In the roadside tourist business, "roadside" meant everything. There were no good ideas distant from the highway.

Every year since 1937, Earl had invested in the expansion of the Gardens. He had purchased the land before the war. He rebuilt after the war. He planted a beautiful flower garden. He designed the rock façade on the postwar building and, with Ed

Westin, personally made the bricks from his own handcrafted brick molds. He added alligator and crocodile pools and expanded the snake house. Then, after two decades at the same location, he learned that State highway engineers planned to reengineer Highway 16 south of Rapid City and move it a quarter mile east of the Gardens, leaving Earl stranded just out of sight of the fast lane to Mount Rushmore.

Anyone who operated a second-tier attraction in the Black Hills understood that they lived in the shadow of the Shrine of Democracy. Earl was incensed that the engineers treated Reptile Gardens like an afterthought, but their job was to straighten and shorten the route to Mount Rushmore. Earl barely warranted consideration. Reptile Gardens was collateral damage.

Hoping to convince the State that a new highway didn't need to bypass the Gardens, Earl commissioned his own survey and took it to the State's engineers in Pierre. He poured out his frustrations to Joe. "I haven't really battled for a long time but it looks like this will turn into quite a challenge, so I am going to take off my gloves and fight for it." After one meeting with highway commissioners, he jubilantly wrote, "I WIN! NOT official, but the odds are 100 to 1 with me now." But his euphoria was quickly crushed when the commission voted to adopt the new high-speed bypass, leaving in the dust both Reptile Gardens and the days when roadside barkers could stand on the shoulder of the two-lane highway waving their cowboy hats at the overheated cars. He had fought valiantly to stay on his hilltop, but there was inevitability to the straight-line logic of the highway engineers.

Conceding defeat, Earl began to cast about for a new location on the new highway. When a 40-acre parcel in Spring Creek valley became available, he grabbed it. The land was six miles south of Rapid City. It was halfway between the old Reptile Gardens at the southern edge of the city and Sitting Bull Crystal Caverns, where the Sioux Indian Pageant had enlivened Earl's teenage summers.

This gorgeous valley was the site that Paul Bellamy had imagined as the home of the United Nations, and Earl stayed true to Bellamy's imagination. He designed the new Gardens to be part world's fair pavilion and part big tent circus. At the center of the valley, he would build a one-of-a-kind 60-foot translucent plastic dome, 110 feet in diameter, designed by German engineers. The local contractor described the dome as "an architectural marvel." Earl bragged that it was "the largest rigid-framed plastic dome of its kind in the country." Inside the dome, he planted orchids and an eclectic tropical forest filled with birds and snakes, and brightly colored macaws and parrots flew from branch to branch. On the inside walls of the dome, a local artist painted murals of elaborate jungle scenes and Mayan ruins. Snakes by the hundreds, deadly venomous, thick as a man's arm, thin as a sleek racer and long as a tree branch, lurked behind the glass walls of cages that spiraled around the interior of the dome building.

The dome signaled a change in Earl's vision for the Gardens and his treatment of the animals on display. Rather than focusing on the display of hundreds of local or regional snakes that would be dead by the end of summer, the dome created a year-round environment in which specimens could survive the harsh South Dakota winters. With the dome, Earl Chace could assemble a more diversified and exotic collection of international snakes and reptiles that could be sustained year-round.

The relocation allowed Earl to make changes that he had wanted to make for years. He closed the Fairyland Zoo in Custer and moved the zoo and the performing animal acts of the Bewitched Village to the new location. He brought Jim Campbell back as general manager of the consolidated enterprise. He built outdoor botanical gardens where children could have their pictures taken while riding a giant Galápagos tortoise.

Construction on the new complex began in the spring of 1964 and spanned a full year. The most difficult problem was not the engineering of the dome, but the three-mile transport of alligators and crocodiles from the old Gardens to the new. After the biggest crocodile had been trapped and caged, it took 12 men to lift the crate out of the pool and load it onto a truck. But then, having safely transported the crocodiles, the Earls (Chace and Brockelsby) became uncharacteristically complacent with a truck load of alligators, which almost resulted in disaster.

"We didn't bother to tape their mouths shut," Earl remembered years later. "Earl Chace and I climbed into the back of the truck with forty gators who were perfectly quiet until the truck started to move—then they went crazy, snapping at each other and at our feet dangling in the truck. Chace and I tried to balance on the sides of the truck, with our feet in the air, while the jaws were snapping all around us." Fortunately, neither man nor beast was seriously harmed in the melee.

With alligators safely ensconced in their new home, Reptile Gardens opened in June 1965. A double-page advertisement in the *Journal* offered door prizes and free "rattlesnake sandwiches" to opening day visitors. The new complex was electric with a spirit of entertainment. Guides swung on ropes like Tarzan and dropped into snake pits where they walked among the snakes and gave "rattlesnake milking" exhibitions. Muscular young men, stripped to the waist, "wrestled" alligators in large pens with shallow pools and sandy beaches. The wrestlers approached the alligators from the front, tapped their nose and opened the upper jaw, revealing huge teeth. With its top jaw opened wide, the gator could not see what was happening in front of him. The wrestler moved close, reached underneath the bottom jaw, drew it close and then used both hands to clamp the jaws together. If the gator weighed 150 pounds and the wrestler 200, the young man might raise his arm in triumph.

All the wrestlers knew which gators were cantankerous and which were most likely to snap at human contact. One false move and an agitated alligator could whip its open jaws across a forearm or thrash its tail and sprint back into the pool. The crowds loved the action. It took a certain kind of personality to stand in the middle of a dozen alligators and talk to the crowd as if there was no risk.

With these attractions in place, Earl had faced the adversity of a new highway and doubled down. He sold his interest in the Colossal Cave to Joe, went heavily in debt and bet his future on his own creativity. The new Reptile Gardens was not just a tourist site in the shadow of Mount Rushmore. The valley of the dome made it a grand spectacle.

MILKING RATTLERS, WRESTLING GATORS

One thing stayed the same at the new Reptile Gardens: the cult of youth and adventure. Inside the walls was an enduring Neverland. If children were the driving force behind a family's visit, it was important that they make a personal connection with the young guides and staff. Thousands of children passed through the Gardens and returned home with dreams of someday milking the snakes or wrestling the alligators themselves. One of those dreamers was Nick Hall.

A 130-pound immigrant from England with a thick accent, Hall was scrawny and uncoordinated. By his own admission, he was "the last boy picked" for any playground game, and it didn't help that he had grown up in the culture of soccer and cricket. He landed in Rapid City because his stepfather was in the Air Force and had been transferred from England to Ellsworth Air Force Base in the fall of 1958.

When he was 12 years old, Nick took a summer job selling ice cream throughout the city from a freezer attached to the back of his bicycle. One day, he had the bright idea to push his cart to the top of Skyline Drive and sell his wares in the parking lot of Reptile Gardens, where his mother worked in the gift shop. The hill was steep, but his initiative paid off. He sold out by noon. After a few weeks, Earl offered him a fulltime job as a bumper boy. It was the starting job for almost every young boy who came through the Gardens, and in midsummer it could also be miserable.

"On your knees all day in the gravel," Nick remembered. "The strong smell of the radiator and tires. Sometimes insects were plastered to the bumpers so thick that the gum of the bumper stickers would not adhere." Some tourists loved the bumper stickers, but some screamed at the bumper boys and shooed them away from their cars or demanded that the bumper stickers be peeled off.

After two summers, Nick's father was transferred to the East Coast, but each summer for a decade, Nick boarded a bus and headed west to work at Reptile Gardens. He lived in the makeshift basement dormitory and gradually worked his way up the food chain from bumper boy to cleaning the bathrooms and sweeping up in the gift shop and hamburger stand. At night, when he thought no one was watching, he would sneak into the snake pit and handle the snakes.

One day, Bob Armstrong, a snake guide, was bitten on his foot. Earl took out a razor, cut an X across the fang marks and let the wound bleed. But Bob's leg swelled, and he went into a coma. Doctors wanted to amputate his leg, but Earl argued for patience. He had seen many snakebites, he told the doctors. The pain would be excruciating, and the wound would take months to heal, but Bob would recover. It was better than amputation.

Meanwhile, back at Reptile Gardens, Earl confronted young Nick Hall. "Are you ready to milk the rattlesnakes?" he asked.

Nick's first instinct was to say no, but he was caught off guard by Earl's casual demeanor. "I don't know how to do it," he replied.

Earl said, "Yes you do. I know you go into the snake pit at night."

Hall denied it, but Earl knew the truth. "I have to get my parents' permission," Hall said.

"I've already called them."

Hall didn't know that Earl was lying. "When would I start?" he asked.

"In fifteen minutes."

After practicing on one snake, Nick went into the snake pit in front of the crowd. That's the way things happened at Reptile Gardens. When Earl called on you, no matter how scared you were, you stepped up.

With a pat on the back, Earl offered Nick one last vote of confidence: "If you get bit, don't worry. Chace and I will be in the crowd with our razors."

In a flash, Nick Hall's place in the universe changed. He had new status around the campfire in the badlands. Girls looked at him differently. He had gone from timid to daring, from a nerd to a poisonous snake handler. "Earl gave me the greatest gift anyone could give me," Nick remembered. "He gave me the gift of confidence. If he thought I could do something, I thought I could do it."

Sometimes Earl's confidence inspired reckless, mischievous behavior in the tradition of his infamous pranks. One 4th of July, Nick invited his girlfriend to watch the fireworks on the beach at Pactola Lake. Worried that the beach would be too crowded to spread a blanket, Nick came up with a scheme to milk a prairie rattlesnake of its venom, put it in a sack and release it on the beach when no one was looking. He had hoped to impress his date and create enough space to put down his blanket, but the crowd screamed and scattered, and the entire beach emptied. The rangers were furious. They threatened to arrest him and unceremoniously threw him off the beach. With the snake in the sack and his girlfriend in tow, Nick drove to Joe's Bar in Rapid City. After he dumped his snake on the bar, the crowd panicked and ran for the door. Nick repeated this stunt at several other bars and then called it a night. When he returned to his bunk at the Gardens, he found Earl sitting on a stool in a low boil.

"Where have you been?" Earl asked.

Nick told him that he had taken his girlfriend to the fireworks at Pactola. Then they went to a bar in town and had a few drinks. Then he came home.

Earl stared at him. "No you didn't. I know where you've been." He recounted every detail of Nick's night on the town. "Parents are furious at me. The bartender is threatening to sue me. You've ruined my reputation," Earl scolded.

Nick apologized. He insisted that he had milked the snake before putting it on the beach, but Earl was unimpressed. "I thought I was going to be on the next bus out of town," Nick remembered.

Disgusted, Earl began to walk away, but then he turned back to Hall. With a glint in his eye, he said, "If it had been me, I wouldn't have milked the snake first."

From that moment, Nick knew that he wasn't going to lose his job. More importantly, he knew that Earl understood him.

Two years later, in 1965, Nick's job took a new twist when one of the alligator wrestlers was bitten. Once again, Earl came to him, this time with the impeccable logic of a tightfisted businessman. "He explained that the insurance for snake handlers and alligator wrestlers was so expensive that it made sense for one person to do both jobs," Hall said.

Earl Chace was Nick's guardian angel, and he opposed the idea. The alligators outweighed the teenager. Besides, Nick may have mastered rattlesnake milking, which had more to do with a steady hand than brute strength, but he was still uncoordinated, and the alligators had lightning-fast reflexes.

As usual, Earl saw the situation differently. Nick might be small. The alligators might be bigger, he told Nick, but, "Wow, wouldn't that be incredible if he was eaten! The tourists will love a fair fight." True to his faith in Earl's judgment, Nick embraced the challenge. After all, he reasoned, tourist girls loved the alligator wrestlers.

One day, as he often did, Nick fixed his sights on a pretty girl in the crowd and waded to the edge of the pool to grab a particularly feisty alligator and drag it onto shore. Each time Nick approached the gator it thrashed its way loose and ran back into the pool. After three attempts, Nick was losing patience and his own strength. He missed a beat in his timing, and when he tried to grab the alligator's jaw, its teeth sunk deeply into the joint of his right thumb. The wound began to bleed. Nick shook off the pain, but he was experienced enough to know what lay ahead.

Alligators were often fed road-kill deer delivered to the backdoor of the Gardens by rangers. The bloated carcasses made for great meals, but they were also rank with bacteria. The alligator that bit Nick did not follow with an attack. It shook its head and retreated toward the pond. Nick could see the spit and chunks of deer meat in its teeth. His arm began to swell and turned deep shades of blue and black. Earl grabbed a nearby brush and began to scrub the sand from the bite. The doctor complained that it would have been easier if Nick had been bitten by a rattlesnake— at least then he would know how to treat it.

Waiting out the pain was a less than optimistic course of treatment, but Hall returned to Reptile Gardens to face a more immediate problem than his mortality. There were hundreds of billboards on roads all across South Dakota inviting people to come to Reptile Gardens to see the alligator wrestlers, but with Nick's right arm frozen in pain from thumb to shoulder, there were no wrestlers left.

Jim Campbell had an idea. If Nick couldn't actually wrestle an alligator, perhaps he could use his one good arm and create the illusion of wrestling. Rather than approach the gator from the front, Nick practiced jumping on the gators from behind—

the way Seminole Indians did it at tourist attractions in the Everglades.

Nick learned to grab both jaws and hold them clamped together. The alligator might buck him off, but if he could hold the jaws closed and cover the gator's eyes with a towel, he could ride out the panic. One-armed Nick was back in business. Over the weeks that followed, the pain subsided and the swelling declined. But even 50 years later, after a career as a neuroscience professor, his right thumb ached from chronic arthritis—a mild pain and a vivid memory of a young life at Reptile Gardens.

A PERFECT LIFE

— Chapter 14 —

Rapid City in the 1960s was not, by any measure, a class-conscious community. Hard work was the community ethic, and wealth, especially inherited wealth, was modest. In a community of 42,000, the number of millionaires could be counted on one hand. The children of the richest sat side by side with the poorest in school. The absence of a class of inherited wealth and the celebration of individual enterprise were both essential to the emerging mythology of the postwar American West.

Earl and Maude were, by force of personality and social status, among Rapid City's elite. But neither they nor their friends were ostentatious about their wealth and influence. They preached a gospel of modesty. And yet there was an understated, distinctly Western elegance to Brockelsby family portraits: Judee and Janet, perfectly dressed, poised, beautiful, even as teenagers; Johnny and Jeff, scrubbed pink, hair slicked back with Brylcreem, wearing matching pairs of cowboy boots, sport coats and bolo ties; Earl with an effervescent "Come into my home" smile, as if he was greeting Edward R. Murrow and the cameras from *Person to Person* at the door; Maude, the matriarch—less spontaneous, more cautious, but clearly in charge.

A HOME ON RAPID CREEK

In 1952, the family moved into the home that Earl had designed and built on the Rapid Creek property. Judee was ten. Janet was five. Johnny was a baby. Postwar tourism had been so explosive that Earl paid cash for the construction. It seemed like forever since the debacle on Devils Tower, a decade earlier, when Earl had lost all of the money he and Maude had saved to buy a house.

The design of the creekside home reflected Earl's midcentury modern taste. The living room was a 40-foot-long open space. Broad windows looked out on Rapid Creek. An expansive deck ran the length of the house. It was elegant in its details, but it was not a large or pretentious house, and Earl seemed more preoccupied with the meadow of wildflowers than a manicured lawn.

As the children became teenagers, the house exerted a gravitational pull on the neighborhood, which may have been the result of its proximity to the creek or the smell of Maude's cookies wafting from the kitchen. A greenhouse attached to Earl's den allowed him to grow orchids and flowers year-round. When the flowers bloomed, Earl gathered them in bouquets. The scent filled the living room and provided color for the whole winter.

Maude enforced the morals of the household. She took the children to church. She ensured that Earl made annual contributions to the local foster parents program, the Presbyterian Church, the Boys and Girls Clubs. If she had any reputation at all for extravagant behavior, it was her commitment to prepare a home-cooked, sit-down family dinner every evening. "Mom did all the laundry, the shopping and the cooking," Janet Brockelsby remembered. "Meat, potato and salad. Every night. And we were expected to eat every bite." Dinner was mandatory and participation in dinner table conversation was required. Reta Mae and Joe Jr. were frequent guests who required no invitation. The children's friends were also welcome at the table. "We love coming to your house," Judee's friends told her. "Your father talked to us, and your mother cooked."

One of the most important seats at the table was reserved for Eloise Hall, the mother of Earl's friend, Bob Hall, who had given Earl a home on his 1936 trip to Los Angeles. In the years after Earl returned to Rapid City, the Hall family fell victim to unspeakable tragedy. Bob was accidentally killed by a neighbor who mistook him for an intruder while walking his dog. Soon thereafter, Bob's father died. Before the Depression, the Halls had been a wealthy family. By 1950, Eloise was a widow with no secure source of income. Earl took over her mortgage and paid her debts. Toward the end of her life, Earl moved her to the Black Hills. Maude integrated her into the life of the family. "She must have lived near us for several years," Judee remembered. "Dad called her Mrs. Hall. We called her Aunt Eloise. She was always invited to holiday dinners, and we loved her like she was one of the family."

In every way, the life that Earl and Maude created on Rapid Creek represented the triumph of the postwar generation: from homestead to prosperity, from war to security. Part of the security was the freedom to be slightly disdainful of the dull conformity of the 1950s. Rapid Creek was no Hyannis Port, but the Brockelsby family had a Kennedyesque character suited to the optimism and boundless energy of Camelot.

Earl and Maude had been founding members of the Arrowhead Country Club, but Earl put a strict limit on the time that Johnny could idle at the side of the pool. "Golf," he explained, "is a good way to ruin a great hike." Rather than sit by the pool, the children were expected to work at Reptile Gardens, where he insisted that they "set a standard" by working harder than everyone else. What he demanded in discipline, he happily gave back in freedom. He took them camping in the badlands and allowed them to sit on the wheel-well of the truck as he bounced through the rugged terrain. He challenged them to fitness competitions: who could hike the farthest or do the most pushups? He encouraged them to read, to become debaters and to engage in community activities. He sat Judee on his knee and read Spinoza. He hung prints of Monet and Van Gogh masterpieces on the wall of the breakfast room and taught the children about art at the breakfast table. He filled the house with music: the popular songs of George Gershwin— "Rhapsody in Blue," "I've Got Rhythm," "They Can't Take That Away from Me"—classical music, and the exotic melodies of Peruvian-American singer Yma Sumac.

Acutely aware of the repressed emotional life of their own childhoods, Earl and Maude resolved to actively engage their children and raise them in an environment of emotional openness. They were romantic with each other. They took ballroom dancing lessons and practiced with the children in the living room. They were joyful. The result was an uncommon intimacy that occasionally blurred the boundaries between child and adult in ways that the children were not prepared for. When Maude casually took the children to a nightclub one evening to see a live band, the culture shock was too much for 14-year-old Janet. "I saw people doing things that night that I would never think of doing and further more if those kids' parents knew they acted like that they would be embarrsed [sic] to death," she wrote to her father. "I also learned that people are much dirtier than pics and I mean this sincerely from the bottom of my liver. Mother left after the second show with the boys, and Liz and I stayed on with the drunk men and women and OH! ICK!"

The open inquisitiveness of the Brockelsby household reflected Earl's personality. He was, simply, the coolest dad in town. He hid his set of *Playboy* magazines in his office (where Johnny promptly, and a bit too easily, discovered them). But at the height of the Cold War, he also subscribed to *Soviet Life* magazine and displayed it prominently in the living room. "He wasn't procommunist," Johnny remembered. "But he would tell us that we were surrounded by a lot of propaganda that just wasn't true. He told us that they have regular people over there and that we had to learn to think for ourselves. He hated the idea that someone would try to tell him what to read and what not to read." When Johnny started an underground newspaper at Rapid City High School, *On the Other Side of the Fence, Where The Grass is Greener*, the front page was adorned with a graphic symbol of marijuana leaves. School administrators asked Earl to shut his son down, but he refused. "I don't agree with most of what's in the newspaper," Earl explained. "But I think Johnny has learned more from putting out this newspaper than he learned in class."

Earl loved learning by doing. He took the children on long nature hikes to the top of Harney Peak and cooked alligator tail over campfires in the badlands. With the thirsty children swatting flies, Earl lectured and lectured and lectured. "By the time I graduated from high school, I knew all the Latin names for plants and animals in Baja," Johnny remembered. "My friends asked, 'How do you know all those things?' I told them, 'That's all dad ever talked about.'"

When Johnny asked for Earl's advice about a "demonstration speech" for school, Earl suggested that he milk the venom from a rattlesnake in front of the class. Johnny dutifully carried a prairie rattlesnake in a flour bag, delivered his speech and stored the rattlesnake in his locker until school was over.

The uncommon intimacy brought with it an uncommon maturity. Both Judee and Janet idolized their father, but even as teenagers, they were also aware of Earl's mental health problems. When Maude could not rouse him from his depression, she did not hesitate to call upon Judee to try to pull him from his darkness. "Dad was so complex," Judee remembered. "He was so generous, so creative. But he was competitive, and he had a huge ego. And then he would go into one of his bouts of depression."

In 1960, Earl accepted an appointment to an open seat on the Rapid City school board and reentered civic life. It was a strange commitment for a man who had disdained formal education as a teenager and who looked with skepticism on textbook lessons when the true value of education lay outside the classroom window. But he had four children in the school system. If ever there was a time to renew his interest in civic life, it was when the children were fully engaged. The school board appointment symbolized Earl's commitment to community and family, his ability to take care of his own and, at the same time, serve the community's larger interests. During his tenure, he laid the groundwork for a second high school on the west end of town and initiated an art-in-the-schools program. He wanted to hang large prints of artistic masterpieces in the hallways of the schools, but the project never gained enough support from the board of education to be implemented. He gave his time generously but remained frustrated that he still could not move the levers of the local bureaucracy.

When the wheels of reform turned too slowly to hold his interest, Earl made his impact outside the school district, in his own living room. He hosted spectacular evenings of slideshows with tales of adventure from his trips to the exotic corners of the world. He organized rugged trips for the children to Mexico and Asia. When Johnny wanted to take his friends to Baja in the summer after high school graduation, Earl assembled the skeptical parents and convinced them how important the adventure could be for their sons. He sponsored African-American jazz ensembles and Chicano salsa bands at the local nightclubs, then invited the musicians to dinner at home, daring local segregationists to complain.

Most of all, Earl provided the coolest summer jobs in the Hills. Get a job at Reptile Gardens when you were 15, and you could be wrestling alligators and winking at tourist girls by 17. Hundreds, and then thousands, of lucky Rapid City teenagers and college students who worked at the Gardens returned to school with tales of adventure and romance. These were the kinds of summers that people told their own grandchildren about 40 years later.

Earl was a tough taskmaster. He could be impatient with the fact that his own generation's work ethic had slipped away in the cultural revolution of the 1960s. He could be withering in his criticism. But if you were lucky and worked hard, if you showed an interest in what needed to be done before you were asked, you might just get invited to go camping in the badlands and spend the night under the stars on Sheep Mountain Table. A summer job at Reptile Gardens could be magical.

A DEEPLY FRAGILE INNER LIFE

Inside the holiday photographs of a perfect life, Earl was a fragile man. By 1960, he had been taking four to five Miltown tranquilizers every day for almost a decade, and he kept a bottle of barbiturates next to his bed. He considered Miltown a miracle drug that saved his life and gave him control over his manic depression. He shared his enthusiasm and his prescription with friends and family who had a headache, woke up depressed in the morning or could not make it through a day of work, but he worried about the long-term consequences of his addictions. Miltown and the barbiturates managed the extremes of his illness, but they did not cure him.

He experimented several times with cutting back, but the only time that he felt confident that he could reduce his dosage was when he escaped into the solitude of nature: the badlands or the desert around Tucson or Baja California, which he began to visit for at least a few weeks every winter. During the intense months of the tourist season, when the phone never stopped ringing and the days were filled with stressful meetings and demanding tourists, his attempts to cut back ended in disaster. "I would get so nervous I was ready to scream at the slightest thing," he confided to Joe.

Still, he could not resist the urge to experiment. "Unless you misunderstand I want you to know I am actually enjoying this," he told Joe at the beginning of one attempt to cut back. "I am kind of a third interested party to see what happens to my body." In the autumn of 1960, he resolved to take himself completely off Miltown and rid himself of his addiction forever.

"Well, the first day my vision got blurry. The next couple of days my left leg and arm were numb." He kept detailed notes. "This was accompanied by pains in the chest and occasional feelings that I was about to explode at any provocation. I spent another day feeling pretty good and then yesterday [November 4, 1960], I awakened with one of those headaches where your brain feels like it is loose inside of a tom-tom." His suffering was accompanied by chills, nausea, dizziness and lack of appetite. After the withdrawal, he reported to Joe, "I awakened my ordinary stupid self but now my left eye won't open and as I tried to hold it open to drive down town the tears ran out so heavily I was almost blinded and doubted if I could make it to the Reptile Gardens."

While his demons ran wild, his life went dark. On the eve of a trip to Baja, he wrote a very private letter to Maude. He sealed it in an envelope with the inscription, "Open in case of Earl's death." He began with a premonition: "I don't know exactly why I am writing this note, but one reason is that a couple of months ago I received a feeling of impending tragedy...I realized that this tragedy would effect more than just myself, but like a sentence of death by the Gods there could be no turning back, just the slow inevitable movement toward the end."

He described himself as having "great curiosity" about death. He explained that he had rewritten his insurance policy to guarantee security for Maude and the children. He confessed his inattention to the marriage and hinted at infidelities. "Should I apologize for my behavior?" he asked. "I don't know." He was considerate but not romantic. "Whatever my past behavior has been, I have always thought the kindliest most gentle thoughts of you. I wasn't all that you deserved or needed. And don't blame yourself for not being my every need."

Whatever side effects Earl suffered from trying to take himself off the Miltown, whatever demons seeped out from his unconscious, he saved the letter in a file cabinet and never gave it to Maude. With the experiment of drug withdrawal complete and the lessons learned, he promptly renewed his prescription and went back to work. But the letter hinted that the addiction to Miltown and the inability to stabilize his depression were having a corrosive effect on his marriage.

A MAN OF LETTERS

Earl spoke his mind. He was self-confident and self-centered. Businessmen in town remarked that when Earl entered a meeting, everyone in the room turned their heads. When Earl spoke, everyone listened. But he was also fragile and developed a dependency on solitude as well as his Miltown prescription. He built a private office behind his public office, where no one dared to enter without permission. In this space, he kept the lights dim and the music soft. When he went home after work, Maude and the children gave him a space for quiet withdrawal. They entered cautiously and only with Maude's permission.

Earl chose a most remarkable way to bridge the distance between his publicly flamboyant egoism and his private depression. He became a writer—not a writer in the traditional sense of an essayist or novelist. He lacked the singular focus. Instead, he became a prolific correspondent in an age when the telephone had become the primary technology of personal communication.

In the Army, Earl had written Maude every day, even when he was in camp and she was sequestered in a hotel only 30 miles away. He wrote from foxholes and battlefields. Maude returned his effort, writing back even when the dull routines of life on the home front could not match the drama of war. The correspondence enriched their marriage, and Earl kept his collection of hundreds of wartime letters in a file cabinet in his study.

In the 1960s, Earl wrote relentlessly—five, ten letters a day. He wrote to vendors and business associates, especially Joe in Arizona. He wrote to his favorite employees when they returned to college, especially the young women who had been charmed by his magnetism and flattery. In his letters, he offered advice on classes, love lives and relationships with parents. They returned his overtures with letters that began with profuse apologies for being distracted by exams and boys their own age and for writing only one letter for every three that he had written.

One can imagine Earl, alone by the dim light of his inner office, scribbling letter after letter to young employees he barely knew who were half his age. The man who had been nicknamed "the virgin of the European Theater," the man who had been appalled by the sexual behavior of American soldiers during the war was going through a metamorphosis. It was the dawn of the sexual revolution, and Earl, like many men of his era, was drawn to the prospect of easy promiscuity and the sense that old-fashioned bonds of monogamy were breaking down. Yet clearly he knew that he was walking the edges of propriety. He encouraged his female correspondents to use first names only. They called him "Brock" or "Earl." In their letters, they confessed their affairs, failed romances, boredom with college and anxieties about money and the future. They returned his attention with innuendo that suggested an awkward intimacy. "Hello Earl, love of my life," one young woman wrote from college. She signed her note, "Lover, XXX." Another young woman to whom he had sent a Valentine's

Day card complained, "I don't know whether I like the Valentine or not! I really didn't like it until I saw the last word scratched out. You'd best watch it boy!" Still another, mixing literary and sexual innuendo, ended her letter, "Mordaciously yours. XXX."

Despite this correspondence with young coeds, Earl reserved his most personal reflections for Reta Mae, Maude and the children. In the early 1960s, he began to travel for months at a time, but no matter how far away his adventures, he wrote home, and he wrote group letters to the "reptiles" at the Gardens. His commitment to emotional honesty with his children was returned in deep, lengthy, intense exchanges about sex, drugs, depression and family life that reflected almost no boundaries.

He scribbled, often illegibly, by the light of a campfire or the overhead lamp of a truck. He sent photographs and detailed reports from pristine beaches in Baja, rain forests in the Yucatan, treasure hunts in Costa Rica and villages in the central highlands of Papua New Guinea. He gossiped. He offered emotional support to Reta Mae, college advice to Judee and ideas for new projects to Joe, Earl Chace and Jim Campbell. He traveled by a strict schedule. At each wilderness post office, he sent a bundle of letters home and received the same from Maude and a dozen notes from the children, all stuffed in an airmail envelope and mailed to the villages on his itinerary.

Judee wrote with perfect cursive penmanship. During her first month in college at the University of Arizona, she sent Earl seven long letters. On September 2, 1960, she worried, "I feel just like the shy and lonely little girl I used to be until I was about 14." A week later, with the thrill of freshman life in the dormitory, she announced that she had made friends and "[I] am not so homesick any more." She was lonely for her boyfriend who had returned to college in Maine. She complained, "The boys down here are fast and loud and obnoxious." In every letter, she tended to Earl's insecurities. "I think of you often daddy and I hope you aren't too discouraged with life," she wrote on September 6. She signed her letter: "Love always daddy dear…I am sure that I have the nicest daddy in the world." Judee could sense Earl's emotional fragility and responded with reassurance and comfort. "Daddy, nothing is wrong and I'm not mad or disappointed with you. I guess my letter seemed so because most of the time I am tired and depressed for no particular reason."

Janet, just beginning high school, was breezy and self-assured. She wrote about her performance on the debate team and her social life. She tagged her letters casually: "take it easy."

Johnny wrote in large block letters reinforced with copious exclamation points. He began his letters, "Dear Old Man." He reported on the successes and failures of the Rapid City High School basketball team and his bowling prowess. He grudgingly reported his grades (A in reading, B's in math and English, C's in science and social studies, D in shop). "It wasn't too bad. But mom was real mad but she always is." He wrote about his date for the upcoming school dance and exclaimed: "I've been busy with the girls!! (Just like you) Ho! Ho!"

Earl's youngest son, Jeff, affectionately nicknamed "Jeep" by the family, scribbled notes on old dinner napkins. Always, the children's letters ended with declarations of love and pleas to "come home, we miss you."

Maude's letters were full of the news of the town. She wrote with little intimacy. Weather, dinner with Reta Mae or Earl's mother, gossip about friends, news from the Gardens. By the mid-1960s, it was apparent that an unspoken distance had entered the marriage.

It was Reta Mae who laid her emotions bare in letters to her brother. In the heat of her separation from Joe Maierhauser, she clung to Earl. "In all my life there have only been two people I could love without misgivings, that I could wholly trust, and that I felt loyal and respectful to," she wrote in January 1962. "Of course they were you and Joe." Like all the others, she worried about him: "you pass out so much kindness and thoughtfulness I hope some of the kindness and generosity comes back to you to give you happiness that you long for—and deserve."

Although Earl traveled for longer periods, spent his weekends in the badlands and retreated into his own seclusion, the children would later remember their childhoods as secure and loving. He was not home for months on end. But the children felt comfortable in the security that Maude created for them and confident that "he was home even when he was not at home."

The correspondence files that survived in the basement of Reptile Gardens for half a century are by no means complete. Sometimes only fragments of an exchange exist. Sometimes it is difficult to interpret the innuendo. Sometimes letters are undated and even unsigned. Thousands of letters, including the complete file of wartime correspondence with Maude, were destroyed in the Rapid City flood of 1972. Nonetheless, by sheer volume, letter by letter, month by month, through the decade of the 1960s, the correspondence offers a remarkably raw, vulnerable, exposed portrait of an American family navigating its way through the turbulence of the times—through mental illness, infidelity, experimentation with drugs, the war in Vietnam, the generation gap and the slow, painful estrangement of Earl from his family.

TRAVELING MAN

— Chapter 15 —

From the time he was a child standing near the railroad tracks in Kadoka watching the brightly painted sides of circus cars rumble down the track, Earl Brockelsby knew that adventure lay beyond the town limits. Skiing the badlands alone or travelling by train to the Chicago World's Fair, he was inspired by the idea of exploring what he did not know and had never seen. He had gone to war in Europe, but unlike his fellow soldiers, he had engaged France and Germany as much as a grand tour of Western civilization as a battlefield. Who else would take liberty in Paris on the eve of liberation and visit the Louvre and Catacombs?

After his mental breakdown, Earl's love of travel became compulsive. He traveled the way a starving man eats—not with patience, but with desperation, devouring his adventures rather than savoring them. He spent months and thousands of dollars preparing for each trip. After each trip, with barely a moment to contemplate or celebrate, he began planning the next adventure. Between the mid-1950s and late 1970s, Earl visited 40 countries, on every continent except Antarctica. His trips grew longer—a month, sometimes three. His search for solitude became more extreme, and his separation from Maude and the family grew deeper.

Each year, when Reptile Gardens closed in the autumn, Earl packed his passport in his coat pocket and traveled. Sometimes for a few weeks, sometimes a month. He always returned home for the holidays and major events in the life of the family, but over the years his trips grew longer and his distance from family life increased. He wrote long letters to the children that came stamped with a hundred far-flung postmarks and received their love and adoration in return in thick envelopes mailed by Maude.

Travelling did not hold the same allure for Maude. She did not come to it naturally or with the same obsession as Earl. She occasionally went with Earl to safe destinations like Hawaii and Mexico City and Havana, Cuba, in the heyday of casinos and nightclubs, but she had less tolerance for uncertainty. Even on small trips, the stress of the unknown and Earl's unpredictable nature outweighed the joy of exploration.

Once, for example, Maude accompanied Earl to Montana to visit friends. Earl hijacked what was supposed to be a social trip, to hunt for rattlesnakes in a prairie dog town. Maude knew she was in for trouble when Earl caught 12 snakes—rattlers and bullsnakes—and tossed them into a cardboard box in the trunk of his car.

Halfway home, driving through the dark of the Wyoming prairie, Maude began to hear strange sounds beneath the seats and behind the dashboard. Earl reassured her that it was just the darkness and sounds of the road playing tricks on her, but he knew better. The snakes were loose in the car, and soon enough, one was curled up comfortably in Maude's lap.

"I slammed the brakes on the car," Earl remembered. "But before it even skidded to a stop, Maudie had jumped from the car and went rolling into the ditch."

Using a flashlight, Earl found only six of the snakes. Some were tangled in the springs under the front seat, in the upholstery or even in the fabric lining of the car top. Earl found one lounging on the engine and realized that the only way it could have gotten there was by crawling between his feet, through the small hole by the clutch and into the engine compartment.

With six snakes still loose in the car, Earl and Maude set out again in uneasy silence. When Earl stopped for gasoline, the attendant discovered one bull snake wrapped around the gas tank cap. At home, Earl left the doors and hood of the car open for the night, hoping that the remaining snakes would be gone by morning.

For Maude, the trip had been a cautionary tale about travelling with Earl. The unexpected was not something that might happen under trying circumstances. The unexpected was bound to happen.

FROM THE BADLANDS TO BAJA

For a badlands boy whose aesthetic sensibilities had been forged in the rugged buttes and wide horizons of a dinosaur graveyard, the deserts of northern Mexico were paradise writ large—a seemingly endless wilderness of solitude.

Scale made all the difference. A man could disappear into the badlands for an afternoon, camp on Sheep Mountain Table for a weekend, photograph the same gnarled cedar tree at sunrise over and over again, in every season, and still be home for Sunday dinner. But Baja and Sonora, in the days before drug cartels, time-share condominiums and off-road motorcycle races, was a real escape. In the complex ecology of mountains and forbidding desert, estuaries and ocean shoreline, a man could get lost forever.

The idea intrigued Earl. He spoke frequently with his closest friends, even his teenage daughters, about escaping his life, his responsibilities and his addiction to tranquilizers. There were only two places he dared to imagine throwing his bottle of Miltown out the window and being free: the badlands and the deserts of Mexico.

Beginning in the early 1960s, using his annual business trips to Colossal Cave as an excuse for fleeing the South Dakota winter, Earl began travelling into Mexico. He crossed the border 14 times in ten years. Sometimes he entered from Mexicali, navigated the estuaries of the Colorado River and explored south down the mountain spine of Baja. Some years he crossed at Nogales and drove his old Chevy Suburban through the Sonoran Desert, past Copper Canyon—*Barrancas del Cobre*—and down the western shore of Mexico proper. He gazed across the Sea of Cortés at the specter of the Baja desert. While tourists flocked to the Pacific coast resort towns of Tijuana, Rosarito Beach and Ensenada—all within a half-day of the U.S. border—or the mainland resort cities of Puerto Vallarta and Acapulco, Earl preferred to take his Hasselblad camera and drive deep into Baja or Sonora, where his only companions were roadrunners, blue whales and warrior tribes who had struggled for four centuries to protect their desert from outsiders.

No matter where he went, Earl traveled light, indifferent to comfort. Companions learned quickly that Earl hiked in the spirit of Teddy Roosevelt—line of sight to his destination, with no idling along the way. He once took Pulitzer Prize-winning war correspondent and newspaper columnist Hal Boyle on a daylong trek into the badlands to discover a place where humans had never walked. Boyle recounted the story for his readers. "Before we even reached the picnic site—hobbling from three cactus spikes that had pierced my loafers—I knew I had blundered." He begged to turn around and go back, but Earl pressed ahead. "For three hours we climbed terrifying crags or dried silt, slid down embankments, crawled through poison ivy beds on hands and knees and inched through canyons too narrow for a gazelle,"

Boyle wrote. "'Let's go back,' I said. 'But first show me this place where the foot of man has never trod.'"

"Right where you're standing," said Earl.

Earl took hundreds of trips into the badlands alone, but he also longed to find someone who could share his adventures. Like Boyle, most people couldn't keep up. They spent their first hours in the wilderness wanting to turn back to the familiar, while Earl wanted to forge ahead toward the unknown. Few had the fortitude to hike through the pain, to eat hotdogs cooked on a snake stick coated with sand and to sleep on the ground with spiders and snakes and curious mice.

Hiking in the badlands was one thing, but spending a month in Mexico presented an altogether different challenge.

In the early 1960s, Earl finally found a companion to travel with—someone who grasped his obsession with solitude and did not need the constant reassurance that Earl was just about to turn back in the face of adversity. Marshall Young was a true child of Rapid City. He had not been born on a homestead or raised on a ranch. He was a town boy. He had lost his father as a child, and the most influential man in his life was his grandfather Paul Bellamy. Young's childhood aspiration was to drive tourists through the Black Hills in one of Bellamy's luxury convertible buses. He had grown up at Bellamy's Sunday table, where Rapid City's civic leaders plotted the development of the local economy. Guests were as likely to include Frank Lloyd Wright, Gutzon Borglum, Lord and Lady Halifax or even President Calvin Coolidge as well as family and neighborhood friends. But of all the civic leaders around the table, Young was most drawn to the man who called himself the Snake King of Reptile Gardens.

Marshall Young went to work for Earl in 1948 at the age of 12. He earned a dollar a day as a bumper boy, tying the handcrafted Reptile Gardens bumper signs to the fenders of tourist cars. He was employed at the Gardens every summer for a decade.

He worked his way through the organization from gardener to snake guide to gift shop manager. Every time Earl announced to the crew that he was planning a camping trip into the badlands, Young was the first to sign up. On hikes, he never fell behind, even as a 12-year-old. He had the ability to keep his complaints to himself and the innate, unschooled wisdom to stop talking when the birds sang.

Twenty years younger than Earl, Marshall Young was, in his own way, just as ambitious. His summer employment at the Gardens helped pay his tuition through college at the University of Iowa and then law school at Iowa and the University of Arizona. In 1964, not long after he returned to South Dakota, he practiced law and was elected a district court judge at the age of 27. His relationship with Earl deepened with time, and when Earl considered who might be able to handle explorations deep into Mexico, Marshall Young was his choice.

They took their first trip together in 1961, driving Earl's old pickup truck with a camper top. They carried a small propane cook stove and sleeping bags. They packed the truck with hand-me-down clothes, gifts for village children and tools for village craftsmen.

Earl planned his trips to the smallest detail. He memorized topographical maps of the Baja landscape where there were no roads. He felt truly free when he had passed the last road sign and the last road. Day after day, they traveled at five miles an hour.

"We never thought about food," Young remembered years later. "We ate hot dogs and boiled noodles. Sometimes along the coast we would get some fish. But the trips weren't about food. They were about adventure."

When the trails became impassible for the truck, Earl arranged for pack burros to take him even deeper into the wilderness. For centuries, treasure hunters had roamed into the Sierra Madre and the deserts of northern Mexico in search of gold or ancient cave paintings. Earl went in search of pure solitude.

At night, they unrolled their sleeping bags on the ground and slept under the stars. When it rained or the wind blew gritty and cold, they huddled in the camper. Earl could go a week without a solid meal and sleep in dirty, wet clothes. But every morning, he shaved. Then he hiked in the wilderness, carrying his Hasselblad with its heavy lenses—including a 15-inch telephoto—in his backpack.

"He thought nothing of hiking 10 or 12 miles into the desert, just to take a picture of a wild flower or cactus whose shape caught his imagination," Marshall remembered. When he did not carry his camera, Earl filled his backpack with rocks, as if he were doing some kind of penitence.

For days on end, the two men sat on the rocky beaches and watched whales calve in San Ignacio Lagoon. They fished with local fishermen and spent hours by the campfire communicating in broken Spanish and broken English. Marshall sat quietly, listening to the pidgin conversation, while Earl chatted away with his new friends as if they were having breakfast together in Rapid City.

Marshall marveled at the audacity. "Earl couldn't speak Spanish. But he was a great listener and he could piece together a conversation with words and gestures and patience."

Some of the fishermen became lifelong friends to whom Earl gave money, tools and even a small fishing boat that he carried into Baja on the roof of his camper.

On the west coast of Sonora, Earl became a patron of isolated bands of Seri Indians. Coronado had discovered the Seri in the sixteenth century while he was lost in the desert. The tribe had fought Spanish colonialism with handcrafted weapons and survived, retreating with each generation into more remote coastal and island sanctuaries. Inhabitants of a harsh desert environment, the Seri had a reputation for being aggressive warriors who were deeply suspicious of outsiders, and Earl had been warned to stay away. Instead, he drove straight into their villages and muddled along with hand gestures and broken Spanish until he became an intimate friend of the tribe.

He took gorgeous photographs of village life, collected rough sculpted ironwood crafts and traded carving tools and sandpaper for fish and sustenance. For years, he funneled money through missionary linguists Ed and Becky Moser to pay for life's simplest necessities: blankets, food for the elderly, bicycles and tire repair kits, shovels, chisels, crowbars and medicine.

Anthropologists from the University of Arizona marveled at the speed with which Seri crafts became more sophisticated and refined, unaware of the patron from South Dakota and his truckload of modern tools.

When Earl discovered that a large portion of elderly fishermen had cataracts from a lifetime of staring into the water, he mobilized a team of eye surgeons to set up a portable eye surgery clinic. He loaned money to poor cattle ranchers to buy feed for starving cattle and to fishermen to mend their nets or send their children to the city for medical emergencies. He kept detailed ledgers of his contributions, but he had no interest in being repaid. He had so much and they had so little, he told friends. He helped in any way he could.

He left Mexico exhausted, speeding indifferently through the American landscape, returning home with new photographs, pockets full of colored minerals, seashells, turtle eggs to woo his children with exotic omelets, tribal crafts and an accumulation of dirt and scrapes from months on the road. He came home to Maude and the children, new construction at the Gardens, invoices for new snakes and alligators, debt, Reta Mae's insecurities and his tranquilizers. Each spring, the cycle would begin anew, with maps and a plan to explore another remote corner of the desert the following year.

RACING NICK HALL THROUGH BAJA

Over the years, Earl's trips to Baja became mythological. He organized slideshows and told rousing stories of where he had been, what he had seen and whom he had camped with on unnamed beaches. He told the tallest tales and stretched the veracity of his stories to their breaking point. Family and staff huddled on pillows in the living room of the Rapid Creek house and were thrilled by his performance.

One night in the fall of 1967, Nick Hall dared to challenge the pulpit. At age 19, Nick was no longer the nerdy kid who had peddled his bicycle up the steep grade of Rockerville Hill to sell ice cream in the Reptile Gardens parking lot. He had matured into an experienced snake handler and alligator wrestler, and he developed his own taste for adventure. After the 1965 season, he had ridden his bicycle 2,000 miles back to home and school on the East Coast rather than take the bus.

As Earl was recounting the travails and dangers of a recent trip and the hyperbole grew thicker and the dangers more captivating, Nick interrupted, "It can't be that bad. I could ride Baja on my bicycle."

Nick's brash claim unleashed Earl's own instinct to meet bravado with a dare. Years later, Nick remembered the evening in detail. "Now, what you have to understand about Earl is that what made him so charismatic was that he never grew up. He had no boundaries at all. He was old enough to be my father, but he would dare us to do anything. He would gamble about everything. He was more competitive than anyone I ever met."

Earl's dares could be trivial and childish. "He would wave my paycheck over his head and smile and say, 'flip you double or nothing,'" Nick remembered. He would take a group camping in the badlands and wager who could go the longest without drinking water. Then he would take off running down the trail and dare his young initiates to keep up.

Earl was incredulous at Nick's boast that he could endure the wilds of Baja on a bicycle. "He bet me that I couldn't make it." As Nick considered the rigors of a 2,000-mile ride through shifting sand, he began to walk back his boast and make excuses. He reminded Earl that he was due back at school.

Earl would have none of it. He upped the ante. In front of everyone, he told Nick that he would pay for the trip and that Nick wouldn't have to pay him back unless he failed to reach his goal. Nick took the bet. In late October 1967, he began the 2,000-mile trek from Rapid City, down the spine of Baja, Mexico, to Cabo San Lucas.

Despite his impulse for gambling and the appearance that he recognized no boundaries, Earl had a keen ability to judge human capacity. He had known, years earlier, that Nick was ready to wrestle alligators. He had followed Nick's reports the summer before, when he rode his bicycle across the United States. He knew that Nick could make it, and that's what made their relationship so special. Far from abandoning Nick to the wilds of Mexico, Earl followed a few days behind in his truck and met Nick halfway down the length of Baja under the light of the November full moon. For the rest of the trip, Earl camped and hiked at his leisure but followed close on Nick's tracks.

When Nick finally arrived in La Paz, he discovered hundreds of off-road enthusiasts and a ragtag fleet of dirt bikes and dune buggies. They had just finished the first-ever Baja 1000 Race. He quickly became the toast of La Paz and was given a trophy by the race organizers for being the first bicyclist to cross the finish line in a race that included no other bicyclists.

Nick was well hungover the next morning when Earl pulled into town. "Well, I finished the ride," he proudly exclaimed. "Not so fast," Earl responded. "You said you could ride the whole length of Baja, and Cabo San Lucas is still a hundred miles away."

Nick rallied his energy and rode the last hundred miles in two days, with a proud Earl Brockelsby close on his rear fender. "I never considered not finishing," Nick observed, years later. "I would never let Earl down."

THROUGH MEXICO AND CENTRAL AMERICA

— Chapter 16 —

Earl and Marshall Young had driven 1,200 miles through Baja in 1961. In 1962, Earl planned a 14,000-mile trip through Mexico and Central America. He was fascinated with the volcanoes that surrounded Mexico City and wanted to climb Popocatepetl. He wanted to visit the Diego Rivera murals at the National Palace and photograph the Mayan pyramids, especially the ones that were still under a cloak of jungle, whose mysteries were just beginning to be studied by archeologists. He anticipated watching local boys catch iguanas in the coastal swamps of British Honduras (Belize). He wanted to visit the highlands of Guatemala, the lakes of Nicaragua and the hidden caves and cloud forests in Costa Rica. He wanted to do all of this in three months, before the 1962 season opened at Reptile Gardens.

The trip would be an arduous forced march, and he picked his team carefully—six stout souls packed into an old Suburban that had been dubbed "the Monster" by the crew at Reptile Gardens. He invited Marshall Young. He invited John Evans, a strong, 21-year-old reptile enthusiast from Mansfield, Ohio, who had caught a bus to Rapid City at the age of 14 and worked summers at Reptile Gardens ever since. He would soon become a world-renowned mountain climber, who spent his life climbing and exploring the highest peaks in the world.

Earl invited Jon Oldham, another Reptile Gardens summer staffer. Oldham was a reserved, thoughtful, academically inclined son of New England, who had a passion for herpetology and an eye for Judee Brockelsby. Jon worked under Earl Chace as an assistant curator and was the obvious heir apparent when Chace retired. Earl also invited his daughter Judee. She had little interest in reptiles or mountain climbing but a real interest in Jon Oldham and spending time with her father. Maude's last words to Judee on the eve of the trip were, "Don't let your father talk you into doing anything you don't want to do."

That made five. There was one open seat, and Earl offered it to anyone on the staff who could get parental permission to go. Two people applied, and Martie Kuehn won the coin toss. Four men, two women, camping gear, clothing, Earl's precious Hasselblad and, as ever, paltry food supplies were jammed into the Monster, and the crew headed south.

They spent a few days searching for a way into the deep and inaccessible Copper Canyon. They enjoyed a deep-sea fishing expedition in Guaymas. They spent a night at the tourist hotel in Mazatlán. For the first week, the trip had the feel of a comfortable, if modestly crowded, family vacation. Then Earl's secretary, Francie Armstrong, joined the group, and Earl turned the Monster south and east toward Mexico City.

Now the group was seven—far too crowded even for the Monster. The original five had voted not to add Francie, but Earl vetoed the opposition. She was having nervous problems, he explained, and needed a break from work. For the rest of the trip, the two were inseparable.

With the exception of a few days in Mexico City and occasional low-end motels in Belize and Guatemala, the explorers camped, with women in one tent, men in another. Earl's food supplies were so spartan that the women rebelled after the first week and refused to allow him to cook. They began to buy rice by the kilo and divide the cooking responsibilities among themselves.

They camped outside Mexico City at the base of Popocatepetl to acclimate themselves to the altitude, and on the third day, they began their ascent of the volcano. John and Jon struggled to the summit. Marshall followed a dog "who looked like he knew his way" and ended up at a sheer cliff from which he had no choice but to turn around and climb down. Earl never made it. John and Jon were 22. Earl was 46. All the badlands hiking in the world could not condition his middle-aged legs for an 11,000-foot vertical climb. The women never tried. John and Jon's heroics were short-lived. They returned to base camp and proceeded to spend the night vomiting from altitude sickness.

Everyone in the group battled turista, and soon the whole group suffered from a respiratory fungus. By the time they reached the Mayan jungles of eastern Mexico, they were covered with ticks and lice and chiggers. At the hotel in Mérida, Earl claimed the record of 44 chiggers, which he painstakingly dug out of his skin. The women wore skirts and suffered the most. Their legs were covered with bites. Nothing seemed to relieve the pain, until an elderly woman along the road observed the women scratching the welts on their legs and suggested that they wash the infected bites in lime juice. It was a miracle cure.

No matter the travails, Earl offered no reprieve from the schedule, only the challenge to suck it up and press on. "Oh, it was just miserable," Judee remembered.

Earl had a saying, which he shared over and over with friends who suffered from the delusion that it might be fun to travel with him. "Adventure is an experience so dangerous or so miserable that one is thrilled to return to the monotony of everyday activity." Few people, including his daughter, understood beforehand that he took quite literally the idea that what didn't kill a person made them stronger.

Occasionally, the difficult and painful were offset by the spectacular. Miserable days were redeemed by splendid nights around the campfire. The painful bites of mosquitoes and sandflies were forgotten when the group camped on beaches where the sky was full of stars and the ocean was radiant with phosphorescent algae.

In Honduras, the group set up camp in the dark, only to discover that they had pitched their tents next to an army base. Earl had driven the Monster to town, when soldiers from the base arrived at camp. John and Marshall had grown full beards in the Castro guerrilla tradition. All three men were promptly arrested as spies and spent a night in jail before Earl showed up with their passports and bailed them out.

The intrepid explorers made their way back to Belize City, which had been virtually destroyed by a recent hurricane. The population was still struggling with the task of rebuilding. Earl booked the group into a bed and breakfast, but the conditions were miserable, with overflowing toilets that were emptied twice a day by a boy who cleaned the waste and then poured a new bucket of water into each toilet.

"The odors rise and rise," Earl wrote home. "If only I had taken up pipe smoking so I wouldn't notice. Of course my eyesight would be the same and it's quite a mess that greets the eye as you lift the lid."

Repelled by the conditions, the group retreated into the forest and camped near a beautiful waterfall. The women spent the next day washing clothes, bathing in the river and celebrating the natural beauty before them, while the men went hiking. But even in the presence of paradise, the trip was so difficult that Jon and Judee found no time for romance.

After almost a month in rugged terrain, the Monster was badly dented and crippled by a busted shock absorber, but there was no place to make repairs. Rather than drive the tortuous roads from Belize into Guatemala, Earl decided to load the Monster onto a small shallow-draft freighter and ferry it to Guatemala. *The Heron Hunter* must have been a beauty in its day, with a polished mahogany hull and brass fittings, but by the time Earl's group boarded the ship, it was 60 years old and had taken its share of abuse and more.

Loading the Monster onto the *Heron* required both calculus and courage. "The boat was only about 40-feet long and 14-feet wide, so our Suburban was probably a third of the boat," Marshall remembered. "They had to lay out these huge mahogany planks from the dock to the boat and John Evans drove it onto the front of the boat."

It was a windy night. The waves were perilous. None of the cargo was tied down, and as the waves tossed the boat, the cargo rolled across the deck. Earl, Marshall and Jon stood guard against myriad pending disasters. When a calm between the swells created an opportunity, they waved and shouted to John who gunned the Monster up the makeshift ramps and onto the boat and then jammed on the brakes to keep the truck from cascading over the far side.

The bumpers of the Monster were suspended two feet off both sides of the boat when *The Heron Hunter* set to sea for the three-day journey to Puerto Barrios on the coast of Guatemala. The voyage was nothing compared to what awaited them in Guatemala.

At the dock in Puerto Barrios, they discovered a revolution in progress. Ever since the CIA had overthrown the democratically elected government of Jacobo Arbenz in 1954, Guatemala had been suffocated by a seemingly never-ending civil war. Earl's undaunted but naive crew arrived in Guatemala City in the middle of a riot against the US-backed conservative government. Protestors had torn paving stones from the streets to throw at police and government soldiers.

Marshall Young was told that the protestors had already killed two Americans and were looking for more. John was behind the wheel and deftly followed an ambulance, with its sirens blaring, through the middle of a rock-throwing mob outside the presidential palace, until the travelers were safely at their hotel for the night.

The next morning, the Monster limped out of town as quickly and quietly as it could. "I was so naive, so inexperienced," Judee remembered. "I just thought if we waved out the windows and smiled everything would be fine."

The group traveled on to El Salvador, Nicaragua and Costa Rica. It rained for three straight days in Costa Rica, and the Monster was stuck in mud to its chassis until a farmer used his ox team to drag the 7,000-pound truck and its cargo a half-mile to solid road. The farmer invited the crew to share a dinner of fried bananas and agouti, a local gourmet sweetmeat that is commonly mistaken for bush rat. Soaked and miserable, the crew ate with abandon and pronounced the meat delicious. The fire was warm, and after all they had been through, sleeping on the dry floors felt like staying in a five-star hotel. They climbed the Poas volcano and explored caves. Earl reported that Costa Rica was "the best" country in Central America; "certainly," he added, "it is the most prosperous, best educated and in some respects the most beautiful."

The trip had been educational and exciting but also exhausting. Earl had made contact with reptile dealers at every stop, and by his measure, the trip had been a spectacular adventure that got better with each telling.

"It definitely was the trip of a lifetime," Martie Kuehn remembered. It set her life on a new course. On the way back to

Rapid City, the Monster stopped at Colossal Cave, where Martie met Joe Maierhauser. She fell in love with the cave and the desert. The two began to date. After the difficult drama of his separation from Reta Mae, Joe was finally ready to settle down—with Martie. The couple married and managed the Colossal Cave together for 50 years.

THE TREASURE OF COCOS ISLAND

— Chapter 17 —

On the eve of a 1967 treasure hunt to the remote island of Cocos, off the Pacific shore of Costa Rica, Earl left a handwritten note for Jim Campbell and scribbled on the envelope: "Open only in case of death." Like many entrepreneurs who held tight control over their businesses, Earl had never formally outlined his views on succession or the future of Reptile Gardens in the case of an accidental death. He had been in many tight situations in Baja, but he always escaped. The 1967 trip to Cocos, however, promised to be so unpredictable that he finally put pen to paper.

As usual, there was a hint of morbid melodrama between the lines of practical information. "Jim! I rather hope that you don't have reason to open this letter," he began. "On the other hand eternal sleep does have a certain appeal, at least Nature prepares us with age to meet the end…I went to the bank…and explained that you could and should run the show—with Chace in the snake house, Gerry [Wagner] on the Gifts, Ret in the office, (Jonny O[ldham] if Chace should as he did in '66 want to quit.)." Earl went on to speculate that his son Johnny would someday want to "take an active part in the Operation and should be switched from job to job so he knows a little of everything."

The letter is remarkable for two reasons. First, there is no mention of Joe Maierhauser. Unable to keep the secrets between Joe and Reta Mae or hold their marriage together, Earl had chosen Reta Mae and sold his interest in Colossal Cave to Joe. Second, Earl seemed to finally understand that Reptile Gardens could survive without him. If he was in town, of course, he would have a hundred ideas for the crew to implement, but after 30 years at the helm, he was confident that a combination of Jim Campbell, Earl Chace, Jon Oldham and, of course, Reta Mae would keep the ship on course during his travels. The freedom from responsibility led Earl to venture even farther from home and for longer periods.

For centuries, tales of hidden gold and silver and pirate's treasure had ridden the waves from the strange tropical island of Cocos 340 miles across the Pacific to the shores of Costa Rica. When he was approached by a friend who knew a friend who knew a friend who had seen the treasure maps, Earl became convinced that a man he had never met could lead an expedition straight to the treasure that no one else had found in 200 years of exploring. All the expedition needed was for Earl to pick up the tab.

Cocos is an ecological wonderland. Deep ocean currents created an oceanic landscape of spectacular coral reefs and deep-sea food chains—300 species of fish, with thousands of hammerhead sharks at the pinnacle of the pyramid. Jacques Cousteau described Cocos as "the most beautiful island in the world." Literary scholars speculated that Cocos might have been the inspiration for Daniel Defoe's *Robinson Crusoe*.

On the Galápagos Islands, the average rainfall was less than 12 inches a year. On Cocos, just 500 miles north, ocean currents created a tropical microclimate, where the annual rainfall averaged 276 inches. Rivers flowed in every direction, pulsing with

200 waterfalls and countless deep, clear ponds. Forests reached to the sky. The interior jungles were an ecological treasure in their own right, with 235 known flowering plants, 90 species of birds and 400 species of insects. Darwin had painstakingly developed his theory of evolution on observations made in the evolutionary hothouse of the Galápagos. How different his research might have been if the *HMS Beagle* had landed at Cocos.

After exhaustive study of the legends, Earl confessed to John Evans: "The more I read the more convinced I am that anyone who says he saw treasure on the island is a dreamer or a four-star fraud."

It was an ignominious beginning to a treasure hunt, especially one that would cost him tens of thousands of dollars, but it did not dampen Earl's enthusiasm. So why did he go? Why did he *pay* for an expedition with so little hope of success?

In the brain of a gambler, there is precious little difference between putting a fat hundred down on a dog race, losing $50,000 on the commodity markets, searching for hidden treasure or hiding a rattlesnake under your hat. Earl did it all. Besides, he had a sliver of an idea of where the treasure might be that no one had considered, and the idea spawned his hope.

Dozens of expeditions had explored Cocos, but they had kept to the shoreline caves on the assumption that pirates would not carry heavy wooden crates of treasure into the thick jungle. Earl approached the quest from a different angle. No one had explored the Cocos interior. He was confident that if he hiked inland, he would find ecological treasures to photograph. If he discovered gold, so much the better.

"He probably would have given it all to a museum," Marshall Young reflected years later. "He wasn't interested in the gold. He was interested in the adventure."

When his expedition landed, Earl's partners, true to tradition, surveyed the shoreline caves. Earl took off for the interior, lugging his Hasselblad through the tropical heat and humidity. After several days of hiking, he concluded that if there was treasure buried on Cocos, it had probably been dumped into one of the deep emerald pools at the base of one of the island's waterfalls—but there were hundreds of pools.

Although the expedition found no treasure, Earl returned home satisfied with stories to tell and slides of waterfalls and Cocos flowers that only a few had ever photographed. He counted it an even trade.

FALLING IN LOVE WITH PAPUA NEW GUINEA IN 1968

Earl's fascination with Baja's deserts was easy to understand, but Papua New Guinea was halfway around the world. It was different in ways that Earl did not understand until he arrived at the primitive colonial capital of Port Moresby. In every way imaginable—the aesthetic of the rain forest, with no horizon line; the cascading waterfalls of the highlands; and the wide, turgid rivers of the tropical lowlands—it was opposite from the barren, cactus-studded deserts of Baja. But against this natural drama, there was also malaria, a riot of bacteria and viruses, the tightly woven tapestry of ancient tribal civilizations and the heavy-handed colonial authority of Australia. Why, other than wanderlust, would he ever choose this destination?

Earl left no record of his 1968 trip to Papua New Guinea, but one of his companions, John Clifton, kept a diary in which Earl's posturing and ego come into full focus. "[Earl] travels by himself for eight months out of the year and, as he says, the only time he is homesick is while at home," Clifton wrote. "He is determined not to become a millionaire, although he's having a little trouble at the moment since his current assets are around $900,000 and he owns 1 ¼ million pounds of cocoa, the price of which has risen to the point that he has gained another $100,000 or so. One of his many projects consists of helping boys, orphaned or otherwise. He has made several trips to Baha, Mexico and seems to have adopted an Indian tribe there…He has served a term as mayor of Rapid City. Also owns a dog track and the pari-mutual machines at two other tracks. He has an interest in a gambling casino in Las Vegas."

It was rare for Earl to attach himself to a formal tour party when he traveled, but Papua New Guinea was a new adventure, and as a hedge against his inexperience, Earl booked himself on an international birding expedition.

He had a mild interest in birds, but the trip was no vacation for Earl. Given his penchant for center stage, it is easy to imagine him holding court at dinner parties about his true purpose: to one-up Arthur Jones and purchase three of the largest crocodiles in the world! He had made a deal with a reclusive Australian crocodile hunter named George Craig, who lived on the New Guinea island of Daru in the delta of the Fly River. Craig was a legend in the international crocodile trade. Like Arthur Jones and Earl with his rattlesnakes, Craig had put his life on the line and become a celebrity among wildlife adventurers.

When the Australian army withdrew from Papua New Guinea after World War II, Craig had stayed. He made his living hunting crocodiles for the market. He had slaughtered thousands. But he had become disgusted with the waste of the slaughter and put down his gun. It was more dangerous and more of an adventure to capture a crocodile than kill it from a distance with a high-powered rifle. Craig pledged to capture and protect the last giant survivors of the species.

As difficult as the deal had been with Arthur Jones, the 14- and 15-foot crocodiles he brought home from Africa had been a bonanza for Reptile Gardens. Craig's crocodiles were three feet longer, 17 and 18 feet from nose to tip of tail, and more than half a century old. In his mind, Earl could see the new roadside billboards: "Visit Reptile Gardens and see the *largest* crocodiles in the world!"

Earl spent $10,000 building a new pond and shelter for the crocodiles and thousands more on export permits from Australia and import licenses into the United States, which required that Craig escort the crocs from Daru Island to Rapid City. Earl never revealed the actual purchase price of the crocodiles, but friends estimated that he had invested $40,000 in the animals (almost $260,000 in 2015 dollars).

After he made arrangements with Craig to ship the crocodiles to America, Earl went exploring with Father Robert Jilek, a Catholic priest whose mission included the Sepik River and the old haunts of anthropologists Margaret Mead and Gregory Bateson. In the rainy season, the Sepik could be a raging torrent, lapping against the raised timbers of ceremonial houses and village homes, six feet up the ladders that led to people's living quarters. But in the dry season, the river receded and became a languid swamp of switchbacks and 15,000 lakes. Europeans described the Sepik as the Amazon of Asia, a wonderland of egrets and hornbills, with jungle to the shoreline of the river. It was a world without electricity, where villages went pitch dark at sunset.

Jilek's boat, an *African Queen*-type diesel trawler, coughed its way upriver at a pace fast enough to power through the current but too slow to outrun the swarms of mosquitoes that fed at sunset in hoards that hummed like a squadron of bombers. It chugged past the floating islands of hyacinths, serrated spines of crocodiles lounging on the surface and narrow fishing canoes that lined the banks of the river. It cut through black water tributaries stained by millennia of rotted plants. Malaria, yellow fever and Japanese encephalitis were endemic to the river.

Villagers were wary of outsiders. Colonial Australians kept a rough, unsentimental, absolute order, but every European who ventured up the Sepik understood that the tribes were only a generation removed from cannibalism and murder as a young man's rite of passage.

Priests and anthropologists were intruders, and by 1968, both had left scars on the cultures of the Sepik. Earl was neither. He was an adventurer, come to *see*. He did not have the patience for scholarship or the conversion of lost souls. He counted himself a curious neighbor, not an authority.

When the boat docked at villages like Ambunti, Angoram and Yangoru, Earl took stock of the intricate carvings that told the stories of each village—its ancestors and its spirits. The craftsmanship was superb, even with Stone-Age tools. Earl reasoned that the trade in native crafts could be a profitable business: the enormous masks mounted at the entrance to ceremonial houses, the ornate woven grass penis gourds that could bring a Nebraska farmer to sheepish boasting, the ancestor totems, the crocodile heads carved onto the bridge of canoes. Crocodiles were at the center of creation stories. Snakes, on the other hand, all snakes—large and thick or slender and harmless—were taboo, mercilessly slaughtered and publicly displayed.

In Angoram, Earl met with art dealers and began to buy—a dozen of this, 20 of that. He had a good eye, but he bought in bulk, indifferent to the fine points of sculpture or craft or meaning. "Airport art" the Port Moresby locals called it. He bought gifts for the family. He bought stock for the gift shop. He knew there was more to be made from the canoes full of village crafts that floated down the Sepik each year. He had come to New Guinea to buy giant crocodiles. He had come on adventure. But the art gave him a new reason to return.

Earl caught up with his birding group at the Mount Hagen Sing-sing in the western highlands. The festival had first been organized by Australian authorities as a way to stanch the endless cycles of tribal warfare and channel ancient tribal antagonisms into games: spear-throwing, running, team competitions, dance and music performances, cooking exhibitions and food booths. Thousands of tribal people descended out of the jungle to participate, along with ten or fifteen foreign tourists, all held in a fragile peace by the strong arm of Australian authorities. Australian colonialism had brought security to the jungle wilderness. Tourists could be forgiven for stepping cautiously into the highlands.

Archeologists hypothesized that the highlands were first settled 50,000 years ago. The forest canopy was so thick that it created the illusion of solitude and wilderness. In reality, the highlands were settled into hundreds of distinct agricultural communities. Whole cultures and whole languages were separated by slender valleys, thick forests and the legacy of tribal war. Survival in the highlands was all about who you knew and which side of any given valley you were on. Earl knew no one and barely knew where he was, but he was unrestrained.

He loaded his backpack with his Hasselblad and lenses, a few days of rations and a canteen of water. He said his goodbyes to the birding expedition and hiked into the forest. For three days, he traveled off the grid. He walked into villages, took out his Hasselblad and asked to take a picture. His personality was infectious. As he had in Baja, he engaged people with sign language, pidgin English and uninhibited enthusiasm. Soon he was invited into the men's ceremonial lodges—the stilted long houses where men conducted their rituals, shared tribal stories and prepared the next generation for manhood.

When he reemerged, he had hundreds of photographs of village life. Among the villagers of the Waghi Valley, Earl had found a new love. He couldn't wait to go back.

TO NEW GUINEA WITH JANET

While he was still in the air, flying home across the Pacific, Earl began to plan his next trip to New Guinea. He could count on Marshall Young, who would jump at the chance to join the expedition. When he considered which of his children to invite, he settled on his second daughter, Janet, a graduating senior at

Colorado College. Jeff was too young and too preoccupied with school and learning to play the drums. He was the Boy Scout who marched through his merit badges with focus and determination. He was squeaky clean, studious and interested in politics and justice. He loved libraries. He dutifully fulfilled his responsibilities at Reptile Gardens, but he showed little interest in mud, slime and giant reptiles.

Johnny was too deeply entrenched in the social life of high school: girls, cars and sports. Judee had married Jon Oldham and had a family of her own. She was the mother figure among the siblings, the responsible older sister—more like Maude than Earl. Earl was hesitant to draw comparisons, but it was undeniable that Janet had Earl's instinct for adventure. In the late 1960s, she had embraced the experimentation of the cultural revolution more than any of his other children. She loved Earl's intimacy, his willingness to talk about anything, including his own failings. She marveled at his creativity, his fearlessness, and she dreaded his disappointment. She kept Earl on a pedestal.

One day in the spring of 1968, Earl's two daughters were talking about their father's unhappiness. Judee offered the judgment that Earl was having an affair and had taken his new romantic interest to Africa.

For Janet, nothing was ever the same. She had known too much for a teenager, but not everything. In one casual comment by her older sister, the pedestal crumbled. All the innuendo, all the veiled gossip of her youth, was laid bare and made real. She began to pull away from her father.

For Earl, nothing symbolized reconciliation like an invitation to travel together. To travel with Earl was like being invited into his inner sanctum. As a graduation gift, he suggested that Janet join him on a trip to New Guinea. As a hedge against the distance between them, Janet asked if her best friend from college could join the expedition. Earl did not hesitate to say yes. He paid all the expenses.

As usual, Earl did all the planning. He wanted to retrace the route of his 1968 trip by taking the girls to the Solomon Islands and Fiji, then on to Daru Island to visit George Craig's crocodile retreat, up the Sepik River and into the highlands for the Mount Hagan Sing-sing. From New Guinea, he planned to travel to Cambodia and the ruins of Angkor Wat and then continue to Nepal and hike the Himalayas. It would be an around-the-world extravaganza, a healing balm for his relationship with Janet.

Janet spent the summer in a torrid romance with a fellow worker at Reptile Gardens. Earl's dealings with the young man were tense and provocative, perhaps even threatening. Earl came to believe that the upcoming trip might be a way to break up the romance.

By the end of the tourist season, Janet was not at all sure that she still wanted to go, but inertia and the fear of disappointing her father kept her from backing out. "Dad had spent so much time and so much money planning every detail of the trip. I didn't want to go, but I couldn't say no."

The highlight of the trip was supposed to be a visit to George Craig, but the crocodile camp was so deep in the jungle that the pilot could not find it. The small plane spent hours meandering down the Fly River and into the delta, searching for Daru Island and any sign of Craig's camp, but every island looked like every other. Finally, the pilot confessed that he was lost and handed his topographical maps to Earl, who strained to identify the shape of a recognizable shoreline beneath the clouds.

When the group finally landed at the primitive runway and was taken to the crocodile pens, Janet could not contain her wonder. "The crocodiles were huge, probably twenty feet. Bigger than the biggest crocs that Arthur Jones had brought back from Africa. We stood separated from them by a short wooden fence. They were prehistoric, awe-inspiring. They were so ancient. And I was convinced that I could make a connection with them, tune into their reptilian brains. That's how crazy it was."

Earl had been deeply frustrated by Craig's failure to deliver the crocodiles as promised, and the majesty of seeing them once again, up close, compounded his disappointment that the animals were still in their pens at Daru Island and not at Reptile Gardens. Craig had broken his collarbone and been incapacitated only weeks before his planned departure for the States, and the delay had given him time to think. He had already made a decision to leave New Guinea and move his entire operation to Green Island, a small atoll in the Great Barrier Reef.

Craig did not tell Earl that he was having second thoughts about the sale, but he began to think it was a mistake to part with his crocs, no matter what the price. As the months dragged on, and the export permits expired, Craig was increasingly inclined to cancel the deal. Earl grew more and more frustrated that his newest spectacle was slipping away. Face to face with George Craig and the crocs, Earl hoped that the deal could be salvaged, but Craig wouldn't budge. Even though he returned all the money that Earl had paid for the crocodiles, a cloud of disappointment was cast over the trip.

Earl took solace on a slow trip up the Sepik River on Father Jilek's missionary boat. Village by village, the group made their way into the interior of New Guinea. Again Earl was fearless. The boat would dock, and Earl would begin to greet the villagers. He pointed to the lens of his Hasselblad camera, nodded his head, grinned a broad, endearing smile and began taking pictures of the villages—hundreds of pictures of naked women's breasts in the uninhibited tradition of *National Geographic*, dusty children, grizzled elders, brightly colored, wildly decorated costumes, thatched roof huts, ceremonial houses and river sunsets. The natives, many of whom had never seen a camera, stood silently bewildered. A decade behind the shutter of his Hasselblad had turned Earl from an amateur into an expert. The strength of his photographs was his willingness to get close. And his landscapes captured cultures in nature that had only just begun to be seen by the outside world.

Earl led his ragtag expedition into the highlands. It was hardly a secure vacation for the untutored four from Rapid City. And yet, it was so exotic, so different, that Janet was swept into the spectacle of the Mount Hagen Sing- sing. "We flew for hours over the jungle in this little airplane. The mountains were all around us, above and below. And we were in the middle of the clouds. And then, below us in the Wahgi Valley, hundreds and then thousands of people were walking on the trails leading to Mount Hagen. They were all dressed in their most colorful clothing."

Janet endured the long days in New Guinea, but her heart was not in it. She could not dispel the tension with her father. She wanted to return to her boyfriend in Rapid City. After weeks of hiding her feelings, she finally confessed. "The hardest thing I had ever done in my life was to tell my father that I didn't want to hike the Himalayas. I wanted to go to Cambodia and then go home."

Earl did not object. She suspected that he understood and did not want to continue either. The group held together through war-torn Cambodia and then headed home. Only Janet's college friend continued to India, fulfilling her dream to trek through the Himalayas—alone.

THE DARK SIDE OF PARADISE

— Chapter 18 —

The rupture between Earl and Janet rippled through the family. Her reaction was to escape. When she returned from Asia, she flaunted her independence and moved in with her boyfriend. She announced to the family that she wanted no further contact, even though the entire family lived within a few miles of each other. Earl did his best to oblige. As the tension deepened it became clear that reconciliation, at least in the short term, was not possible. Janet moved to Seattle, married her boyfriend, took a job as a teacher and became pregnant with her first daughter. Despite her desire to separate, there continued to be occasional letters and phone calls.

Earl reacted to Janet's self-imposed exile with anger and a sense of betrayal. As he always did, he took his frustrations out with his pen. On January 5, 1970, he scrawled a hand-written letter to Janet. He described her voice on the telephone as "crisp bitterness." He wrote about loving her, but used the past tense. Under the circumstances, he wrote, he resented being asked for money. He concluded with a declaration that he did not have a $1,000 in all his accounts. It was a brutal, manipulative letter, an expression of anger and frustration over his inability to control events within his family. But in the end, he pulled himself back from the brink and never mailed it. He folded both the carbon copy and the original inside an envelope with no name or address and filed it away in the cavernous basement of Reptile Gardens. On some level, Earl resisted the temptation to burn bridges. He hoped Janet would come back. When she did, he would be there to embrace her.

In the broadest sense, the break between Janet and Earl was a sign of the times. The years 1969 and 1970 brought a cascading drama of social upheaval in the nation. American families were torn apart. The fact that a rupture could happen to such an all-American family, in a place like Rapid City, to a man who claimed a special ability to understand young adults, signaled how deeply the generational conflict of the 1960s had cut into mainstream American life.

In quick succession, Johnny graduated from high school, went off to college and also rebelled against his father. Janet returned to Rapid City with her daughter and joined a commune that was mocked by the family for its dysfunction as the "The Uncooperative Cooperative." Her search for independence led her to the frontier of Paraguay, where she and her second husband bought land and lived with her daughter under primitive, frontier conditions. In different circumstances, it was exactly the kind of adventure that Earl might have encouraged.

Judee and Jon Oldham tried to hold the extended family together. When Earl Chace retired, Jon was named curator at Reptile Gardens. Jon was more interested in science and education than tourism. After two years it became apparent that Earl would always hover over his decisions, and Jon would never have an opportunity to be his own man. He and Judee decided to leave Reptile Gardens and move to Boulder, Colorado, where Jon began a Ph.D. program in biology under the direction of the esteemed herpetologist Hobart Smith. Judee enrolled in a master's degree program in school counseling.

Only Jeff remained at home. While the older children had been influenced by Earl's charisma, Jeff had been influenced by Maude's steady hand. He had done his family duty by working at the Gardens, but in high school he threw himself into music, debate and scholarship. He trusted his own interests in community service, journalism, progressive politics and the church more than the "free spirited" youth culture at the Gardens.

Earl's social status in the community and his international travels masked the entropy at home. He was finally a millionaire, even if it was mostly on paper, but his wealth did little to calm his mind. He traveled to escape his depression and his addictions. He was cast adrift. "He was a seeker who never found what he was looking for," Judee later concluded.

Maude blamed herself for not being able to make him happy. "I spend a great deal of time thinking about you and about how much you mean to me and how wonderful you are, and about how much I want you to know all these things," she wrote on the eve of Earl's 1970 trip to Baja, "only the sad thing is—the thinking just stays in my head and you never know. I don't know how to say it except you mean so much to me—and I love you. There! Simple and true.'" She promised to try harder. "I want to see you before you leave—and I want to write to you at every mailing address…*will you let me please?* It would mean a lot to me."

It was a curious ending to a sad letter. Earl had held his relationships together, through time and distance, with a routine of vigorous correspondence. He had used correspondence to express his most creative thoughts, his most intimate feelings and to confess his sins. Had he told his wife that he did not want to correspond with her?

None of the children understood the depth of the break. Socially, Earl and Maude kept up appearances, but Maude bore the stigma when Earl moved out of the house and into his private office at Reptile Gardens.

"I am sorry I gave you the impression as to be worrying about what people think," Maude wrote to Earl, "but I don't ever go any place that someone doesn't inquire, and I just wonder what to say. If I only had nerve, I would put a big quarter-page ad in the *Journal* saying: 'To Whom it may concern: This is to inform anyone interested that Earl Brockelsby has left my bed and board because of my many inadequacies (too varied and numerous to mention here) and will not return." She confessed that she was "too meek and weak" to post the advertisement.

THE CHANGING FACE OF TOURISM

In the early 1970s, social science researchers paid little attention to the tourism economy in America. Individual entrepreneurs, including Earl, counted the cars that passed on the highway and made rough calculations about how many pulled into the parking lots of their roadside attractions. But nobody knew where the cars had come from or where they were going. Nobody knew how many people were in the cars or what they wanted from their vacation. Businessmen had a thumbnail understanding of the attractions in their region, but few people understood tourism on a national scale.

When the price of gasoline doubled in the wake of the 1973 Arab oil embargo, Congress considered the national security implications, the inflationary implications for the economy, the consequences for United States relationships with Israel and the Arab nations, but the government paid almost no attention to the impact on automobile tourism. Everyone knew that the tourism economy was enormous, but for the most part, people like Earl still made decisions based on experience and instinct. That's what made operating a roadside attraction an art rather than a science.

Nonetheless, some enterprises had advantages. Walt Disney's fantasy world had access to a major population center. The cultural zeitgeist of Southern California was anchored in fantasy. Disneyland was open every day of the year, and going to Disneyland was a rite of passage for every Southern California child and family. If tourist families planned their vacations to feature a day or two at Disneyland, they could round out the week at Knott's Berry Farm, the beach, a baseball stadium, the theater or one of a seemingly endless array of public and private golf courses.

By contrast, Black Hills tourism entrepreneurs could never escape the lean reality of a bitter, unpredictable winter and a five-month tourist season. The Black Hills were too small to be developed into destination ski resorts. The national parks were too small and too undeveloped to attract visitors interested in staying for more than half a day. Neither Badlands nor Wind Cave had park hotels. There were only a handful of golf courses in western South Dakota, none of which were championship quality. There were small town rodeos and tourist attractions that celebrated the frontier cowboy mythology of the Wild West, but there was virtually no effort to revive the spirit of the Sioux Indian Pageant or include Native American culture in the tourism economy. The days when Lakota families danced with tourists in the streets of Kadoka on summer weekends were long over. If anything, Lakotas were more segregated from the mainstream economy in the 1970s than they had been in the 1920s.

One summer event in the Black Hills drew national attention. In 1938, only a year after Earl started Reptile Gardens, motorcyclists began travelling to the town of Sturgis to race and camp, blow off steam and escape the boredom and constraints of their lives in the cities. By the early 1970s, rally organizers claimed that several thousand cyclists attended the rally every summer. By

Black Hills standards, it was a large and rapidly growing event, but the rally was the farthest thing from a family vacation. Local law enforcement officials described the era as a time when "gangs and hardcore bikers" dominated the campgrounds, and the attitude of local citizens was "batten the hatches and lock up your daughters." The motorcyclists spent as little money in the local economy as they could, and with the reputation for gang fights that surrounded the late summer event, the kind of tourist families who might visit Reptile Gardens were more likely to stay home than venture out to the Hills.

Beyond the natural constraints of winter and geography, Black Hills tourism suffered from an even greater cultural constraint. The western ethic of rugged individualism and competition worked against the development of a coordinated, regional approach to tourism. Among owners of Black Hills tourist attractions, the whole was *not* greater than the sum of the parts. The owners of each attraction viewed a dollar spent down the road as a dollar lost from their own pocket. In the 1930s, when Earl had first built Reptile Gardens, there were only a handful of roadside attractions in the shadow of Mount Rushmore and Custer State Park. By the 1970s, there were dozens, each competing against the other for the tourist dollar.

The go-it-alone culture extended to the approach that towns and civic organizations took to their own tourism promotion. In the late 1920s, businessmen from many towns in the region formed the Associated Commercial Clubs of the Black Hills and committed themselves to work together to coordinate events and promote tourism. These early efforts failed due to small town rivalries, envy of the larger economic clout of Rapid City and a general undercurrent of jealousy and resentment. In 1939, after more than a decade of failure and missed opportunities, businessmen in Rapid City ramrodded a new organization into existence—the Black Hills, Badlands and Lakes Association (BHB&L)—to promote regional tourism.

Officials at BHB&L approached Governor Harlan Bushfield for a subsidy, but the governor flinched at the idea of using state funds to subsidize economic development for only one half of the state. Undeterred, the leaders created a convoluted scheme to launder a small grant of $2,600 through the South Dakota Departments of Publicity and Transportation. The governor was still nervous about the potential for political blow back. "All references to activities of the Highway Commission on your behalf must be off the record and not for publication," Bushfield wrote to the new president of the association, "due to the fact that I fear political retribution in other parts of the state."

The idea of coordinating the promotion of Black Hills tourism found a more receptive audience among the leaders of the post-war generation, whose world views were more expansive and less isolationist than prewar tourism boosters. BHB&L delegations began to travel to national tourism conventions and travel shows. In 1947, the entire budget of the organization was used to promote Paul Bellamy's effort to bring the United Nations to the Black Hills. Just as they had taken over local governments, the postwar generation began to take over Chambers of Commerce and tourism associations. Prewar jealousies fell to the side. Earl's friend Ted Hustead, founder of the world famous Wall Drug, became president of BHB&L in 1962. Earl took over the presidency in 1966. Al Mueller, the owner of Al's Oasis on the west bank of the Missouri River at Chamberlain, became president in 1969. Lloyd West, the owner of Black Hills Gold in Deadwood, became president in 1979. These men, along with Lester "Si" Pullen, the owner of Rushmore Cave, and Josef Meier, the owner of the Black Hills Passion Play, became vocal advocates of regional tourism planning. Among this group, Earl was the first among equals, the leader most willing to step forward and argue that blind competition and a lack of cooperation between the different tourism businesses had hurt the overall economy.

By the early 1970s, Reptile Gardens had matured into a highly successful business. It had the largest privately owned collection of reptiles in the world and a steady stream of summer customers. Earl increasingly turned his energies toward the region. While he accepted the philosophy of highway beautification, he fought the federal government's attempt to limit highway billboards in South Dakota, where they were essential to tourism advertising. He became a friend and an advocate of Korczak Ziolkowski, the Polish-American sculptor whose vision to carve a monumental bust of the Lakota warrior Crazy Horse on his war pony rivaled Mount Rushmore in both scale and romance. Time and again, Earl met with young entrepreneurs and shared his knowledge of Western tourism. Each meeting began with the two questions: "How close to the road can you build your attraction?" and "Do you have a reserve fund to survive the winters?"

THE PENDULUM SWINGS

Peter Norbeck's original vision for tourism in South Dakota had featured nature, camping and wildlife. His efforts led to the creation of Custer State Park, one of the largest and most successful state parks in the nation. Gutzon Borglum's plan for Mount Rushmore complemented Norbeck's vision, as did the creation of Wind Cave and Badlands National Parks. All of these parks celebrated education, conservation, spiritual enlightenment and the "See America First" ethic of prewar tourism.

Earl's Reptile Gardens and the proliferating roadside attractions that multiplied in the shadow of Mount Rushmore followed a different course. They adapted to the postwar automobile revolution and the changing psychology of family tourism by featuring entertainment rather than education. In the 1970s, the pendulum began to swing back. Many roadside attractions were poorly prepared to deal with the change. The local economy was still based on a ten-state market and family automobile vacations, but there were subtle shifts in the psychology of tourists.

Earth Day in 1970 coincided with a new interest in conservation, bird watching, wildlife photography and ecotourism. Families wanted to experience nature, not a contrived spectacle. They wanted to learn from their vacation, not simply be entertained. Earl began to receive letters complaining that children should not be allowed to ride the giant tortoises.

In February 1973, several hundred activists from the Pine Ridge Indian Reservation and their supporters from the American Indian Movement (AIM) occupied the site of the 1890 Wounded Knee massacre and demanded a federal investigation into abuses by the Pine Ridge tribal government. The occupation lasted 71 days. It drew national media attention, the intervention of the FBI, and long negotiating sessions with South Dakota's congressional delegation. When the occupation ended on the eve of the tourist season, AIM leaders announced that they would set up roadblocks to limit travel onto the reservation and called for a boycott of tourist attractions in the Black Hills. The AIM boycott had little real effect, but it highlighted the fact that the postwar tourism economy had made little effort to integrate "cultural tourism" into the regional economy. Tourists could buy rubber tomahawks at local curio shops. They could have their picture taken with Earl's friend, Ben Black Elk, at Mount Rushmore, but few tourists ever attended small town powwows or Indian rodeos or traditional Lakota ceremonies.

For his part, Earl had deep connections with individual Lakota families. He was generous with private charity to Indians. But in the wake of the Wounded Knee occupation, neither he nor the other leaders of the tourism economy attempted to integrate Lakota culture into a regional tourism strategy.

DAKOTA POLITICS

For as long as Earl could remember, the Brockelsby family had been neatly wrapped in a cocoon of pro-business, progressive Republican politics. Maude was a Republican. His closest friends were Republicans. In Rapid City, Republicanism was a way of life. As president of the Black Hills, Badlands and Lakes Association, Earl had influence in the higher reaches of the Republican Party. He had access to the governor, members of the state legislature and the state's small congressional delegation. All he had to do was pick up the phone.

He also had his differences with the Republican Party. On civil rights he was an integrationist in the urbane, progressive tradition of Nelson Rockefeller. Except for a handful at Ellsworth Air Base, there weren't many African Americans in Rapid City. But when Earl got the opportunities, he made subtle statements of principle.

He had a long tradition of using family for promotional photographs. In 1965, he chose Judee's son Jon-Jon to sit on the back of Methuselah and grin for the camera. Judee and Jon Oldham were living in apartments owned by Earl in downtown Rapid City. Their next-door neighbors were an African-American couple from the air base. Earl had hired the man as a part-time property manager. The couple's daughter, Shirley, was just a little older than Jon-Jon. Earl hoisted Shirley onto Methuselah's back, she held Jon-Jon around the waist like they were riding bareback into the great American future, and Earl snapped the photograph. By his reckoning the photograph made a great postcard. He ordered several thousand for the gift shop.

The gift shop could count on one hand the number of African-American patrons who came through the doors of Reptile Gardens each summer, but the few who did were drawn to the photograph and thought it was charming. By the hundreds, however, white patrons complained that a little black girl had no business sitting on a tortoise with a white boy. Earl had made his statement, his way. He could care less what the segregationists thought.

He attended Republican fundraisers in Rapid City, but there were aspects of Republican partisanship that rankled. He liked to tell people that he was too independent to vote a straight Republican ticket. He voted the man, not the party, and he was particularly proud that he had not voted for Richard Nixon in the 1960 presidential election. Earl was not a Cold Warrior in the tradition of South Dakota Senator Karl Mundt. He had no patience for saber rattling. He was not a pacifist in the religious tradition, but he had seen his share of blood and war and wanted no part of a new war, especially in the poor nation of Vietnam, half a world away.

One afternoon in 1963, Maude and Earl were visiting the sculptor Korczak Ziolkowski and some of his friends at Ziolkowski's home near the construction site of the Crazy Horse Memorial. Earl had been too young to know Gutzon Borglum, but he had embraced Ziolkowski as a kindred spirit. He was a fellow World War II veteran who had been wounded on Omaha Beach. They shared a belief that Black Hills tourism should be built on the back of private enterprise, not government subsidy. Over the years, the two men had become close friends. During the visit, Earl stepped onto the balcony to get a breath of fresh air and soak in the view.

Over his shoulder, he heard a soft voice. "Would you like some company?"

The two men started a conversation that would continue, off and on, for the rest of Earl's life.

George McGovern had grown up poor in Mitchell, South Dakota, the son of a Wesleyan Methodist minister, who often took his pay in vegetables and waste-cuts of meat. His parents were Republicans, but George was heavily influenced by the social justice values of the Wesleyans, and he embraced Franklin Roosevelt's New Deal. By South Dakota standards support for

FDR made him a wild-eyed radical, but he had built a political base through relentless grassroots organizing and particular attention to farm policy.

Earl had followed McGovern's ascendance for almost a decade, since the studious history professor had first run for Congress in 1956 and been red-baited as a communist sympathizer. McGovern's most effective rebuttal was his own record as a bomber pilot during World War II. He had flown 35 missions over German-occupied Europe. As a Republican, Earl had not voted for McGovern, but he admired the way that McGovern fought back tenaciously and won.

McGovern served two terms in the House before challenging the popular Cold Warrior, Karl Mundt, for the Senate in 1960. He lost. But true to his tenacity, he ran again in 1962 for an open seat and squeaked out a victory over his Republican rival by only 597 votes. Once again, Earl had voted against him.

When McGovern walked onto Ziolkowski's balcony, he had just taken his seat as the junior Senator from South Dakota, and he knew better than anyone that South Dakota was a small state where personal relationships crossed partisan divides. He desperately needed friends in the conservative business community of Rapid City. From Earl's perspective Black Hills tourism needed an advocate in the heavily Democratic Congress. In addition to political motives, the two men genuinely liked each other. They shared the experience of World War II. They were internationalists. They were intellectually curious. And they both felt estranged from the deepening United States involvement in Vietnam that both their parties supported.

Earl began a slow drift to the left. His new political outlook was reinforced by his world travels and the fact that his own sons and the young men who worked for him spent their early twenties under threat from the draft. But the main impetus for Earl's movement toward the Democratic Party was his personal friendship with George McGovern. In the late sixties, McGovern led him to a new relationship with a prairie populist who was, in his own way, even more radical than McGovern.

Jim Abourezk was born and raised in Maude's hometown of Wood, South Dakota. His parents were Lebanese Christians who had immigrated to the United States at the end of the nineteenth century and set up a trading post in Wood. Abourezk was a true populist—rough, plain spoken and fearless on the stump. He could walk into a meeting of the most conservative South Dakota ranchers, look them in the eye, call their bluff and walk out with a handful of votes from men who did not agree with him on a single matter of policy, but believed he understood their problems and would fight for them.

Abourezk was too young to serve in World War II, but he was eager to get away from the Great Plains and enlisted in the Navy during the Korean War. He was 39 when he ran for Congress in 1970, but he was more sympathetic with the spirit of the sixties generation than his own. "With the history of Republican party domination in South Dakota, especially in the Second Congressional District, no one cared to invest in a sure loser," Abourezk wrote in his autobiography. But fate had a way of supporting his campaign that he could have never anticipated.

In May of 1970, as part of the widening War in Vietnam, the United States invaded Cambodia. College campuses erupted in protest. At Kent State University four students were shot and killed by National Guardsmen, many of whom were the same age as the protesters. Hundreds of colleges, from the prestigious Ivy League to small community colleges in the Midwest, went on strike and shut down. Students fled the campuses and flooded into political campaigns across the nation. McGovern recruited hundreds to work for Abourezk's populist, but seemingly hopeless, congressional campaign. They came to South Dakota with no money, no place to sleep and no idea where they were.

The students overran Abourezk's campaign headquarters and his home. They overflowed into the homes of his friends. The idealistic but starving students ate their way through the campaign's resources until, two weeks before election day, Abourezk was despondent that he had no way to feed his own family.

"As I sat in my law office staring at the wall and wondering how to carry on with the general election campaign, and at the same time, how to buy groceries so that my family could eat, Earl Brockelsby walked in and plunked down $300 in cash on my desk."

"I figure you could use this about now," Earl said.

"It was an amazing gift," Abourezk wrote, "made with perfect timing. I thanked him profusely, and after he left, I went straight to Safeway and stocked up on food."

Abourezk rode his bologna sandwich brigade to victory in 1970 and took his seat in Congress as an outspoken anti-war congressman from a conservative Republican state.

Earl did not like making formal political contributions. He hated the paperwork and the paper trail. Like other contributors in his generation, he preferred working in cash. The way he looked at it, he wasn't making a "political contribution" to Jim Abourezk. He was just giving a little cash to a good friend to get him through a rough spot. Things would even out. That's the way it was between friends. He would get his money back—someway.

Two years later, Abourezk was considering a run for the Senate. Karl Mundt had suffered a severe stroke in 1969 and was forced to retire. Some suggested that the Senate was too big a reach for the one-term Congressman and that he should run for re-election to the House. Besides, George McGovern was the Democratic candidate for President, and South Dakotans didn't know whether to cheer their favorite son or run away in shame from McGovern's liberal anti-war politics. If Abourezk decided to run for the Senate, McGovern's coattails would be of little use.

When Abourezk decided to run anyway, Earl and Maude hosted a fundraiser for their underdog friend at the house. The comedian and television personality Danny Thomas was the guest of honor. Thomas was Maronite Catholic from Lebanon. Born Amos Muzyad Yakhoob Kairouz, his stage name had been Americanized to Danny Thomas. At the dinner party, Reta Mae asked for Thomas's autograph. Earl searched the living room for a suitable surface for the autograph and settled on the old Indian skull he had offered to Joe Maierhauser for the Colossal Cave. Thomas signed his name and commented that he had never signed such a unique autograph.

A month before the election, Earl called Abourezk with an oddball question. A group of Republican farmers in Mellette County, men who played the commodity markets with Earl, wanted to make a friendly wager on the election. They agreed to put up $25,000 against Abourezk, if Earl would put up $25,000 for Abourezk. The $50,000 pot was all cash—winner take all. Earl wanted to know what Abourezk thought. Friend to friend, should he take the bet?

Abourezk knew Earl's penchant for gambling, but $25,000 was a fortune to a congressman. Besides, the race was too close to call, and Abourezk didn't have the stomach to throw his friend's money away on a wild political gamble. He counseled patience until the tracking polls showed something firm.

Two weeks before election day, Abourezk felt confident that a victory was within reach. "Make the bet," he told Earl.

Both men won big. Abourezk was elected with a whopping 57 percent of the vote, and Earl pocketed the cash.

Earl's support for George McGovern's presidential campaign in 1972 was public and enthusiastic. To the amazement and exasperation of state Republicans and tourism officials, Earl had "Vote for McGovern" painted on the large Reptile Gardens' billboards along Interstate 90. In the presidential campaign, Earl made no brown bag contributions. His donations were publicly recorded, for everyone to see, including Richard Nixon.

After the election, the IRS audited each of Earl's businesses. No payments were due. Nothing was amiss. But the audits cost Earl thousands of dollars. When records of the Watergate investigation were released in 1973, it became apparent that Earl had been on a list of 600 political enemies compiled by the Nixon White House, many of whom were McGovern contributors or confidants. Nixon's staff had turned the names over to the IRS with instructions to audit their taxes and make their lives miserable. After his impeachment and resignation, it became a badge of honor to be on Nixon's "Enemies List." Earl was number 113 on a list that included the artist Georgia O'Keeffe, the actor Paul Newman, the musician Herb Alpert, the Harvard economist John Kenneth Galbraith and hundreds of politicians and business leaders.

Earl's political activism had never been ideological. Party registration was not important to him. He campaigned for friends with whom he had personal relationships. His opposition to the war in Vietnam and nuclear proliferation grew from his own personal experience in World War II. His support for racial integration was a personal belief, not born of any real struggle in his own community. After the McGovern presidential campaign and the Nixon Enemies List, Earl registered as a Democrat.

Like their father, all the children, each in their own way, became politically active in the Vietnam years. Maude became a Democrat. But it was Jeff who went to work on Capitol Hill, first for Senator McGovern, and later for Senator Tim Johnson. Jeff found his true calling in politics, and through politics Earl found a way to build a relationship with the one child who had been too young to experience the glory days when Reptile Gardens was the center of the family universe, and Earl was its king.

BRENDA ADAM

Earl had a talent for compartmentalizing his life. He was dismissive of Maude's preoccupation with what other people thought. He just didn't care. He had no problem with being one of the wise men of the regional economy, speaking before a crowd of hundreds of businessmen, and then retreating to his lonely bed at Reptile Gardens. Few people, other than his close friends, knew that he was manic depressive or addicted to Miltown. His private life was nobody's business. But as his estrangement from the family grew, Earl became more reckless with his romantic adventures.

In the summer of 1971, he developed a crush on Brenda Adam, a college student from Iowa employed as a guide at the Bewitched Village trained animal show. She had long legs, golden blond hair and a flat, long face and thin smile. She was a year younger than Johnny, ten years younger than Judee. While she was working at Reptile Gardens, she had a brief summer romance with Jeff's high school debate partner, but considered herself, as a college student, too old for the boy. Instead, she turned her attention to Earl, who was more than twice her age.

At first, Earl played the role of elder advisor. He took her camping in the badlands. He listened to her plaintive, youthful complaints about boys in her dormitory and boys she dated. After the 1971 tourist season ended, Earl invited her to join his next trip to Baja.

Brenda was ecstatic. "Thank you for opening me up to the endless excitement of life," she wrote Earl. Then she explained that she would have to ask her parents' permission to make the trip.

Earl also invited Johnny to join the trip and Brenda's estranged boyfriend. It was an odd group. From college Brenda wrote to Earl almost daily in anticipation of the adventure. Gradually, the letters became more intimate. In November, she sent Earl an envelope with locks of blond hair and exclaimed how much she was looking forward to being in Rapid City for the holidays. By January of 1972, she was signing her letters, "Oodles of love."

In Baja, Earl took a series of nude photographs of Brenda, artfully set against driftwood on the beach, but he wrote nothing about his infatuation. He gave no hint that he was falling in love. Many of Earl's closest friends believe that Earl had expected Brenda to let go as soon as the group returned from Baja. Earl had faced the music before. He had written his share of goodbye letters. After the tears dried, reality always set in—he was too old, there were too many other boys at college, the girls had their whole future in front of them. Most young women recognized the affairs for what they were—summer flings. Brenda was different. She returned to college in the fall of 1972, but she refused to let go. She looked far beyond the age gap and turned her attention to the task of becoming Mrs. Earl Brockelsby.

In the middle of the Baja trip Earl received a letter from Maude. Rapid City was abuzz with gossip that Earl was a drug dealer, she reported, and he was about to be arrested. To the suspicious, it all added up. He traveled to Mexico every winter. He knew the border and its security. He imported huge crates of plants and reptiles. It would be so easy to slip a hundred dollars to the same border agents he had bribed to get his reptiles across the border.

Maude was frantic. "Please, please tell me the truth," she implored.

The rumors were malicious gossip, but whatever the motive, the gossip fed a narrative that Earl had created. It was only a small leap of the imagination from swash-buckling adventurer to international drug dealer. The problem was not that Earl might actually be a drug dealer. The problem was that Maude no longer trusted that she knew her own husband.

THE FLOOD

— Chapter 19 —

On Friday night, June 9, 1972, Earl and Brenda were camping in the badlands when it began to rain. It had been a wet spring in the Black Hills. A series of thunderstorms over the prior week had left the ground saturated. Thunderstorms in western South Dakota are like gray-black, tumultuous shape-shifting spirits that pass in twenty minutes and do not linger. Stand on a hilltop, and a person can see blue sky on both ends of the storm as it races across the landscape. The storms last just long enough for people to take a break from work, have a beer and then go back to work. But something was eerily different about the rain on June 9. It began in the late afternoon, and it didn't stop. The winds blew in from the east, rose against the Hills, and the skies opened. But in the upper atmosphere, the winds were calm. The powerful currents that normally pushed a storm east were idle. The storm cells stacked up and collided into each other. After six hours the Hills and all its creeks were soaked with 15 inches of water. It was pitch black, and no one could predict when the storm might relent.

The National Weather Service office in Rapid City watched the flood gauges on Rapid Creek with increasing alarm, but their data was slim and they were understaffed. Earl and Brenda had watched the sunset sky from the badlands and knew there was a storm brewing, but expected it to blow over like storms always did.

In 1907, a storm had flooded Rapid Creek and pushed 13,000 cubic feet of water per second through town and onto the eastern prairie. In 1920, a flood had pushed 8,000 cubic feet per second. Both storms had been devastating, destroying houses, flooding businesses and killing a handful of people. But by 10:00 pm on June 9, Rapid Creek was pushing 50,000 cubic feet—four times the largest flood in recorded history.

Mayor Don Barnett scrambled to stay ahead of events. The city issued emergency warnings throughout the evening for everyone who lived along the creek. For the city, one question rose above all the others. Would the old Canyon Lake dam hold? Could it withstand the rising water and the debris that was being pushed against it? If the dam was breached, the flood would rise exponentially. As the situation became more desperate, city officials drove to the home of the city ranger who lived closest to the dam at Canyon Lake, relieved him of his post, and evacuated his family.

The Brockelsby home, the anchor of their stability and style, was only a quarter mile away. Earl had understood that he was building in a flood plain. He boasted that he had overbuilt the foundation and set his pilings 20 feet down to rock. The wood paneled living room and bedrooms were upstairs, ten feet above the flood plain. The ground floor included Johnny's bedroom, a guest bedroom, a ping pong table, pool table, Earl's office and a den with files of Earl's correspondence—his literary legacy, including the letters he had written to Maude every day during the war. Cabinets held slides from Earl's world travels all the way back to the early 1950s and a large collection of ammonite fossils that he had collected in the badlands. There was no hundred-year-flood on record that the house could not shrug off, but this storm was creating a thousand-year flood.

Just as it started to rain, Johnny Brockelsby and a few high school buddies were headed out of town into the Black Hills on a camping trip. Like everyone else, they thought the clouds would burst and the sun would be shining before they reached their campsite. But a mile out of town they were stopped by emergency vehicles and turned back. After clearing his own belongings from his ground floor bedroom, Johnny decided to drive to a friend's house to get plywood panels to nail over the windows. He became trapped on the north side of the Creek and never made it back to the house until the next morning.

Maude and 17-year-old Jeff were home alone. They had been through the exercise of prepping for a flood many times. After the 1962 flood, they had mopped up almost a foot of water from the ground floor. It had been a nuisance, but the family had learned their lessons and considered it a reasonable price to pay for living on a flood plain in paradise.

As the rain continued, Maude and Jeff swung into action. They moved Jeff's drum set and amplifiers to the upper floor of the house. They took Earl's precious collection of first edition books off the two lower shelves in his study and piled them onto the top shelves where they were confident the flood waters would never reach. Worst case, they calculated, two feet of water and a week of clean up. They went upstairs to watch *The Tonight Show Starring Johnny Carson*. Jeff's buddy came over to gawk at the rising creek. It was 11:00 pm when local anchors broke into NBC programming to announce that the Canyon Lake dam had been breached by the floodwaters.

Jeff looked downstairs and saw the door burst open. Water began to flood the ground floor, "like filling a bathtub." Their neighbor, Martin Schroeder, ran across Jackson Boulevard, hoping to carry Maude on his back to the high side of the road, but before the little group could run to safety, Jackson Boulevard became an impassable torrent.

"We stood on planter boxes in the front yard and watched a house float by," Jeff recalled, years later. "And then I saw a body float by in the water. It was pitch black. There was no electricity, no street lights, and it was still raining heavily."

Dozens of homes burst under the force of the flood and people who had been hugging their children in bed at one moment were catapulted into fallen trees the next, screaming in the dark for their lost loved ones. As trees hit the power lines, transformer boxes exploded into fireworks for a second, maybe two, and then the sky went black again. Maude and Jeff realized there was no hope of returning to the second-floor living room.

"We could have stayed inside and sat in the living room and never gotten wet," Jeff remembered. "But once we were outside, there was no going back."

The ground floor was flooded ten feet deep. Earl's library was destroyed. Maude and Jeff huddled on the planters in the front yard for an hour until the National Guard arrived, out of the darkness, with ropes that were stretched across the road to guide the four soaked and stranded citizens to safety. Maude and Jeff spent the rest of the night at the Canyon Lake Methodist Church.

Within a day, the floodwaters receded, and Rapid City began to calculate the damages. The Red Cross reported 238 deaths. Six bodies were discovered buried in the silt of the Brockelsby yard. Five people were missing and never found. Another 3,057 people were injured and 1,335 homes were destroyed. Five thousand automobiles had been swept downstream. In some places they were piled on top of each other like an accordion, filled with mud and driftwood. Thirty-five businesses were destroyed and 236 damaged.

Rumors spread that crocodiles had escaped from Reptile Gardens. Spring Creek had flooded, but the Gardens had ridden out the storm with almost no damage. The crocodiles were secure in their concrete ponds. The heavy nine-foot carved crocodile coffee table from the Brockelsby living room, however, was discovered in a children's park ten blocks away.

Earl and Brenda returned to town the next day. When Earl walked into the house he saw Maude stretched out asleep on the couch, exhausted, and thought for a moment that she was dead.

Earl's absence during the crisis weighed heavily on the survivors. At the moment he had been most needed to defend his home, to save his own treasures, to protect his family, Earl had been away on a romantic tryst.

Jeff and Joe Maierhauser, Jr., with a crew of workers from Reptile Gardens spent the rest of the summer making repairs to the house and trying to salvage whatever could be saved. The flood had wrecked the tourism season, but Earl had promised jobs for his crew, and he kept his word. The crew removed 150 tons of mud and silt from the lower floor of the home. Earl's library was destroyed. The downstairs ceiling was marked with ghostly rectangular images of books that had been soaked in mud and slammed against the ceiling by the raging current.

He could not stand to sort through the file drawers of letters and slides, and even though Jeff believed that many could be saved, Earl instructed him to throw all the letters away. Joe, Jr. collected what slides he could find with the improbable hope that he might one day salvage Earl's photographic legacy.

Ten days after the flood, Earl wrote a "Dear Friends" letter in response to the hundreds of phone calls and letters that poured into the office. He reassured his readers that the family was safe and that the city would recover. But his writing betrayed an odd structure that revealed his own inner turmoil. The first paragraph that described his absence, his camping trip to the badlands and his intention to spend the weekend photographing wildflowers was written in the third person: "Expecting sunny skies, Earl took off for the Badlands late Friday afternoon, planning on spending Saturday photographing wild flowers." Of course, no mention was made of Brenda or the fact that Earl was no longer living at home. In the second paragraph, after realizing the danger of the impending flood, he switched to the first person. "I stopped at the first telephone and tried to call my home but there was no answer and fearing for the safety of my family I drove into Rapid City as fast as the truck would go." It was as if he was describing two men: one, the badlands camper and photographer who had no responsibility to be home, and the second, a frantic, concerned father and husband who rushed to save his family.

Years later, Judee cast her judgment on the flood. "I think it changed everything. Jeff was going to college. Janet was living in Whitewood, South Dakota. We had moved to Boulder. It was a natural time for my dad to say, 'I want a new life.'" At Thanksgiving in 1972, Earl pulled Judee aside and told her that he was divorcing Maude.

Maude was heart-broken but stoic. She moved to Boulder where she picked up the pieces of her life and became matriarch to Judee's family—giving Judee space to focus on her new job as a school counselor. As she had done for her whole life, Maude baked cookies for her grandchildren, took care of them after school and cooked family dinners on Sundays. Earl discreetly sent her money for car repairs, dental work and taxes. He informally managed her small investments in the stock market and counseled her on money market investments.

Maude sent Earl dutiful thank you notes, but her dependency made her resolute in the advice she gave her daughters and grandchildren. She had never taken her chance to go to college. She had turned down a scholarship and gone to work at Woolworth's to support her family. Then she had married Earl. "Finish college," she told her family. "Build a career that will make you independent. It's your insurance policy."

Earl and Brenda married in the spring of 1973 and moved to a small abandoned ranch south of Tucson, close to the Mexican border. In the nineteenth century the landscape had been exquisite with knee-high native grasses and groves of cottonwood trees that drew their sustenance from tiny springs beneath the sand. Cactus stood among the giant rocks like sentries of the last American wilderness. But a century of overgrazing had reduced the ranch to gravel and weed. Earl didn't seem to mind. He and Brenda moved into the dilapidated bunkhouse, and he poured his energy into remodeling the century-old adobe home. It was a small house, but once again Earl turned it into an elegant masterpiece, a perfect setting for what he imagined would be his retirement.

ROLLER COASTER '70s

— *Chapter 20* —

Earl told his friends that he had retired when he moved to his ranch in Arizona. He was happy to be done with South Dakota winters and to be in the desert he loved. But it was a half-hearted retirement. He busied himself with projects to develop the ranch, including a scheme to restore his denuded pastures with an expensive irrigation system and pay for it with profits from a wheat commodity trade. He made $50,000 a day for three straight days, then lost it all three days later and cancelled the project.

He developed another plan to breed alligators. Johnny hauled the first batch of small gators from Reptile Gardens in a stock trailer. When he stopped for the night he unloaded the gators into the bathtub in his motel room—to the terror of the morning housekeeping crew. When it turned out that zoos and tourist attractions were awash in alligators that could be bred in Florida and Louisiana for a lot less than Earl could breed them in Arizona, he scrapped the plan.

One problem above all others held Earl's attention in 1973. He was a thousand miles away from the office and Jim Campbell's day-to-day management, but he continued to hold complete ownership of Reptile Gardens and the authority to intervene whenever he wanted. It was an unworkable structure that kept Jim under the stress of trying to anticipate Earl's decision-making and Earl in a state of anxiety about what was being done in his name and absence.

For 35 years, Earl had held tight control of the reins. Now Reptile Gardens faced an existential crisis. Like so many family businesses, there was no formal plan of succession and no clear heir to his life's work. Did Reptile Gardens have a future if he actually retired? Who would own it? Who would manage it? Who would provide the creative spark? And who was willing to do the mind-numbing work of holding a family enterprise together day after day, year after year in the face of fickle tourists and unpredictable economic forces?

In Earl's absence, Reta Mae managed the office. She made payroll, filed the taxes, kept the paperwork flowing and handled Earl's personal accounting. Since childhood she had been Earl's closest confidante, but she had little knowledge of reptiles and was most effective behind the scenes rather than as the public face of the company. Johnny managed the gift shop, but Johnny was in full rebellion, much of it directed against Earl. Neither Judee, Janet, nor Jeff wanted to take over the Gardens.

The steady, indefatigable Jim Campbell had assumed greater and greater duties as general manager. After Earl Chace's retirement in 1968, a number of curators came and went. It fell to Jim to provide continuity. He ran the physical plant and hired the staff. He handled the advertising and made trips across the state to repair, repaint and install highway billboards. He tried his best to translate Earl's distant advice into practical, cost-effective solutions. He was widely respected, but he had none of the authority of ownership.

By the mid-1970s, friends worried that Campbell was working himself into the grave. One of the people who worried most was Joe Maierhauser, Jr., Reta Mae's son, who was a student at the University of Colorado. Like each of Earl's children, Joe had worked summers at Reptile Gardens since he was nine. He considered Jim a mentor and a surrogate father. He could read the weariness on Jim's face. "Jim worked 24 hours a day, 7 days a week, all year. And he was never satisfied," Joe remembered. "I knew he couldn't keep doing it forever."

Jim worked himself to exhaustion each summer, then spent the winter months in San Diego. The heavier his responsibilities became, the more his burdens followed him. He hated the idleness of winter. He began to paint to fill the void, but painting did not restore his spirit. He complained to Earl that he could not shake an upper respiratory virus. He could not sleep. He had been born with one leg shorter than the other. He had worn orthotic shoes his whole life, but under the stress of intense physical labor at the Gardens, his hips and legs were always in pain.

Earl may have tried to build a new life in Arizona. He may even have wanted to retire. But until he had a plan of succession, he knew he could not. If Jim became seriously ill or the economy was hit by a sustained downturn, he would be sucked right back in.

One day when Earl was passing through Colorado, Joe, Jr. pulled him aside and told him, "Jim is killing himself. You've got to come back." The bluntness of Joe's comment was persuasive, but Earl had already been thinking the same thing.

Earl also had other reasons for coming home. His impulsive marriage to Brenda had not liberated him to create a "new life." It had only deepened his isolation from the family. At Reptile Gardens, he had nurtured a free-spirited culture of extended family, but in Arizona he felt isolated with Brenda as an unsentimental gatekeeper. Close friends had warned him that a marriage to a woman less than half his age would never last.

Increasingly, he understood that Brenda contributed every day to his estrangement from his children and grandchildren.

THE ENERGY CRISIS

The state of the American economy provided another powerful reason for Earl to return to the Black Hills. The Arab oil embargo of 1973 had triggered a crisis of confidence among American consumers. All across the American West, roadside tourist attractions dependent on the automobile were buffeted by the volatility of global energy markets and the unpredictable constriction of gasoline supply. Odd-even rationing at gas stations resulted in dramatic front-page photographs of lines around the block, with occasional fistfights at the pumps. In 1974, the American Automobile Association reported that 20 percent of the gas stations in America had no gasoline to sell.

Most roadside attractions did not keep detailed statistics about visitation, but attendance at national parks in the West told the story. In 1972, 2,698,300 people visited the Grand Canyon. Two years later, only 1,888,600 entered the park—a decline of over 800,000 people. In 1971, 2,281,200 people visited Mount Rushmore. By 1975, the number had dropped to 1,533,500—747,700 fewer people were eating at restaurants in Kadoka, visiting the gift shop at Wall Drug or stopping at Reptile Gardens.

Disney World in Orlando, Florida opened in 1971. But spending on Florida tourism dropped 15 percent in 1973 and another 22 percent in 1974. California's $4.8 billion dollar tourist economy lost $500 million in 1974 (almost $2.5 billion in 2015 dollars). The California Chamber of Commerce reported, "the hardest hit were areas wholly dependent on automobile visitors."

In June of 1974, national unemployment held at a nervous 5.4 percent, but jumped 3.6 percent between June 1975 and May 1976, topping out at 9 percent during the worst of the recession.

People who feared for their jobs did not take summer vacations.

In 1972, inflation was a modest 3.2 percent, but by 1974 it was 11 percent. The tourism economy of the West had been built on the optimism of the post-war years. President Ford declared inflation public enemy number one and wore Whip Inflation Now (WIN) buttons to rally the public, but no amount of sloganeering could counter what President Jimmy Carter described in 1979 as the "malaise" that had settled over the nation.

For a local tourism entrepreneur distant from the locus of power, the unpredictability of global events made even the most basic planning difficult. Earl and Jim Campbell struggled to calculate how many employees to hire for the summer. How much money to spend on advertising? How many postcards, stuffed dinosaurs and T-shirts to buy for the gift shop? How many hot dogs for the concession stand?

Earl's best hope in the mid-1970s was the unique regional economy of the Black Hills. Isolation and slow growth could be frustrating for an entrepreneur, but they insulated businesses like Reptile Gardens from the worst of the nation's woes. Families in Minnesota and Iowa and Nebraska who cancelled their plans to fly to California or Florida chose to drive to low-cost vacations in the Black Hills.

With deep pockets, a large reserve and high name identification, Earl believed that Reptile Gardens could ride out the energy crisis, but he couldn't lead his staff from his adobe in Arizona. The crisis required his full attention.

MAUDE STARTS OVER IN BOULDER

While Earl struggled to find his way back to Reptile Gardens and back to his children, the focus of family life shifted to Boulder, Colorado. Judee and Jon Oldham had been the first to leave Rapid City and begin a new life at the University of Colorado. They were followed by Joe, Jr. in 1972. After the divorce, Maude moved to

Boulder. She built her life around church and grandchildren.

"We had no money," Judee's second son, Jeff Oldham, remembered. "My parents were graduate students. Maude lived in our basement. I remember when I was just a little boy, I actually slept with her every night. Grandmother was my stability. She made breakfast every morning. It was just unconditional love. Even when I was in junior high school and I rode my bicycle to school every day, she would make my lunch, and I would stop by her house and pick it up on my to school."

Just as she had done in Rapid City, Maude volunteered in the community, baked cookies in the afternoon, encouraged her grandchildren to do their homework and prepared Sunday dinner for the extended family and friends.

Earl's response to the growing distance between himself and his family was to reach out to Janet. No matter how frustrated he had been with his daughter's life choices, Earl must have smiled at the thought of Janet living a homestead life on the Paraguay-Brazil frontier. By the spring of 1974, his feelings of abandonment had softened, and he dispatched Johnny to Paraguay to check up on his sister.

For two days Johnny and a friend flew deeper and deeper into the landlocked forest of central South America. From the last airport at Pedro Juan Caballero, they took a two-hour bus trip to an outpost on the Brazilian border, where they had agreed to rendezvous with Janet. They waited three days, unsure whether she would ever show up. On the fourth day Janet emerged out of the forest leading two packhorses. Johnny and his friend traded off walking and riding for ten miles on a narrow wildlife trail that meandered back and forth along the border to the clearing where Janet's home had been carved out of the jungle. They lived with her family for three weeks.

The homestead had a hand-dug well, and Janet washed the family laundry in a nearby stream. The house was a primitive four-post frame wrapped in a thick gauge, black plastic sheeting—a late twentieth-century version of the tarpaper shack of the American frontier. Janet cooked over an open fire. The family survived on beans, rice, pasta and an occasional rooster who pecked too eagerly at the strawberries in the garden.

Janet had taken her two-year-old daughter, Suzy, into the wilderness. She became pregnant with her second child. Whatever privilege she felt by growing up wealthy in Rapid City was wrung out of her in Paraguay. She was a dirt-poor homesteader, much like her grandmother on the barren plains of Cottonwood, South Dakota.

The land was beautiful, and Johnny understood the allure, but he was tormented by mosquitoes. He slept without a mosquito net, and one evening counted 50 bites on the back of his swollen right hand. He drank himself into a stupor each night on homemade gin and passed out so that the whining of the mosquitoes would not wake him.

Janet and her husband may have hoped that Johnny's trip would inspire others to follow their trail and file for their own homesteads, but it was a harsh, difficult life. Johnny left Paraguay more worried about his sister's health than inspired by her courage. He had no intention of returning home as a booster for the Paraguayan homestead movement. To the contrary, Johnny thought it was time for Janet to come home.

In the wake of Johnny's trip the correspondence between Earl and Janet intensified. Her letters were longer and more loving. His letters were marked by his characteristic generosity. She described the growth of his granddaughter Elandra. She invited Earl to visit. She confessed that she had lost weight on the frontier and was down to only 120 pounds but wasn't complaining.

She chronicled the family's illnesses and injuries and battles with local pests, "Suzy was burned by a caterpillar and cried for twelve hours."

Janet described her garden—squash and strawberries. She described her relationships with local Indians and her growing fluency in Spanish. She thanked Earl for his money and letters. She told her father she loved him, and in the family tradition she handed the pen to Suzy to scribble a signature at the end of each letter.

For his part Earl encouraged Janet to write a book about her adventures and promised to come for a visit. By the autumn of 1974, the adventure had run its course. Two years on the frontier was longer than most American homesteaders had lasted. Janet and her husband decided to sell their farm and come home.

BACK TO WORK

Under the cover of his concern for Jim's health and hopeful that his long, sad estrangement from family might be near an end, Earl and Brenda moved back to Rapid City in time for the 1975 tourist season. He purchased a mansion on a hill less than a mile north of Reptile Gardens that was popularly known around town as the Pink Palace. The house had originally been built by Peggy Keenan, the owner of the Holy Terror Mine in Keystone, South Dakota. She shared Earl's love of Black Hills minerals and had covered the exterior of the house with pink rose quartz that lit up the walls in the afternoon sun. The masonry that framed the fireplace was purple lepidolite, and the living room carpet was purple to match.

The Pink Palace was far too big for Earl and Brenda, but its sprawling living room was elegant, and the large windows looked to the Black Hills and prairie in all directions. It had the feel of an eagle's nest built in a cluster of trees looking down on Reptile Gardens. Earl could sit on top of the hill and survey the valley below. He could count tourist cars on their way down the hill.

He could see if anyone had accidently left the light on at closing time or take a casual walk down the hill and catch the young staff having a party after midnight.

Earl threw himself into work. His reunion with Jim Campbell gave both men new energy. He drove his old truck to the Gardens early, stayed late, and as he had done when he was young, he worked seven days a week. He did not step on Jim's authority, but found his own niche planting and tending specular flower gardens around the complex. Visitors could be forgiven for believing that the slender 60-year-old man on his hands and knees, digging in the soil, was a gardener—not the owner.

Brenda posed a more complicated problem. She had originally worked as a show presenter in the Bewitched Village. When she returned to Reptile Gardens as Earl's wife she made little effort to relate to his children or the staff. She insinuated herself into the business in a way that infuriated and demoralized Jim Campbell. She held herself apart, claiming knowledge she did not have and authority as Earl's wife that she had not earned.

Earl had always had a streak of pessimism that ran to the morbid. If something could go wrong, it would. In his first months back in Rapid City he began to consider what would become of his life's work if he died suddenly and the family lost control of the Gardens to Brenda. Since the war he had never had a partner at Reptile Gardens. He had refused to give Maude an ownership stake in the company as part of the divorce settlement. If anyone else deserved to be a partner, it was Jim Campbell, but Jim had never insisted, and Earl had never offered.

Now it was time to consider the future. Earl created a privately-held corporation, putting a legal patina on a company he had run out of his hip pocket for 40 years. He gave shares to each of his four children and to Reta Mae. He gave shares to Jim Campbell for a lifetime of loyalty. He gave Brenda one-seventh of the company and kept the majority of the stock for himself. The children rebelled at his decision to leave Maude out. It was petty. They pooled their shares and divided the total by five, each keeping one fifth and giving Maude the final fifth.

Midway through the 1976 tourist season, Earl had every reason to believe that he had solved his most challenging problems. Janet and her family had come home. He had put the company on a solid legal foundation and guaranteed that it would stay in the family. Tourists arrived early and kept coming. The crowds grew in May and June. Inflation had declined steadily over a year to 5.4 percent. Perhaps the American people were finally shrugging off the effects of the oil embargo. The heart of the summer of 1976 felt like 1946. All the pent up desire to explore the open road was let loose. It promised to be a blockbuster year. And then, in the dark morning of August 22, with a month left in the tourist season, smoke began to rise from the dome.

FIRE

Jeff and Johnny Brockelsby lived together in Rapid City in the summer of 1976. Johnny was manager of the Reptile Gardens gift shop. Jeff was a cub reporter for KEVN News, the local ABC affiliate in town. Early in the morning of August 22, Johnny received a panicked call from a friend. The electric wiring in one of the python cages had shorted overnight and sparked a fire.

The heat was so intense that it melted the dome and its metal frame into black clumps of plastic and twisted steel. Trapped inside, the animals could not escape. Thousands of reptiles in the second floor display cases, nearest the dome, were burned or suffocated in the dense smoke. Tropical birds flew into the updraft and were vaporized. Crocodiles and tortoises on the ground floor survived, but the indoor tropical forest was reduced to charcoal. Delicate orchids left black shadows of ash on the linoleum floor.

Jeff raced to the scene, the first newsman to report on the column of smoke rising out of the wreckage of his own family's business. When Earl and Brenda pulled into the parking lot Jeff stepped back momentarily to give his father time to take in the devastation.

"I interviewed Jim Campbell about the losses," Jeff remembered, "but I just didn't feel like I could interview my own father. It was too soon."

Earl was stoic.

"He had a deadpan expression on his face," Jeff remembered. "I was trying to think of something to say to break the ice, and I said, 'It could have been a lot worse.' Dad was the kind of person who always expected the worst, and situations like the fire vindicated his pessimism. He had no emotional reaction at all. He just stood there."

Brenda's response was bitter. She did not seem to understand the emotion that passed between Earl and Jeff; the unspoken family conversation, the gentle son determined to give his father space to grieve. She had no memories in the dome. She had never held the snakes in her hands. She had never planted orchids.

"I told them, 'At least no one was hurt,'" Jeff remembered.

Brenda yelled at him, "What do you mean, nobody was hurt? We were hurt. It will cost us money."

Money was the last thing on Jeff's mind.

Reptile Gardens did not close down after the fire. Earl and Jim and the crew doubled down, as they always did in difficult times. Earl cut the entrance price. The snake and alligator shows continued even as salvage workers cleared the rubble and the acrid stench of melted plastic hung in the air. But the record-breaking summer evaporated in the smoldering wreckage.

Amidst the disaster, the creative side of Earl's brain began to spin. Crisis created opportunity. Instead of retrenching and cautiously rebuilding, he used crisis as an opportunity to expand: to improve the visitor experience, add new exhibitions and innovate with design and display. He ordered a new, clear dome that allowed the natural light to filter through the indoor forest. He scraped the linoleum off the floor and replaced it with Vermont slate. He ordered new orchids and tropical trees. He spent $300,000 to rebuild after the fire and paid off the mortgage four years later when a commodity position in gold turned a huge profit.

Reconstruction of the dome was the easy part. More painful and heart breaking was the tedious task of restoring the reptile collection. To do the job, Earl did not call his son-in-law Jon Oldham in Boulder. Jon had already moved on to an academic career in biology. He did not turn to Jim Campbell, who was overwhelmed with the challenge of keeping the doors open. He did not call Earl Chace or any of the half dozen curators and assistants who had passed through since Chace's retirement. Earl called his nephew, Joe Maierhauser, Jr. and asked him to come home and rebuild the reptile collection.

Earl said the job was temporary. He made no permanent commitment. But he also understood that his nephew was the one person in the family who could be groomed to take over the company when the time was right.

JOE MAIERHAUSER, JR.

Reta Mae's son was tall and lanky, like his father. He had been born a cousin to Earl's children, and raised as a brother. He was treated like a son by Maude and Earl. But there was no denying the hole in his life. The Brockelsby children had grown up with the coolest father in the neighborhood. Joe had grown up without his father. The Brockelsby children had grown up with a mother who was a rock of stability. Joe had grown up with a mother who loved him dearly, and did her best, but as he got older it seemed that she depended more on Joe than he depended on her. By the time he was in high school, Reta Mae suffered from seizures and periodic black outs. It was Joe who took care of her.

"On Jan. 30th I had a blackout and came to and found myself on a stretcher in an ambulance—cost me $30 for that single ride," Reta Mae wrote to Earl in Mexico when Joe was seventeen. "Boy Joey really put the restrictions on my activities…He said he was sick and tired of being so scared and thinking I was dead." Joe demanded that she stop drinking, go to bed early, and improve her diet.

When Joe's personal problems became too great he found refuge at Reptile Gardens. No matter how lonely life got, he knew that Earl and Chace and Jim Campbell watched over him. Earl sent him presents every Christmas, took him to the badlands on camping trips and mailed him personal letters from exotic places around the world. Joe reciprocated by loving what Earl loved. He loved Reptile Gardens. He loved photography. He loved the exotic photographs from the villages of Papua New Guinea.

Joe started working at the Gardens in 1963 at the age of nine, and he couldn't wait to get to work. Like each of Earl's children, he started at the bottom. He earned $4 a day cleaning up after the tourists, scrubbing toilets, dumping trashcans and restocking soda pop machines. Over a decade, he learned to do every job imaginable. He was a carpenter and snake guide. He worked in the gift shop. He studied Jim Campbell's work ethic. He became assistant curator and listened intently to the way Earl Chace told snake stories that mesmerized the tourists. He absorbed it all because instinctively he understood that Reptile Gardens would be his life.

When he was 17, Joe wrote a note to Earl on the back of a postcard of Frederic Remington's painting *The Night Rider*. "I was just thinking and I realized that I have never really thanked you for all that you have done for me. I hope you don't mind, but I will always think of you as the only real father I have ever had."

Like his cousins, Joe had emotionally distanced himself from Earl and Maude's troubles. He visited Earl in Arizona but kept his distance from Brenda. Joe graduated from the University of Colorado, Boulder in 1976. He took a job in the cost accounting department of the Head Ski Company, but when Earl called, he jumped at the opportunity to return.

The Joe Maierhauser who came home in December of 1976 was different than the shy teenager who had gone off to college four years earlier. His work at Head Ski Company had given him confidence, but it had also taught him that he did not want to spend his life as a "corporate drone." He had grown up in the free spirit culture at Reptile Gardens, and he knew that he could never be happy in a button-down corporate job.

As Joe set about his work, he resolved to change the way Reptile Gardens purchased and raised its snakes. It turned out to be far more difficult to rebuild the international collection in 1976 than it would have been just five years earlier. The Endangered Species Act had been signed by President Nixon in 1973. The Convention on International Trade in Endangered Species of Wild Flora and Fauna (CITES) had been put into force in 1975. The fire had killed priceless five-foot long giant Chinese salamanders and huge Blomberg's toads from the rainforests of Colombia, but Joe could no longer cold-call Earl's old friends and order replacements. They were banned for export, and even if they could be smuggled out of third world countries, the U.S. Fish and Wildlife Service would block them from being imported into the United States. They could never be collected again.

In the new regulatory environment, Earl's old habits created new problems. When an unknown broker in Africa reached out to Earl and wanted to establish a relationship, Earl ordered a sample shipment and wrote a check. The investment was small. If the dealer delivered what he promised, Earl said he might place a larger order. That's the way he had always done it. When the shipment arrived in Chicago, Fish and Wildlife agents discovered banned baby Nile crocodiles in one of the storage compartments that had not been listed on the manifest.

Earl insisted that he had not ordered the crocodiles and did not know they were in the shipping container. But African crocodile populations were being decimated for the European skin market, just like the Asian populations had been in the 1950s. Earl's shipment was exactly the kind of illegal activity that the new laws were designed to stop. The Fish and Wildlife Service confiscated the entire shipment, threatened to prosecute Earl and blacklisted Reptile Gardens.

It would be impossible for Joe to rebuild the collection without the cooperation of federal agencies and Earl had just made his job far more difficult. Only 20 years earlier Earl had subsidized Arthur Jones's "anything goes" expedition to the Caprivi Strip. Now he was being blacklisted for having done far less.

Earl was furious, but the incident was a cautionary tale. Joe could no longer trade reptiles on a handshake or smuggle snakes and lizards under the front seat of a truck. The next generation of zoo curators would have to operate in a more complex bureaucratic environment that stressed conservation and restoration rather than entertainment. The mini-scandal never became public, but it was a small and significant signal that Earl's way of doing things was passing.

PASSING THE TORCH

— Chapter 21 —

The years that followed the fire were golden years. The nation shrugged off the energy crisis and tourists put their foot to the pedal. The new dome opened in the spring of 1977 and was an immediate sensation. Visitation rose 28 percent. It was the greatest one-year increase since 1946, and to accomplish such growth in the shadow of the energy crisis made the profits even sweeter. The only cloud in the picture was Earl's marriage. He could not escape Brenda by planning a trip into the wilderness. Unlike Maude, Brenda loved to travel. She insisted on going everywhere with him.

After the 1977 tourist season, Earl took Brenda to Papua New Guinea, hoping to recapture the magic of their early romance, but he wasn't the same man who had trekked alone into the highland forest a decade earlier. When a village headman offered to buy Brenda, Earl laughed dismissively at the offer, but wrote home to the crew at Reptile Gardens that on second thought he should have taken the offer more seriously.

In early November 1978, four years after the end of the Arab oil embargo, 37,000 Iranian oil workers went on strike to oppose the rule of the Mohammad Reza Pahlavi, the Shah of Iran. To tourist operators in the Black Hills, it seemed like an inconsequential international event, one of hundreds of strikes and public demonstrations that the Shah had squashed with severe police and military action.

Reptile Gardens was going into its annual hibernation. Earl and Brenda were on their way to Baja. Jim Campbell was headed to San Diego. Joe Maierhauser, Jr. had completed the job of rebuilding the reptile collection. He was newly married to Carole Foster, a young Reptile Gardens summer worker from Selby, South Dakota. The couple intended to spend the winter in Arizona before Joe enrolled in graduate school at the University of Kansas.

The Iranian oil strike was a foreshadowing. Two months later the Shah of Iran fled his country. The Iranian Revolution swept new leadership and an entirely new worldview into power. The dictatorial power of the Shah was replaced by the dictatorial power of the Ayatollah Khomeini. In the chaos, Iranian oil production plummeted from 6 million barrels of oil a day to just 1.5 million barrels. In global terms, the loss of the Iran supply was small. Saudi Arabia stepped into the breach and increased production. The West Texas oil fields increased production. But the fragile psychology of the American consumer was shaken. Attendance at national parks declined precipitously and gas lines returned. In a matter of months the confidence that had taken half a decade to restore was crushed.

The tourist season in 1979 was dismal. Seven hundred thousand fewer people visited Mount Rushmore in 1979 than 1973. At Reptile Gardens, Earl calculated that attendance dropped 33 percent in one year—a net loss of $230,000 at the turnstiles. Once again, the roller coaster took its toll. Earl survived by tapping into a million dollar safety reserve that he had accumulated in the boom years. But it was not a reserve that could cover 33 percent losses for more than a few years.

A NEW GENERATION

At the end of 1978, Joe Maierhauser, Jr. was at a crossroads. He had successfully re-established the new reptile collection. He had proven himself to Earl and Jim Campbell. In Earl's mind, Joe was the obvious heir apparent when Campbell retired. Everyone except Johnny had already moved away, and Johnny's relationship with his father was so tense and argumentative that he was ready to quit his job as gift shop manager and move to Colorado. Only Joe had the breadth of experience to succeed Jim as general manager.

There was another option for Joe. His father had strongly advised him to leave Reptile Gardens, escape Earl's influence and go to graduate school. As dysfunctional as their relationship had been growing up, Joe felt a strong desire to please his father. He had been accepted into a Masters program in anthropology at the University of Kansas for the fall of 1979. He intended to study American Indian art and culture. A graduate degree would create opportunities. He could teach. He could travel and do research. If the right opportunity presented itself in four or five years, after Jim retired, he could return to Reptile Gardens. An advanced degree would give him the gravitas to escape Earl's shadow and be his own man.

Joe and Carole took six months to think about their options. They moved to Arizona and went to work with Joe's father on the construction of a small museum at Colossal Cave. The museum would feature the geology of the cave, the archeology of local Native American tribes, wildlife, and the cowboy history of the region. It was a short-term job, but it was an opportunity for Joe to develop his own instincts about museum design, display, and interpretive resources.

From Tucson, Joe and Earl began a steady correspondence—not as uncle and nephew, not as a series of holiday greetings, or birthday cards, or thank you cards, but as equals. As he built the museum, Joe wrote about the business of tourism in just the language that Earl respected. "I have ordered 25 price lists. At this point the postage for them is about all we can afford, but it is still a great deal of fun. I get so involved in all this and spend hours reading price lists and books." Later he suggested, "I think they could boost sales by at least 10-15 percent if they improved their displays and changed a few items…The diorama display needs plex…The mineral display needs lights." Joe's attention to the details, the small daily tasks of the tourist business, must have been music to Earl's ears.

Joe and Carole left for the University of Kansas in the fall of 1979. Carole enrolled as a freshman and loved her new life. For a small town girl from South Dakota, the university was an exciting, stimulating playground of new relationships and new ideas. Joe, on the other hand, was miserable and depressed. He discovered that he was not a scholar, and the program did not give him the freedom to pursue his own interests. He began to realize that four years of graduate school was a high price to pay for pleasing his father. Meanwhile, Jim began to signal that he wanted to retire, and Earl hinted that he was ready for Joe to come back.

Like all graduate students, Joe and Carole lived poor, and one day Joe found himself painting the house of a senior professor who had taken pity on his poverty and offered the odd job of house painting to help make ends meet. Joe was venting his frustrations when the professor's wife reflected on her husband's own career and offered Joe an important insight: "If this is the only thing you want to do in life, then do it. But if you have any doubt at all, don't stay."

That was all it took. He knew he wanted to come home.

Joe had no interest in being Earl's assistant. He accepted that he would spend the first summer learning from Campbell, but when he became general manager he did not intend to run Reptile Gardens in Earl's shadow. He wanted to make changes, and he was willing to push back against Earl's sense of prerogative.

The world of zoos and tourism was in transition, and Joe wanted to emphasize a new conservation ethic. He wanted to stop purchasing rattlesnakes that had been poisoned during Oklahoma roundups. He filled in the old snake pit. Earl complained that Joe was ruining a major tourist attraction when he got rid of hundreds of water snakes that were free roaming inside the dome. Joe argued that it had become a nightmare to keep the water snakes alive through the summer. Besides, there was no thrill in seeing dozens of water snakes. Tourists wanted to see the deadliest snakes in the world, not timid water snakes that died every night and had to be screened out of the pond every morning.

Joe did not want to fight the U.S. Fish and Wildlife Service. He wanted to work with it. He wanted fewer snakes with longer life spans and more exotic appeal. He didn't want a hundred prairie rattlesnakes piled on top of each other. He wanted the biggest timber rattlesnake he could find. He wanted one inland taipan, the most venomous snake in the world, and he wanted the snakes beautifully exhibited and accessible to tourists. He wanted a boomslang from southern Africa. He wanted reptiles that no one had ever seen. He wanted a blue poison arrow frog from the Amazon, and he wanted specimens that would make Reptile Gardens an authentic conservation mecca as well as a popular tourist attraction.

Earl argued with Joe, but he did not resist. No matter how contentious an argument became, Earl knew when to pull back. "You are in charge now," he told Joe. "Do what you think is right."

One thing both men agreed on was the need for something new. It was a curse to have tourists drive by in the belief that they had visited last year and there was nothing new to see. A large percentage of Reptile Gardens patrons were repeat visitors, and it was critical to have something new each season to entice old friends back to the park.

Earl proposed a new spectacle, a show with powerful, stately birds of prey like bald eagles, owls, and hawks. Joe agreed, but he had no idea how to find someone with the skills to put such a performance together. On the same day as their conversation, at closing time, Joe heard the phone ring as he was walking out the door. By chance he stopped and answered.

Scott Shupe had a lilting, soft southern accent that Joe found immediately engaging. He had been curator of reptiles at the Ross Allen's Reptile Institute in Silver Springs, Florida, in the early 1970s, and knew his way around the tourism business. He had even visited Reptile Gardens on vacation. Looking for something new, Scott had developed a birds of prey performance that had become quite popular at public schools across the south, but he wanted a steady summer venue. He was calling on the off chance that Reptile Gardens might be interested.

Joe was skeptical. "Our schedule is very demanding," he said. "Can you do 14 shows a day, 7 days a week, all summer?"

"That wouldn't be a problem," Scott answered.

When Scott sat down with Earl for a face-to-face interview, he confessed that he had no advanced academic training in ornithology. It might lose him the job, he thought, but he might as well get it out in the open at the beginning.

"Most employers want to see your credentials," Earl answered. "I go more by [the] look in your eye."

Scott was sold, and so was Earl. Scott brought his menagerie of owls, eagles, vultures and hawks to Reptile Gardens in the summer of 1982 and stayed for five years. Because there was no place designed for the bird show, Scott performed from inside the alligator pen, with curious alligators brushing their tails against his leg. He built a box with a sliding door at the top of a telephone pole that opened with a pulley cord and placed a bird inside the box at the beginning of each show. He lectured about the birds: their magnificent eyesight, their ability to hunt at night, their speed, their talons, and their migrations. When the time was right he pulled the rope, the box opened and a hawk or eagle came screaming through the crowd and on to Scott's fist. The crowd gasped in amazement and cheered.

HEART ATTACK, DIVORCE AND RECONCILIATION

Earl hated whiners. A blister was the kind of thing that a man walked through. Thirsty? Run a mile in the summer sun. Pain in your chest? Take a hike. Above all, don't let your body conquer your mind. In the summer of 1982, Earl and Jeff went hiking together in the badlands. Jeff was not a highly trained athlete. He was more comfortable in a library than the wilderness. He was a dutiful son, but he spent most hikes looking at Earl's denim rear end. On this day, Earl couldn't keep up. Jeff could not help but notice how often Earl stopped to catch his breath. Falling behind did not come gracefully to a man who bragged about his fitness.

After Christmas, his exhaustion deepened. The pain in his arm nagged at him. He could not catch his breath. Was this the same exhaustion that had preceded his breakdown in 1949? Had he lost control of his mental illness? After Christmas, he checked himself into the hospital, but doctors could give him no clear answers other than to recommend rest.

At 4:00 am on January 21, 1983, Earl had a heart attack and was rushed to the hospital in Rapid City. He spent ten days in recovery and was sent home. Four hours later he had a second heart attack and returned to the hospital. After a week in the care of local doctors, he was flown to Porter Memorial Hospital in Denver where cardiologists discovered that two arteries were completely blocked, a third was blocked 90 percent, and two more were 50 percent closed. Surgeons performed a quintuple by-pass operation.

Rather than recover, Earl grew weaker in the month after his surgery until doctors discovered embolisms that were constricting the flow of blood to his lungs. Recovery from a quintuple by-pass was hard enough. With the new complications, he recognized that recovery would come to dominate his life.

"They tell me it will take a full year to recover," he wrote to Jeff, "so I am learning the meaning of patience. Maybe I can squeeze out another 5 or 6 years of enjoying life. At least that is my goal."

In the aftermath of his heart attack and surgery Earl no longer came early to the Gardens and worked late. He was only 67, but he was housebound. Occasionally, when he had the energy, he would drive down the hill and walk the gardens with Joe. It made him proud.

"I have been down to the Reptile Gardens a couple of times for a few minutes," he wrote Maude a month after his surgery. "There isn't much I can do or want to do. Reta Mae and Joe pretty much take care of everything I used to do. I certainly don't know what we could possibly do without them."

Brenda made no effort to participate in the family business. She continued to travel internationally. Earl did not go with her. He preferred to visit the family in Boulder, and he invited his grandchildren to spend time at the Pink Palace. He longed for reconciliation, and Janet received his overtures with graceful enthusiasm.

He became more introspective. He recorded his memoirs into an audio recorder for Reta Mae to transcribe. He made one last effort to hike Harney Peak and gazed east toward the badlands.

Maude had kept a cordial but measured distance from Earl's life for over a decade, but she took no satisfaction in his misery. When he had his heart attack, she offered condolences and told him that she would pray for his recovery. She had spent her adult life attending to Earl's physical and psychological fragility.

Even in divorce she ended her frequent letters with prayers for his health and peace of mind.

The more he came to Boulder, the more his generosity came to the fore. His arrogance receded. His financial gifts increased, and he turned his generosity to the grandchildren. He amended his will to make Maude heir to the Arizona ranch. It was a valuable asset, but a cruel irony. She thanked him for his attention to the family and for his weekend visits.

After Sunday dinners they sat on the porch of Judee's home and talked about the past. But Maude was cautious about becoming emotionally vulnerable or accepting responsibility for his well-being. She signed her letters "…as ever," and he did the same, as if there had once been a foundation of love that they both kept as a fond memory.

In the spring of 1986, Earl and Brenda divorced. As part of the settlement, he demanded that Brenda return her shares in Reptile Gardens. He believed his offer was generous and considerate, but when Brenda insisted on keeping Earl's cat he reduced his offer. He was victorious in court and kept his cat. It was a petty ending to a bad marriage.

Shortly afterwards, Earl asked Maude to move home to Rapid City and live with him. She asked for patience. "I appreciate your offer and truly can't make any decision at this time. I am giving it much thought."

When Earl visited the family at Christmas, Jeff overheard his parents negotiating their future in whispers. "I was listening behind the door of my bedroom, and they were talking about how it would work. Dad kept saying that she could keep her apartment in Boulder if she wanted to. And then he asked her to marry him."

Two months later, Maude still had not made up her mind. "I try to think about what it would be like to live in Rapid City again," she wrote. "It's been 14 years this month since I came here, and it seems even longer…You have been more than kind and fair and I want to do what I feel is right for all. I hope you can understand my indecision (and not get mad at me!)" She seemed to be truly searching for what would make her happy. For the first time in fifteen years she signed her letter, "My love."

CONCLUSION

Maude and Earl Brockelsby married, for the second time, on May 30, 1987, at a ceremony in the chapel of the First Presbyterian Church in Rapid City. Their youngest son, Jeff, was Earl's best man. Reta Mae was Maude's maid of honor. At first, the new marriage was greeted with skepticism within the family. Maude had made a new, fulfilling life in Boulder. She was close to her grandchildren and active in her church. The prospect of returning to Rapid City to serve a man who was in poor health seemed an unfair bargain.

The children were baffled by the reconciliation, but as the years passed each came to realize that the love and commitment their parents had for each other had deeper roots than the hurt. As Maude came back to Earl, the children made their peace and followed.

Maude made no demands, other than marriage. She knew what awaited her: Earl's congenital heart condition and deteriorating health, his lifelong battle against depression, his addiction to tranquilizers. Maude balanced it all against her overriding desire for the family to be whole and her appreciation for his amazing creativity and generosity. There was also a practical consideration. She believed that marriage was an insurance policy that would secure Earl's commitment to keeping Reptile Gardens in the family.

The couple retreated to the Pink Palace and lived a quiet life. Earl remodeled the master bedroom, lining the walls with thick carpet to reduce the noise from Highway 16. The colors of the bedroom were muted. The space became a den of solitude. He read voraciously and eclectically—mystery novels, philosophy, natural science, psychology and politics.

He paced at night and kept notebooks filled with single-spaced notes about his health. Maude sat with him for hours at a time. Three or four times a week, Joe Maierhauser or Jeff would visit. Only rarely did Earl drive down the hill to Reptile Gardens. When he did, he went to celebrate rather than judge or give directions.

In the last years of his life, Earl did what is so difficult for entrepreneurs to do. He let go of his life's work to the next generation. Over a period of a decade, beginning with Jim Campbell's retirement and Joe Maierhauser, Jr.'s promotion to general manager, he slowly and steadily distributed stock to the family, increasing the next generation's stake in the company as he aged. He convinced Johnny to return to the Gardens in 1989 to become the director of communications and public relations. Johnny became the voice of Reptile Gardens in the community. In 1996, he was elected president of the Black Hills, Badlands and Lakes Association, 30 years after Earl had held the same position. In 2015, Johnny also won the prestigious Ben Black Elk Award for his contribution to South Dakota tourism—33 years after Earl won the same award.

At a family shareholders meeting in 1991, Earl appointed Jeff to be the treasurer of the family corporation. Jeff had shown no particular interest in the management of Reptile Gardens, and Earl did not consult him before making the announcement. He simply said, "I think Jeff should be the treasurer. He knows how to handle money."

Jeff had been born the same year as his cousin Joe, and the two boys had grown up together. They were twelve years younger than Judee and seven younger than Janet. Jeff and Johnny shared Joe's perspective about the need to adapt Reptile Gardens to the demands of twenty-first century tourism, and in their own way the three young men steered Reptile Gardens in a new direction. Most important, Earl shared their view that the Gardens could not stand still. The Interstate corridors of Florida, Arizona and Southern California were littered with boarded up reptile attractions that could not innovate and stay abreast of the interests of passing tourists. The survival of Reptile Gardens depended on its ability to offer something new to each generation.

"Don't worry about how I might have done things," Earl reassured Joe. "Do what you think needs to be done."

In the weeks before his death from a sudden, fast moving cancer in 1993, Earl made his way down to the Gardens for a final visit. He walked the grounds with Joe, thrilled at the expansive gardens, the petunia mountain, the manicured lawns, the towering cottonwood trees that cast shade over the walkways and the orchids that were his personal passion.

"I think it is a finished product," he told Joe.

"No it's not, Earl. It will never be finished," Joe responded. The answer could not have been sweeter.

ONE LAST CRUSADE

Earl could be criticized for not supporting individual projects that he knew were undercapitalized or located too far from established tourist routes. But when he found an idea that he liked, he became a supportive, even zealous advocate. In the mid-1970s,

Earl met two graduate students at the South Dakota School of Mines, Peter Larson and James Honert, whose passion for science and the badlands equaled his own. They were geologists and fossil hunters. They loved rocks and they loved working outdoors—just like he did.

They had a big vision of how they could turn their passion for science into a profitable consulting business. They set up their business in the abandoned alligator pit of the original Reptile Gardens building at the top of Radar Hill.

The young men had Earl's appreciation for the spectacular. They imagined the discovery of giant fossils—*T. rex* and sea turtles, but they did not see themselves as tourism entrepreneurs. They were serious researchers and seasoned in the craft of fossil excavation and preparation.

Like so many westerners, including Earl and the crew at Reptile Gardens, Larson and Honert and their friends lacked advanced academic degrees. But in the field, where patience in extreme heat and dexterity with a dentist's tool often trumped a Ph.D., they were creative master craftsmen. When the fossil of a giant sea turtle (*Archelon*) was discovered in the Pierre shale south of Rapid City in 1977, Larson assisted European fossil experts with the cleaning and stabilization of the skull, tail and rear feet. The fossil was gigantic, 13 feet by 16 feet, and Larson worked both in his own laboratory and in Switzerland to dig the fossil out of its rock tomb. Today, the original fossil is on display at the Museum of Natural History in Vienna, Austria. The second full-size casting ever made of the fossil greets visitors on the second floor of the dome at Reptile Gardens.

In 1979, an expanded partnership that included Peter's brother, Neal Larson, and Robert Farrar renamed the enterprise—the Black Hills Institute of Geological Research. They became part of the international fossil trade, working with museums, universities and wealthy collectors around the world. In 1990, they found the fossil of a lifetime—the most complete, well-preserved *Tyrannosaurus rex* skeleton ever discovered—embedded in a prairie rock formation on the Cheyenne River Indian Reservation.

Earl appreciated the passion that the Larsons and Farrar had for paleontology, but he loved spectacle more, and a 40-foot long, 13-foot tall dinosaur fossil was a gargantuan spectacle. It was just the kind of once-in-a-lifetime discovery that could transform the museum at the Black Hills Institute into an influential tourist attraction.

For two years, the team at the Black Hills Institute cleaned and prepared the *T. rex* fossil. Then, in 1992, federal agents descended on the Institute laboratory and confiscated the fossil and hundreds of other fossils collected on public and Indian lands. The arrest outraged Earl. To his mind, Larson and his colleagues had done a great public service by discovering and professionally preparing the *T. rex* fossil.

All of Earl's passions aligned: his love of the badlands, fossils, and geology; his belief in young entrepreneurs who had turned their own sweat into a successful business that straddled the line between science and tourism; his disdain for academic snobs who postured about credentials but had no idea how hard the work was in a place as severe as the badlands; his libertarian values about land use in the West and his conviction that places like the Black Hills Institute strengthened the regional economy.

"This is my last crusade," he told his family. He wrote his friends in Congress. He formed a defense fund to fight the federal indictment, and he rallied the community to keep the *T. rex* fossil in South Dakota.

Earl did not live to see the final results of the trial. The *T. rex*, named "Sue," was sold at auction to the Field Museum of Natural History in Chicago. Peter Larson was convicted on a series of financial technicalities that arose from the unauthorized collection of fossils on federal land and sentenced to two years in federal prison. The auction and conviction demonstrated that the world Earl had grown up in had finally passed.

LEGACY

Born when the last homestead claims were being filed on the prairie, Earl Brockelsby was present at the creation of the modern American West. He was a sensationally complex man—naturalist, intellectual, international adventurer. He was plagued by mental illness, and yet he was one of Rapid City's most successful and innovative civic leaders and businessmen. He was a showman and a circus barker with a passion for philosophy. Most of all, he was a salesman.

There is a story from the early days of Reptile Gardens that reveals Earl's essential character. On his many travels he had a habit of collecting objects that he believed could be sold in the gift shop at Reptile Gardens. On one trip, he brought home a collection of pottery, but to Earl's unforgiving frustration, the gift shop staff could not sell the assorted items. The unsold pottery languished in the basement. Finally, Earl threw up his hands.

"The pottery isn't the problem," he said, "It's the way you're trying to sell it. It's all in how you make the pitch."

He proposed a bet. "I'll go out in the parking lot and collect some gravel from underneath a car. I bet I can sell it for a dime."

Sure enough, he did. Approaching a tourist, he smiled and engaged with genuine interest. He talked about the geology of the Black Hills. He described how the region had once been a shallow ocean and told how limestone was made from the skeletons of ancient sea animals buried and compressed in the ocean sediment for millions of years. Finally, he made the pitch: "You wouldn't want to leave the Black Hills without a sample of this unique limestone that you can display in a nice bowl on your living room table as a way of remembering your trip." Within a half hour, Earl had sold a bag of gravel and made his point.

Earl had been born in the golden age of the railroad circus, and the spirit of the circus was forever part of his imagination. He designed the great dome of Reptile Gardens to be more than an engineering feat. It was reminiscent of the circus big top. Under the big top, tourist families came not for science or education (except perhaps incidentally) but for spectacle and wonderment, death defying acts of courage and life-long memories. Earl was the charismatic ringmaster.

Earl did not set out to build a natural history museum or a public zoo. In a later era, scientists and zoo curators designed micro-ecosystems that enabled wildlife to hide and camouflage and escape from human contact. Earl created a space where tourists could press their faces to within an inch of the deadliest snakes in the world and ride a giant tortoise. The tension between Earl and the curatorial staff (beginning with Earl Chace) could be palpable at times, but the fundamental purpose of Reptile Gardens was never in doubt. It was important to have an exhibition of endangered Cuban crocodiles, but it was not a spectacle, and it was not as entertaining as watching a bare-chested 20-year old man jump on the back of an alligator.

The legacy of the big top continued long after Earl's passing. Under the stewardship of Joe Maierhauser Jr., Earl's four children and his grandson Jeff Oldham, Reptile Gardens has created a new identity for itself as a force for conservation, science education and research as well as remaining one of the preeminent tourist attractions in the Black Hills. The professional staff regularly consults with leading public zoos and universities on the handling of snakes. But it has not lost its commitment to the grand spectacle.

In 2004, after three months of negotiations between curators Terry Phillip and Ken Ernest and the Australian government, Reptile Gardens finally purchased the giant crocodile that Earl had sought for half a century. Rather than procure the crocodile from a hunter or private broker, curators patiently negotiated with government officials and a private amusement park in Sydney, Australia, that was closing. The crocodile—named Maniac by its Australian keepers—was enormous, 15'8" long and 1,250 pounds. It had been born in captivity in 1970 and had never experienced the "red tooth and claw" of nature.

Earl had not hesitated to fund Arthur Jones's expedition to Africa in 1956 or fly twice to George Craig's wilderness outpost in Papua New Guinea in the late 1960s to purchase a giant crocodile, but he would never have had the patience for protracted negotiations with Australian government export agents. It is also unlikely that Reptile Gardens, under Earl's direct management, would have escaped the informal blacklist of the U.S. Fish and Wildlife Service. It was Earl's vision of the spectacular to have one of the world's largest crocodiles at Reptile Gardens, but in the new conservation culture of the twenty-first century, Joe and Ken Ernest did what Earl could never have done. When he arrived at Reptile Gardens, Maniac was among the five largest crocodiles in captivity in the world.

No child has ridden a giant Aldabra tortoise at Reptile Gardens in 20 years. The decision was a simple but important concession to the changing values of tourist families and curators. The new policy was one of many that marked the end of Earl's era and the beginning of the new. But the spectacle of the giant sea turtle remains. Visitors who climb the interior stairs of the dome at Reptile Gardens find themselves face to face with a bronze casting of the largest sea turtle fossil ever discovered.

The fossil *Archelon ischyros* was discovered in the mid-1970s in the Pierre shale formation of the badlands 45 miles south and east of Reptile Gardens. The sea turtle, measuring 15 feet by 16.5 feet, weighed 4,500 pounds and lived in the shallow sea that engulfed the Great Plains during the Age of Dinosaurs. Earl knew of the fossil, helped fund its preparation by Peter Larson at the Black Hills Institute and tried to keep it in South Dakota. When he failed, it was sold to the Museum of Natural History in Vienna, Austria. The Black Hills Institute won the rights to cast the fossil for reproduction, however, and Reptile Gardens was the first to purchase a full-size casting.

Reptile Gardens continues to be at the center of Black Hills tourism. In 1937, Earl parked abandoned automobiles in the parking lot to attract passing motorists. In the summer of 2015, 300,000 tourists visited the Gardens. A third of these visitors came from South Dakota or bordering states. They were overwhelmingly repeat visitors, often grandparents bringing their grandchildren. Reptile Gardens' location on the highway from Rapid City to Mount Rushmore affirms Earl's original conviction that the key to success for a tourist attraction in the automobile age is to be on the road. In 2015, just as in 1937, being on the road to Mount Rushmore was golden.

Earl created the largest collection of reptiles in the world in the most unlikely place, but his greatest legacy is an army of several thousand teenagers whose lives were transformed by a summer job at Reptile Gardens. They have gone on to become attorneys and judges, doctors, computer engineers, writers and poets, entrepreneurs, real estate developers and scientists. But in the entire history of the enterprise, no one but Earl Brockelsby has ever greeted tourists with a rattlesnake under his hat.

ACKNOWLEDGMENTS

Judee Brockelsby Oldham, Earl's eldest child, once told me, "Dad was a *very* complicated man. If the book reflects how complicated he was, it will be a success." I had no idea.

Judee, and Earl's other three children, Janet Brockelsby Jacobs, John (aka Johnny B) Brockelsby and Jeff Brockelsby, spent countless hours in person, over the phone and by email helping me understand the full dimension and forgotten details of Earl's life. "Growing up in any family on some level feels ordinary," Janet told me. "In reading Dad's biography with the distance of time, we have not only learned more about him, but we can also see his many dimensions more clearly." The project turned out to be as much of a journey for the family as it was for me as the author, and I am forever grateful for their willingness to open the Reptile Gardens archives and give of themselves to tell this story. It was a process that required the family to explore old memories and old relationships and to rediscover their father and mother. "What struck us so profoundly was the love and caring that permeated our lives in spite of the outer turmoil," Janet explained. "Dad and mom were generous with and thoughtful of each of us, our children, their own siblings and the extended family, which included the hundreds of young people who passed through Reptile Gardens. This love was the glue that kept our families close. Our mother often encouraged us to acknowledge gratitude in life, and we are truly grateful to our mom and dad."

Earl's grandson, Jeff Oldham, is assistant general manager at Reptile Gardens and represents the ascendency of the third generation. Jeff gave voice to the extraordinary generosity that Earl showed to his grandchildren in his last years and helped me understand Maude's personality and lifestyle during the time that she lived in Boulder, Colorado. Joe Maierhauser, president and CEO of Reptile Gardens gave both his personal archives and countless hours of his time. What he did not know from personal experience, Joe researched on behalf of the project. He helped make contacts with valuable sources and brought great perspective and balance to the narrative.

Judge Marshall Young played a special role in Earl's life. He began his relationship as a young worker, but evolved over the years into one of Earl's closest friends. He was a fellow traveler in Mexico and New Guinea, personal confidante, legal advisor and counsel to the second generation after Earl's passing. Marshall's numerous interviews were essential to helping me understand Earl from a perspective outside the family.

Joan Pollok Borel, Bob Borgmeyer and Carole Foster worked at Reptile Gardens and had personal friendships with Earl and his family. Their interviews were valuable in understanding the summer youth culture and the way that Earl created an "extended family" at the Gardens. Martie Kuehn Maierhauser generously shared details from her diary of the trip through Mexico and Central America.

Senator James Abourezk helped put Earl's political relationships in perspective. Bill Honerkamp helped me understand Earl's leadership in the regional tourism economy. Stanford Adelstein gave a lengthy interview on the history of Kadoka as a "magical" village on the edge of the badlands. James "Pev" Evans told me great stories of summer nights with Earl at the Black Hills dog track. Kenneth Scissons was one of Earl's life long friends. The two met in junior high school and their relationship extended into adulthood. In his unpublished memoir, Earl described the day in 1948 that he spent with Kenny Scissons trapping 465 rattlesnakes as one of the most exciting days of his life. Ken's daughter, Ruth Ahl, gave a lengthy interview that brought humor and insight to my understanding of Earl and his friendship with Scissons and other Lakotas. Jerre Campbell Jones was the first woman employed by Reptile Gardens as a snake guide. Jerre helped me understand Earl's showmanship and the culture of Reptile Gardens in the years before and immediately after the war.

Nick Hall, Ray Pawley and Charles Peterson all worked at Reptile Gardens as teenagers and went on to careers in science, academics and museum and zoo management. Their intimate acquaintance with Earl and the depth of their knowledge of Reptile Gardens' importance in the culture of zoos, tourism and academic herpetology were vital to the project. Scott Shupe hosted the first Reptile Gardens birds of prey show. His interview helped me understand how Earl balanced the entertainment aspects of Reptile Gardens with science and education. Investment advisor Doug Rogers explained the commodity markets of the 1970s and talked about how Earl managed his investments. Brian Smith, professor of biology at Black Hills State University, gave considerable insights into the behavior of prairie rattlesnakes.

Charles Abourezk, Jake Nordbye, Eric Zimmer and Denise DuBroy read parts of the manuscript, offered valuable comments, and encouraged me throughout, as did all of Earl's children and Joe Maierhauser, Jr. Kyle Read at Badson Studio and Matt McInerney at Motel created an inspired book design. Diana Pavek compiled the index. Amanda Waterhouse organized Earl's correspondence and copyedited the book with the assistance of Lois Facer and Eric Abrahamson. Lois also read the manuscript, compiled and digitized the photographs and managed the project from start to finish. Eric edited the book. He is my anchor, my friend. His encouragement never flagged.

SOURCES

In the late 1970s, Earl Brockelsby made a series of lengthy audio recordings in which he reflected on his childhood in Kadoka, the founding of Reptile Gardens, his experiences during World War II, his efforts to rebuild Reptile Gardens after the war and his struggles with manic depression. Reta Mae, his sister, life-long secretary and confidante transcribed the recordings into three volumes, totaling 413 typed pages. Over the years, the volumes have been circulated among Earl's family and closest friends as an incomplete, unpublished memoir.

Earl's memoir offers an important contribution to the history of western South Dakota in the first half of the twentieth century. The volumes are introspective, especially regarding his family life in Kadoka, his years as a young man in Rapid City and his experiences in Europe during World War II. They also provide valuable unvarnished descriptions of the difficulties that a young entrepreneur faced in building a tourist business after the war.

The recordings were made when Earl was in his 60s. His memory for specific dates and events was sometimes inaccurate. Occasionally, he exaggerated the importance of small events. At the same time, he left out most of the details of his marriage and family life. Nevertheless, his evolving vision for Reptile Gardens and his perspective on the important influences in his life are clear. These volumes form the backbone of the narrative for *Rattlesnake Under His Hat* and have allowed me to give Earl a primary role in the telling of his story.

From childhood, Earl imagined that one day he would be a published writer. He believed it was a path to fame and fortune. Aside from one small booklet on the behavior of rattlesnakes and periodic columns in the *Rapid City Journal* written to promote Reptile Gardens, Earl never published. Nevertheless, he was an obsessive man of letters. He left a treasure of correspondence in the private archives of Reptile Gardens, which were made available to me during research. These letters are personal, including correspondence with his wife Maude, his sister Reta Mae, his children, his romantic interests, the staff and summer employees at Reptile Gardens, political associates and his closest business partners. Reta Mae typed some of the correspondence, but many of the letters are hand-written. They were scrawled at campfires in Baja or late at night when he was obsessing on a problem and could not sleep.

As a whole, the files represent a jigsaw puzzle of his life with a third of the pieces missing. The complete archive of his correspondence with Maude during World War II, for example, was destroyed in the Rapid City flood of 1972. But the sheer volume of letters over 50 years combined with the emotional honesty and frankness of his writing style overwhelms what is missing. The correspondence files provide a valuable complement to his unpublished memoir and helped to ensure the continuity of Earl's voice in this book. These letters are quoted with the permission of Reptile Gardens.

Walter Prescott Webb's seminal history of the region, *The Great Plains* remains the most important piece of historical scholarship on the difficulties that pioneers faced in settling such a harsh environment. *Beyond the Hundredth Meridian* by Wallace Stegner details John Wesley Powell's perspective on the limits of homestead settlement west of the Missouri River. *Dakota Territory: 1861-1889 A Study of Frontier Politics* by Howard Lamar offers a detailed examination of the economic and geographical forces that influenced South Dakota political organization on the eve of statehood. Herbert Schell's *History of South Dakota*, first published in 1961, is still the best general history of the state during the period that Earl came of age and built his business. Gilbert Courtland Fite's biography, *Peter Norbeck: Prairie Statesman*, provides critical perspective on Norbeck's unique brand of progressivism and his influence on the development of Custer State Park and west river tourism.

Paula Nelson's two volume series, *After the West Was Won* and *The Prairie Winnows Out Its Own*, is essential for understanding the economic and environmental forces that constrained the homestead movement and influenced Earl Brockelsby's parents and childhood. Nelson's research on Kadoka, South Dakota, was particularly valuable considering that it was Earl's birthplace and played such a formative role in his life. Nelson's two books parallel the movements of the Brockelsby family and explain the forces set in motion by the Depression that pushed the Brockelsby family from Kadoka to Rapid City. The photography in Nelson's books is a valuable complement to the text.

Hamlin Garland's *Son of the Middle Border* is a great piece of American literature that details both the struggles and romance of homestead life. Edith Eudora Kohl's memoir, *Land of the Burnt*

Thigh, is every bit as dramatic and spellbinding as Garland. *The Circus Age: Culture and Society Under the American Big Top* by Janet M. Davis sets Earl's formative experience with the circus in Kadoka in the context of the larger golden age of the railroad and travelling circus.

Several local biographies helped me understand the world that Earl Brockelsby grew up in: *Homesteading the Badlands, 1912* by Frank Bormann; *Paving the Way: The Life of Morris E. Adelstein* by Howard Shaff and Audrey Shaff; *Duhamel: Oxcart to Television* by Dale Lewis; *Bear With Me: Dennis 'Doc' Casey* by Don Theye and *The Badlands Fox* by Margaret Lemley Warren. The article "Keeping the Faith: Bertha Martinsky in West River, South Dakota" by Orlando J. Goering and Violet Miller Goering, published in the 1995 edition of *South Dakota History,* also provided important context.

In the early days of Reptile Gardens, the inexperienced staff had no formal training in herpetology or the care of reptiles. They relied heavily on Raymond Ditmars's book, *Reptiles of the World*, published in 1936—a year before Reptile Gardens opened. Ditmars was curator of mammals at the Bronx Zoo at the time that Earl Chace began his career in the reptile house. Chace brought Ditmars's broad influence with him to Reptile Gardens. Frank Buck's popular bestseller, *Bring 'Em Back Alive* (co-authored with Edward Anthony) tapped into a different tradition than Ditmars. Buck was a showman and an adventurer who came out of the circus tradition rather than the halls of academe. Several books were helpful in understanding the methods and traditions of international wildlife trade in the post-war period: Lawrence Earl's *Crocodile Fever*; Bryan Christy's *The Lizard King: True Crimes and Passions of the World's Greatest Reptile Smugglers* and Jennie Erin Smith's *Stolen World: A Tale of Reptiles, Smugglers, and Skulduggery*. Arthur Jones wrote a detailed autobiography of his extraordinary life, including his exploits in Africa. *And God Laughs: The Autobiography of Arthur Jones* is available online at *arthurjonesexercise.com*. The website also links to a series of television interviews that reveal Jones's personality and worldview.

There is no single comprehensive study of South Dakota tourism or analysis of South Dakota's place in the expansion of western tourism in the mid-twentieth century. *A Marvelous Hundred Square Miles: Black Hills Tourism, 1880-1941* by Suzanne Barta Julin explores the early days of tourism, particularly in the southern Black Hills. *Looking for History on Highway 14* by John E. Miller was useful in understanding the expansion of the road system in South Dakota. *Dreams and Dust in the Black Hills: Race, Place, and National Identity in America's Land of Promise*, Elaine Marie Nelson's 2011 doctoral dissertation for the University of New Mexico, gives a contemporary perspective on the conflicts between indigenous culture and modern tourism.

Reptile Gardens was built at a time when the American middle class was first able to purchase automobiles and federal government programs supplemented state efforts to expand state highway systems. Several books helped me understand the emergence of the tourist economy in the West: *Animal Attractions: Nature on Display in American Zoos* by Elizabeth Hanson; *See America First: Tourism and National Identity 1880-1940* by Margaret Shaffer; *In Search of the Golden West: The Tourist in Western America* by Earl Pomeroy. Most influential in framing the conflict between tourism as an educational endeavor and tourism as entertainment was Hal K. Rothman's *Devil's Bargains: Tourism in the Twentieth Century American West*.

No review of tourism in western South Dakota is complete without a thorough understanding of the influence of Mount Rushmore on the regional economy and culture. John Taliaferro's *Great White Fathers: The Story of the Obsessive Quest to Create*

Mount Rushmore is the best history of Gutzon Borglum's obsession; it was particularly valuable for this project because it sets the Mount Rushmore sculpture project squarely in the context of tourism development.

Advise and Dissent: Memoirs of South Dakota and the US Senate by Senator James Abourezk provides details on the senator's relationship with Earl Brockelsby and serves as an invaluable memoir of what it was like to grow up in Wood, South Dakota—the hometown of Maude Wagner Brockelsby. *McGovern: A Biography* by Robert Sam Anson is important for its analysis of how a liberal Democrat survived and thrived politically in a conservative state and how McGovern's military experiences in World War II shaped his attitudes about the Vietnam War.

The archives of the *Rapid City Daily Journal,* on microfilm in the Rapid City Public Library, were essential in helping me understand the larger community context in which Brockelsby worked. The archives of the Rapid City Chamber of Commerce, which are partially available on the Black Hills Knowledge Network's website, contain valuable journals and popular illustrated booklets that document efforts to promote Black Hills tourism in the years between the 1920s and the 1950s.

To the authors of all of these works and to the librarians, archivists and family members who have helped to preserve these primary materials, I am exceedingly grateful.

▲ *Early Reptile Gardens brochure. Artist: Lee Logan.*

INDEX

A

Aachen, Germany, *136*
Abourezk, James "Jim," *276-78, 325, 332*
Acapulco, Mexico, *237*
Adam, Brenda, *280-83, 286-88, 291-92, 296-97, 299, 302, 304-5, 311-12*
Adelstein, Morris, *77, 330*
Adelstein, Stanford, *34, 325*
Ahl, Ruth *31, 325*
Alhambra, California, *75*
Ambunti, Papa New Guinea, *258*
American Indian Movement (AIM), *272*
Ammons, Ida Mary, *31*
Angkor Wat (Cambodia), *261*
Angoram, Papua New Guinea, *258*
Armstrong, Bob, *100, 216*
Armstrong, Francie, *246*
Arrowhead Country Club, *223*
Aunt Phoebe, *75-76, 79*

B

Badlands National Park (South Dakota), *31, 271*
Bad River (South Dakota), *18, 23, 28*
Baja California, Mexico, *77, 225, 226, 227, 228, 231, 236-37, 239-40, 242-43, 245, 252, 255, 259, 266, 280, 281, 305, 328*
Barrancas del Cobre, *237, 246* (*See also:* Copper Canyon)
Basham, Marvin, *80, 94, 122*
Bataan, Philippines, *112, 113*
Bellamy, Paul E., *25, 77-78, 84-85, 156-59, 162, 168-69, 171-72, 213, 238, 270*
Berg, Luvine, *158*
Bewitched Village, *206, 213, 280, 297*
Bigelow, Bob, *103, 114, 147, 152*
Billboard, 89-90, 95, 187, 194
Black Elk, Ben, *69, 272, 315*
Black Hills, Badlands and Lakes Association (BHB&L), *270, 273, 315*
Black Hills Institute, *317-18, 321-22*
Bonn, Germany, *136, 149*
Borglum, Gutzon, *50, 56, 83, 96, 238, 271, 274, 331*
Boulder, Colorado, *266, 287, 293-94, 300, 302, 311, 312, 314, 324*
Boyle, Hal, *237-38*
British Honduras (Belize), *245*
Brockelsby, Emma (mother), *31-32, 35, 41, 43, 44-45, 47, 48, 49, 56* (*See also:* Kingsbury, Sara Emmaline "Emma")

Brockelsby, Janet (daughter) *175, 207-8, 221, 222, 224, 225, 232, 259-61, 263, 264,-65, 287, 290, 294-96, 298, 311, 316, 323-24*

Brockelsby, Jeff (son), *221, 232, 260, 266, 279, 280, 284-86, 287, 290, 298--1, 310-11, 312, 314, 315, 316, 323*

Brockelsby, John Earl (father), *25, 27-28, 30, 31, 32, 35, 39, 40, 41, 43-44, 45, 47, 48-49, 50, 51, 52-53, 54, 56, 61, 77, 81-82*

Brockelsby, John R. (grandfather) *26-27, 28*

Brockelsby, Johnny (son), *181, 221, 222, 223-24, 226, 232, 253, 260, 265, 280, 283, 289, 290, 294-95, 298, 306, 315, 316, 323*

Brockelsby, Judee (daugher), *114, 118, 123, 124, 125-26, 139, 147, 152, 221, 222, 223, 224, 225, 231-32, 246, 247, 248, 250, 260, 265-66, 273, 280, 287, 290, 293-94, 312, 316, 323*

Brockelsby, Maude (wife), *72-73, 74, 77, 80, 81, 86, 92, 93, 100, 101, 102, 103, 111, 112, 113, 115, 118, 120, 123, 124-26, 142, 147, 149, 150-51, 152, 153, 154, 160, 164, 165-66, 173, 175, 176, 178, 179, 181, 182, 182-83, 198, 221-22, 223, 224, 225, 228-29, 230, 231, 232, 233, 235-36, 241, 246, 260, 266-67, 273, 274, 276, 278, 279, 280, 280, 283-87, 293-94, 297, 298, 300, 301, 304, 311-15, 324, 328, 332* (*See also*: Wagner, Maude)

Brockelsby, Reta Mae (sister), *36, 46, 49, 86, 87, 91, 92, 93, 111, 115, 147, 165-66, 167, 179, 181, 182, 198, 201-3, 209-10, 223, 231, 232, 241, 251, 253, 278, 290, 291, 297, 300-1, 311, 314, 327, 328*

Brockelsby, William (brother), *57*

Broken Rope, Godfrey, *70, 94*

Buck, Frank, *11, 89, 189, 330*

Buffalo Gap, South Dakota, *80*

C

Cabanatuan prison camp, *113*

Cabo San Lucas, Mexico, *243*

Cambodia, *261, 263, 276*

Camp Fannin, *123, 140*

Camp McCoy, *151*

Campbell, Jerre, *114, 166, 325*

Campbell, Jim, *166, 167, 181, 184, 191, 197-200, 201, 202, 206, 213, 219, 231, 252, 290-91, 296, 297, 299, 300, 301, 305, 306, 307, 315*

Campbell, Lee, *166, 181*

Canyon Lake Methodist Church, *285*

Caprivi Strip, Namibia, *190, 191-92, 303*

Carroll, Iowa, *28*

Chace, Earl, *177-78, 181, 183, 184-85, 186, 193-94, 202, 213-14, 217, 218, 231, 246, 252, 253, 265, 290, 300, 301, 320, 330*

Chace, I.H., *170*

Chadron, Nebraska, *21*

Chamberlain, South Dakota, *28, 43, 270*

Cheyenne River, *16, 18-19, 55*
Chicago, Illinois, *32, 49-50, 52, 55, 56, 63, 72, 74, 95, 134, 157, 167, 168, 197, 302, 318*
Chicago and North Western Railway, *23, 28, 72*
Chicago World's Fair, *234*
Clifton, John, *255-56*
Clinton, Iowa, *26*
Civilian Conservation Corps (CCC), *200*
Cocos Island, *196, 252-55*
Cohen, Beila "Bertha," *31, 33-34, 45, 48, 69, 77, 330* (See also: Bertha Martinski)
Convention on International Trade in Endangered Species of Wild Flora and Fauna (CITES), *302*
Colorado College, *260*
Colossal Cave, *184, 191, 200-1, 203, 204, 205, 206, 209, 210, 215, 237, 251, 253, 278, 306*
Copper Canyon, *237, 246* (See also: Barrancas del Cobre)
Cottonwood, South Dakota, *295*
Coolidge, Calvin, *55-56, 66, 78, 85, 238*
Cosmopolitan Club, *175*
Costa Rica, *231, 245, 250, 252, 253*
Cousins, Alice Ann, *27-28*
Craig, George, *189, 256-57, 261-62, 321*
Crawford County, Iowa, *26-27*
Crazy Horse, *59, 69, 271*
Crazy Horse Memorial, *274*
Custer, George Armstrong, *19*
Custer State Park (South Dakota), *78, 80, 174, 269, 271, 329*
Custer, South Dakota, *184, 191, 199, 213*

D

Dahl, Art, *77, 82, 117, 118*
Dakota State Bank, *51, 52, 54*
Dark Canyon (South Dakota), *58*
Daru Island, Papua New Guinea, *257, 261-62*
Davis, Sam, *30*
De Anza Park (Tucson), *204*
Dean, Robert, *105, 107*
Dean, Roy, *82, 95*
Democratic Party, *275*
Devereaux, Harry, *121*
Devils Tower (Wyoming), *105-12, 115, 207, 222* (See also: Mato Tipila)
Diego Rivera, *245*
Duhamel, Alex, *66, 67*
Duhamel, Francis "Bud," *67, 97*
Duhamel, Helen, *67, 161*
Duhamel, Peter, *66*
Durrance, Jack, *110*
Dusek, Fred, *171*

E

Ebaugh, Franklin, *180*
El Paso Police Department, *187*
El Salvador, *250*
Ellsworth Air Force Base, *116, 117, 215, 273* (See also: Rapid City Army Air Base)
Endangered Species Act, The, *302*
Ensenada, Mexico, *237*
Evans, John, *245-46, 249, 254*

F

Fairfax, South Dakota, *31*
Fairyland Zoo, *184, 191, 197, 199, 206, 211, 213*
Farrar, Robert, *317*
Federal Public Housing Authority, *171*
Figueroa, Jesus, *91*
Fiji, *261*
Fly River (Papua New Guinea), *189, 256, 261*
Fort Laramie, Wyoming, *59*
Fort Leavenworth, Kansas, *122-23*
Foster, Carole, *305, 324*
French Creek (South Dakota), *19*
French Riviera, *149*
Ft. Pierre, South Dakota, *18, 23*

G

Galápagos Islands, Ecuador, *253*
Garrett, Joe, *62, 70-71, 74, 76, 80, 102, 103-4, 112, 119*
Gentzler, Jack, *100, 103, 104, 107, 114, 120, 152*
Great Depression, *51, 63, 65, 164*
Greeley, Colorado, *186*
Grindstone Butte, *18, 23*
Gross, Don, *103, 114, 120*
Guatemala, *245, 247, 249*
Guatemala City, Guatemala, *249*
Guaymas, Mexico, *246*

H

Hall, Bob, *74, 75, 223*
Hall, Cary, *75*
Hall, Eloise, *75, 76, 223*
Hall, Nick, *215-20, 242-44, 325*
Hand, Mr., *52*
Hangman's Hill (Rapid City), *58*
Harney Peak (South Dakota), *181, 225, 311*
Harvey, Bill, *10-11*
Havana, Cuba, *235*
Hawaii, *104, 112, 235*
Hidden City, *12-14, 65, 69, 70, 79, 84, 195, 204*
Himalayas, *109, 261, 263*
Honert, James, *317*
Hopkins, George, *104-12, 115*
Hot Springs, South Dakota, *20, 80, 154*
Hotel Alex Johnson, *67, 154*
Hustead, Ted, *270*
Huy, Belgium, *134, 135*

I

Ice, Clyde, *107-8, 111*
Infantry Replacement Training Center, *123*
Interior, South Dakota, *31*
Iverson, Ole, *16, 21*

J

Jackley, Albert M., *88*
Jackson County, South Dakota, *25, 32*
James River (South Dakota), *17*
James River Valley (South Dakota), *51*
Jilek, Father Robert, *257, 262*

K

Jones, Arthur, *187-88, 190-94, 199, 207-8, 209, 256, 261, 303, 321, 330-31*
Joyner, Newell F., *106, 107, 108, 109, 110*

Kadoka, South Dakota, *9, 31, 32-34, 35, 36, 37, 38, 39, 45, 46, 47, 48, 50, 52, 53, 54, 57, 58, 60, 69, 71, 72, 75, 77, 108, 147, 160, 169, 234, 268, 292, 325, 327, 329-30*
Kadoka Kommercial Klub, *34*
Kadoka State Bank, *32, 39*
Kingsbury, Alton, *31-32, 48*
Kingsbury, Sara Emmaline "Emma," *31-32, 35, 41, 43, 44-45, 47, 48, 49, 56* (*See also:* Brockelsby, Emma)
Kingsbury, Mason, *44*
Knecht, John, *77, 81*
Koers, Juleus, *116*
Kohl, Edith Eudora, *18, 31, 39, 329*
Ku Klux Klan, *33, 34, 97*
Kuehn, Martie, *246, 250-51, 324*

L

La Paz, Bolivia, *243*
Lake Andes, South Dakota, *72*
Land of the Burnt Thigh, *18, 31, 39, 329*
Larson, Neal, *317-18*
Larson, Peter, *317-19, 321*
Leedom, Boyd, *45, 77, 105, 152, 169*
Leedom, Chester "Chet," *32, 45*

Liege, Belgium, *138, 139-40, 143, 145, 153*
Lincolnshire, England, *26, 27, 59*
London School of Cartooning, *60*
Louvre Museum, *138, 234*
Lower Brulé Indian Reservation, *31*

M

Madame Paquot, *134-35*
Maierhauser, Joe, *166, 181, 182, 166, 192, 200, 201-206, 208-10, 212, 215, 228, 230, 231, 232-233, 251, 253, 278, 338, 315*
Maierhauser, Joe Jr., *201, 202, 210, 223, 286, 291, 294, 300-303, 305, 306-9, 311, 315, 316, 320, 321, 324, 326*
Malmedy, Belgium, *138-139, 141, 142-43*
Marburg, Germany, *146, 148, 149*
Mariners Club (Rapid City), *175*
Martinski, Bertha, *31, 33-34, 45, 48, 69, 77, 330* (See also: Cohen, Beila "Bertha")
Mato Tipila, *105-12, 115, 207, 222* (*See also:* Devils Tower)
Mayan pyramids, *245*
Mazatlán, Mexico, *246*
McGovern, George, *274-276, 177, 178-79, 332*
McLane, Merrill, *110*
Meier, Josef, *270*
Mérida, Mexico, *247*
Methuselah, *176-77, 273-74*
Meuse River, *134, 139*
Mexicali, Mexico, *237*

Mexico City, Mexico, *235, 245, 246-47*
Midland, South Dakota, *23*
Minneapolis, Minnesota, *49, 120, 157, 186*
Missouri River, *16, 17, 20, 21, 29, 49, 51, 168, 270, 329*
Moser, Ed, *241*
Moser, Becky, *241*
Mount Hagen Sing-sing (Papua New Guinea), *258-59, 263*
Mount Rushmore (South Dakota), *15, 56, 61, 66, 68, 73, 80, 83, 84, 86, 93, 94, 96-99, 115, 154, 155, 156, 158, 161, 162, 176, 212, 215, 269, 271, 272, 292, 305, 322, 331-32*
Mueller, Al, *170*
Mundt, Karl, *158, 274, 275, 277*

N

Nancy, France, *145*
National Labor Relations Board, *45*
Nepal, *261*
New Orleans, Louisiana, *190, 192, 193*
Nicaragua, *245, 250*
Nicholson, Oscar, *16*
Nixon, Richard, *274, 279, 302*
Nogales, Mexico, *237*
Norbeck, Peter, *16-19, 20, 21-25, 28, 32, 49, 50, 54, 55, 77, 80, 83, 169, 174, 271, 329*
Normandy Beach, *140*
North Africa, *143, 173*

O

Oldham, Jeff, *294, 320, 324*
Oldham, Jon, *246-49, 252-53, 260, 265, 273, 293, 300*
Olive, Ray, *188*
Omaha, Nebraska, *20, 28, 49, 122, 157*
Omaha Beach, *125, 127, 274*
Operation Cobra, *129*

P

Pactola Lake (South Dakota), *217-18*
Palace Meat Market, *118, 150*
Papua New Guinea, *188, 189, 231, 255-58, 259-63, 304, 321, 324*
Paraguay, *265, 294-95*
Paris, France, *133, 138, 149, 157, 158, 161, 234*
Pawley, Ray, *325*
Pederson, Don, *99*
Pedro Juan Caballero, Paraguay, *294*
Pennington County Bank, *67*
Peterson, Carrie, *31, 59*
Petrified Woods, The, *70-71, 73, 74, 79, 80, 84, 160, 70*
Phillip, South Dakota, *48*
Pierre, South Dakota, *17, 20, 212, 317, 321*
Pine Ridge Indian Reservation, *32, 116, 122, 272*
Plumb, Jack, *74*
Poas volcano (Costa Rica), *250*
Popocatepetl volcano (Mexico), *245, 247*

Port Moresby, Papua New Guinea, 255, 258
Powell, John Wesley, 18, 329
Presbyterian Church Men's Club, 175
Puerto Barrios, Guatemala, 249-50
Puerto Vallarta, Mexico, 237
Pullen, Lester "Si," 270

Q

Quinn, Joe, 107

R

Rapid City Army Air Base, 116, 117, 215, 273 (See also: Ellsworth Air Force Base)
Rapid City Journal, 62, 71, 85, 87, 98, 104, 153, 158, 166, 172, 182, 204, 328, 332 (See also: Daily Journal)
Rapid City Chamber of Commerce, 84, 121, 171, 175, 332
Rapid City Chamber of Commerce Aviation Committee, 169
Rapid City Commission, 169
Rapid City High School, 171, 225, 232
Rapid City Junior Chamber of Commerce, 104-105, 168
Rapid City National Bank, 82, 117, 121
Rapid Valley (South Dakota), 173
Raymond, Eugene, 81
Red Tomahawk, Tommy, 114
Redfield, South Dakota 15, 16, 21
Reptile Jungle, 188

Robinson, Doane, 49-50, 83
Roosevelt, Franklin Delano, 66, 78, 103, 138, 158, 169, 274
Roosevelt, Theodore "Teddy", 9, 23, 37, 96, 97, 98, 105, 237
Rosarito Beach, Mexico, 237
Rosebud Indian Reservation, 31, 32, 59, 72, 174,
Rounds, Neil, 52

S

San Diego, California, 77, 291, 305
San Ignacio Lagoon (Mexico), 240
Schroeder, Martin, 284
Schultz-Basken, Retrout, 147-149
Scissons, John, 31, 59
Scissons, Kenneth "Kenny", 59-60, 69, 152, 173, 193, 325
Sea of Cortés (Mexico), 237
Sepik River (Papua New Guinea), 257-58, 261, 262
Sergeant Nicke, 137
Seri Indians, 240
Sheep Mountain Table (South Dakota), 10, 227, 236
Shupe, Scott, 309-10, 325
Sicangu Lakota 31, 59, 72
Sierra Madre (Mexico), 239
Sioux City, Iowa, 21
Sioux Indian Pageant, 68, 69, 71, 80, 97, 98, 211, 212, 268
Sitting Bull, 68
Sitting Bull Crystal Caverns, 65, 66, 68, 80, 84, 212
Sobotak, Ray, 139-40
Solomon Islands, 261
Sonora, Mexico, 236, 237, 240

Sonora Desert (Arizona), *177, 237*
South Dakota Republican Party, *24, 30, 32, 50, 169, 273, 276*
South Dakota School of Mines, *63, 65, 74, 95, 99, 136, 167, 170, 171, 317*
South Dakota Supreme Court, *45*
Spearfish, South Dakota, *61-62, 72, 81*
Spearfish Canyon (South Dakota), *61*
Spearfish High School, South Dakota, *63*
St. Vith, Belgium, *144*
Stanley County, South Dakota, *29*
Stanley County Land Company, *32*
State Game Lodge, *55*
Stavelot, Belgium, *142, 143*
Stone, Pierre, *99*
Sylvan Lake (South Dakota), *181*

T

Thomas, Danny, *278*
Tijuana, Mexico, *76-77, 237*
Trier, Germany, *135*
Tucson, Arizona, *184, 200, 204, 208, 227, 288, 307*
Tyler, Texas, *123, 124*

U

Uncle August, *43*
United Nations, *156-59, 168, 213, 270*
University of Arizona, *231, 239, 241*
University of Colorado, *180, 291, 293, 302*
University of Iowa, *166, 239*
University of Kansas, *305, 306, 307*
U.S. Fish and Wildlife Services, *302, 308, 321*

V

Vail, South Dakota, *26, 28*
Vernon Pottery Works, *76*
Verviers, Belgium, *143*
Vucurevich, John T., *119-20, 122, 152*

W

Wagner, Charles, *72*
Wagner, Gerry, *80, 92-93, 94, 98, 102, 153, 165, 252*
Wagner, Maude Millicent, *72-73, 74, 77, 80, 81, 86, 92, 93, 100, 101, 102, 103, 111, 112, 113, 115, 118, 120, 123, 124-26, 142, 147, 149, 150-51, 152, 153, 154, 160, 164, 165-66, 173, 175, 176, 178, 179, 181, 182, 182-83, 198, 221-22, 223, 224, 225, 228-29, 230, 231, 232, 233, 235-36, 241, 246, 260, 266-67, 273, 274, 276, 278, 279, 280, 280, 283-87, 293-94, 297, 298, 300, 301, 304, 311-15, 324, 328, 332 (See also: Brockelsby, Maude)*
Wahgi Valley (Papua New Guinea), *259, 263*
Wall, South Dakota, *10, 23*
Wall Drug, *270, 292*
Wasta, South Dakota, *23*
Webb, Walter Prescott, *21, 22, 329*

West, Lloyd, *270*
Westin, Ed, *100, 103, 114, 152, 165, 167, 211-12*
White River (South Dakota), *32, 46*
Wilkens, Mort, *117*
Winged Victory of Samothrace, *138*
Wood, South Dakota, *72, 173, 276, 332*
Woolworth's, *71, 72, 73, 101, 287*
World War I, *35, 51, 77*
World War II, *102, 112-115, 153, 157, 170, 171, 256, 274, 275, 276, 279, 327, 328*
Wounded Knee, South Dakota, *69, 272*
Wright, Frank Lloyd, *61, 97, 238*

X

Y

Yangoru, Papua New Guinea, *258*
Yellowstone National Park, *11, 23, 50, 84, 161, 163*
Young, Marshall, *238-40, 245, 247-50, 254, 259, 324*

Z

Ziolkowski, Korczak, *271, 274-75*

Sam Hurst is an Emmy Award-winning journalist and documentarian. In 1993, he was awarded a Neiman Fellowship in journalism at Harvard University, where he studied evolutionary biology. Following his retirement from NBC News, Hurst and his family moved to the Black Hills where he owned and operated a buffalo ranch and continued to produce documentary movies, including *The Coming Plague* for Turner Broadcasting, *Paul Ehrlich and the Population Bomb* for PBS and *Good Meat* for Native American Public Television. Hurst has written extensively about food and agriculture policy and South Dakota culture and politics.